Victor Spinetti up front...

with Peter Rankin

ROBSON
BOOKS

First published in Hardback in Great Britain in 2006 by
Robson Books
151 Freston Road
london
W10 6TH

An imprint of Anova Books Company Ltd

ISBN 1 86105 943 4

10 9 8 7 6 5 4 3 2 1

Printed and bound by Creative Print and Design (Ebbw Vale), Wales

This book can be ordered direct from the publisher
Contact the marketing department, but try your local bookshop first

wwwanovabooks.com

Contents

For Graham Curnow
17. 7. 30 — 29. 7. 97

Nan Beecher-Moore, Peter Benedict, Barry Burnett &
Lindsay Granger, Bertie Burrows, Allan & Iain Campbell,
Eleanor & Neil Connery, Ken & Rita Cooper,
Sandra Dickinson & Mark Osmond, Ronnie Dorsey,
Britt Eckland, Faith Evans, Lauretta Feldman &
Anne Levy, Alfredo Gaggini, John Geiger, Dulcie Gray
Jack McLauchlan, Gordon Rogoff & Morton Lichter,
Bob & Bren Tranter, Burt Shevelove, Steve Walker, Charles Vance
and Mog Smith.
I'm Glad we were in each other's time.

1

Italy comes to the Valleys

Early in 1965 I was back from America after performing in *Oh What a Lovely War*, Theatre Workshop's musical entertainment about the First World War. I'd done the Beatles films, been on talk shows and won a Tony Award. For once, I was feeling quite pleased with myself. The telephone rang. Would I do the *David Frost Show*? Ten-thirty in the evening, live. 'Any other guests?' Yes, Asa Briggs, the historian. I rang home to Wales: 'Watch the telly tonight. I'll wave at you. It's all I can do because I've got to go to Paris tomorrow to start a new film.'

The car arrived at six o'clock. Six o'clock? The show didn't go out until half past ten in the evening. It wasn't like that on *The Jack Paar Show* back in New York, and the talk show, as we know it, was practically invented by him. Hardly had you walked through his studio door than you found yourself standing in the wings, hearing – well, this is what I heard: 'Jack's guests tonight are Robert Goulet, Phyllis Diller, Victor Spinetti!' and, God, there was nothing in my head. On this huge, right-across-America show, Jack Paar simply asked me, 'What are you doing?' and I told him. I didn't spend hours and hours accounting for my life to a researcher. We started to converse. That was it. So what was this six o'clock all about? The car pulled up at the BBC.

'Mr Spinotti?' That's the bloke on the door, eyeing me.

'No.'

He lifted a receiver: 'I've got a Mr Spaghuzzi here. Yeah . . . Yeah . . . Right . . . You're in there.'

I opened a door and found myself in a dining room, looking at a long table, elaborate drapes, and waiters at the ready, all along the walls. But who was sitting there, leaning back expansively? Huw – one chair for his arm, one chair for his arse – Wheldon, Director of Programmes. We had met before. When I was young and he was editor of the TV arts programme *Monitor*, I had been taken to see him by John Wain, Professor of Poetry at Oxford, with an idea of mine that John had been keen to write. 'My dear John,' This was Huw Wheldon, 'Lovely to see you. Work for us? Oh, yes, marvellous. Now then, tell me your idea. Shoot.'

'Actually it's not my idea. It's Victor's.'

'Ah, Mr Spinetti. You have a very interesting Monmouthshire accent, where do you come from?'

'Monmouthshire,' I answered.

'My father was the Permanent Under Secretary to the Ministry of Education for Wales from 1937 until 1949.'

'Well, with the education I got, he should be ashamed of himself.' This was not true but I had to have a comeback. 'And your idea?'

'I'd love to see a programme where you saw the beginnings of, say, when Bette Davis became that mannered or when James Stewart began to do that extraordinary drawl. At what moment did that happen? Was it always there or did they start it?'

'We have those ideas, possibly once a month,' said Huw Wheldon. 'Now John, you must come and work for us.'

'No thank you,' said John and, together, we left. Outside, the Professor of Poetry at Oxford paused and said, 'What a cunt.'

I suspect I disappeared up my own wisecrack with that remark about Huw Wheldon's father. Perhaps I should have said his father had done a wonderful job as the Permanent Under Secretary then I might have been in *Doctor Who*.

At the long table with Huw Wheldon were Donald Baverstock and quite a few other BBC types, all waiting to eat. They were giving a dinner with roast lamb, mint sauce, fresh vegetables and vintage wine. At the end of the table, like a young schoolboy, saying nothing, sat David Frost. Evidently Asa Briggs and I were the excuse for this meal but having a show to do, we could eat nothing.

Huw Wheldon tucked into his Welsh lamb saying, 'Now, David is going to ask you these questions.' He passed bits of paper round the table on which the questions were typed. Nothing so far had come from David Frost himself, stuck as he was somewhere behind the gesturing hand of Huw Weldon, who, referring to Frost always as 'David', had taken charge. 'Question one,' said Huw. 'When were you first aware of a state known as drunkenness?'

My heart sank because I was thinking, 'This is like one of those essays, "What did you do during the holiday?" or "Which do you prefer, the town or the country?"' The dinner was nothing but a rehearsal. What's more, a rehearsal for a talk show.

'A state known as drunkenness?' he repeated.

'Yes, when I was about five.'

'Five? What do you mean, five?'

'I was born above my Dad's fish-and-chip shop in South Wales. That's where I slept as a little boy. On Friday nights I could hear down below in the shop the sound of singing or fighting, sometimes both. It was Friday night when the miners got paid, so I associated singing and fighting with drunkenness.'

'But what about famous drunks? You worked with Richard Burton. You worked with Brendan Be-han.'

'How about Winston Churchill?'

'WINSTON CHURCHILL!?' he bellowed, banging the table and startling poor David.

'My cousin Elwyn was part of his guard at 10 Downing Street during the war. And he told us there were occasions when they used to carry him up to bed at night. My mother said, "Exhausted?" and Elwyn said, "No, pissed out of his mind."'

'Are you going to say that?' Huw asked. 'May I remind you, Mr Spi-ne-tti. Asa Briggs is here for social comment. You're here for the laughs.'

As we came out of the studio later on, I having told those stories, Huw Wheldon said, 'You realise what you've done, Mr Spinetti?'

'No?'

'Well, now the whole of the United Kingdom will know that your father sold fish and chips.'

'Pleased with myself,' I said when I began. It didn't last long. One only remembers the bad reviews. Still, I've introduced my father, Joe Spinetti, a farmer's son from Italy. How did he come to be selling fish and chips in the Welsh mining village of Cwm? If he hadn't, this is where the book would end.

Before the First World War, life may have been rougher and tougher than it is today – no National Health Service, no Social Security – but it was also less restricted. We have a Common Market now but in those days we had a very common market. It was called Free Trade. Raw materials could be sold around the world with no import tariffs and people could move about to find work, no questions asked, no favours given. One such person was my grandfather, Giorgio, a farmer in northern Italy. He needed a new plough but had no money. Villagers round about had gone to Wales because they'd heard there was work there, so he went too. He may not have known it but young men were going there from all over Central Europe – Czechs, Poles and Hungarians. The work they got was coal mining, which had started towards the end of the nineteenth century. The Welsh themselves had been far too busy farming at the time, hence the need for foreign labour. So off went Giorgio – no passport, no permit – he didn't need those, just a sturdy pair of legs to carry him from his home town, Ronchi, across northern Italy and up through France.

Outside Swansea, he found the mining work he'd heard of but as soon as the money for the plough was in his pocket, back to Italy he went. That wasn't the end of it, obviously. Wales and the opportunities it offered tempted younger members of the family. Life, after all, wasn't getting any better in Ronchi. Giorgio had two sons, Francesco and Giuseppe and these boys knew, by now, that other families – the Contis, the Sidolis, the Marenghis – had not only gone to Wales but settled and started their own businesses. That's in catering, not mining. A decision was made: Francesco, the older brother, would go first and, all being well, send word that his younger brother should join him. The message came. Giuseppe needed little encouragement. Being a good Partisan, he spat on the ground to curse Fascism and set off.

The place the two of them wound up in was a mining village outside Ebbw Vale called Cwm. As you would expect, the Italian families already living in the neighbourhood looked out for the boys but so did the Welsh, or some of them, anyway. A young man called Bill Watson took the boys back to his mother's house where she cooked and did their washing. One of her children – she had nine – was a girl, Lily, eleven years old. Lily took one look at the nineteen-year-old Giuseppe and fell. It was the thick chestnut hair that did it but then suddenly the two Italian boys were back in Italy again, taking money home, no doubt. The most beautiful thing Lily had ever seen in her life had gone forever. She was convinced of it.

She was wrong. There was too much in Wales for Giuseppe to ignore – herself, for a start, but also her big family and work. Giuseppe and Francesco returned to Cwm and took odd jobs. One of them was delivering ice cream from a horse-drawn cart. It wasn't the odd job Francesco wanted, not surprisingly, as locals picked the lids off the big wooden tubs and threw in horse dung. With one of those lids, he hit them and they fled but still he left for London. Giuseppe stayed. He knew he was making a beginning but what he really wanted was a business of his own, so he started to look. Of course, while he was working and looking, he was courting Lily too. Unusual that. Other Italian boys in Wales courted Italian girls. Perhaps 'courting' is not the right word for Giuseppe anyway because, to cut a short story shorter, on 19 August that year, he married his sixteen and a half-year-old sweetheart and on 2 September – with Wall Street crashing and Nazism rearing its head – I arrived. Where? Above the Marine Supper Bar, Marine Street: owner, Giuseppe Spinetti. He was twenty-three.

He didn't stay Giuseppe for long. In no time it was Joe and so, for that matter, was the Marine Supper Bar. It was always known as Joe's. While we're on names, I should tell you, I was christened Vittorio Georgio Andrea, not that I was ever called that. It was just that my father wasn't familiar with the English versions. For anyone else, it was Victor George Andrew. Victor, after Victor Emmanuel, the Italian king, George after my grandfather, Giorgio, and Andrew after Lily's father, a Scot. Put that together and you have an Italian Welshman who's entitled to wear a kilt – the Buchanan tartan, to be precise.

My first memory – that's even before the drinking and fighting – is of me lying in bed, very early in the morning, listening. What could I hear? At first, boots on the pavement out in the street; miners off the night shift were walking home. As they got closer, there'd be the odd murmur, a stifled cough, a snatch of a popular song, 'Ama Pola, my pretty little poppy . . .' sung very softly because they didn't want to wake anyone up. 'Every time it rains, it rains pennies from heaven . . .' Sometimes I got out of bed and looked out of the window. Below, I could see the glow of cigarettes, the whiteness of scarves and black, black faces – pithead baths hadn't been introduced yet. The air, cold and clear, was like a refreshing drink. The men gulped it down.

Our shop was on the main street, which was dead straight, so when the sun had risen I could look from one end of Cwm to the other. To the south was the Marine Colliery, which gave its name to our street, and to the north were the steelworks. Those two industries were the entire reason for all of us being there. At regular intervals smaller streets cut across Marine Street as the village was built on a grid system, like Manhattan in fact – but I'm jumping ahead. Nowadays it's considered a perfect, untouched example of a Welsh mining village. The best bit when I was a child, though, was the mountains either side. They shot straight up, so straight you'd have thought they were supported from behind like a film set. When it rained they were at their most beautiful. It was as if an invisible hand were drawing a silvery-grey curtain slowly across from the West, so that one side glistened while the other side remained dry. It was a show I never tired of.

The first person to stir in our house was my father. Very early each morning, he wheeled a porter's trolley up to the railway station. There, on the platform, would be a wooden box and inside it, packed in ice, the fish. They had been in the sea only the day before. On to the trolley the box would go and back he'd wheel it to the shop. When I was older, I used to try and help but either I got in the way or the box fell off the trolley. It was hopeless. Behind the shop was an outhouse where Joe set to work. At his back was a vat full of potatoes and a machine for peeling them. In front of him was a marble slab with water constantly running across it. Because of Dad's demand for freshness, there could be no heating and in the winter it was freezing. There, he scrubbed, scaled and cut up huge great cod and hake. Simply by looking, he could work out how many pieces he could get from a fish and how much money he would make. When it came to the actual cutting, each piece was exactly the same width as the next. Sometimes I watched, intrigued by the little beards under the jaws of the cod. Once I tried to pick one up but to my horror, it burped and I dropped it. The fish was full of air. 'Out!' snapped Joe. As far as he was concerned, a place of work was not a place for children. The business was everything to him and he took it very seriously. Even the batter was unique – it had a special ingredient. Don't ask me what it was, I don't know – it was a secret. As for the chips, they were so dry they rustled like autumn leaves. In his way, Dad was an artist. Those really were very good fish and chips. People came from all over to eat them.

The shop opened at noon and closed at three in the afternoon. At seven in the evening, it opened again – and stayed open until the last straggler from the last dance or the last pub or the last club came out and down the length of Marine Street, because there was always one light on, The Marine Supper Bar. No, there were two lights – the other one was the glow of Joe's cigarette as he stood in the doorway looking up and down the street, in case there was one more customer.

Every night, he took the range to pieces and, using piles of newspapers, cleaned it and shined it, so that if you were passing the shop, you wouldn't know it sold fish and chips because it didn't smell. Nor did he stop there. He changed the oil in the fryer regularly and every day scrubbed out the fish boxes before they got sent back. They were so clean I could sit in one and pretend it was a rowing boat. On the sides were labels – Grimsby, Hull, Fleetwood, Milford Haven – an early geography lesson.

Joe, you can see, was adapting himself to his new life. What he didn't like about Italy, he dropped. What he liked about Wales, he took on. It wasn't an intellectual thing, more a question of making himself comfortable. For a start, his Italian accent faded. '*Mamma Mia! Bella Italia!*' Forget it, and I never called him 'Poppa', it was always 'Dad'. In the house, he made no attempt to keep up a home-from-home look. Some Italians in the area sent away to Italy for their furniture – heavy baronial stuff, not the elegant tables and chairs of today – Joe didn't. If anything, his favourite chair was at the British Legion, where he sat in a flat cap, sipping pints of 'flat, warm, thin, Welsh, bitter beer' as Dylan Thomas called it. He played darts there too; so well, in fact, that he was a team member for the *News of the World* darts competition. At billiards he was an ace, at tennis he was a wow and he wasn't bad at draughts either. As for the whole business of being a Roman Catholic, that went right out the window.

Back in Italy, picking mushrooms had been an early morning activity for him; in Wales, it still was. There was a feast up on those hills for anyone who could be bothered, and no one else could. I thought I'd make myself useful and asked him if I could go too. 'This one looks good, Dad,' I said, once I was up there.

'No, poisonous. Throw it away.'

When I was older, I tried again with shooting. This time, it wasn't early morning foraging but a social occasion. Dad was respected in the village, so when he went out looking for rabbits and pheasant, it was often with a member of the local constabulary. 'You'll only get in the way,' fretted Dad and sure enough, I did, despite being a good shot.

A cafe, for an Italian family, was a livelihood. For the Welsh, it was something else. The huge, shining espresso machines pushing steam through freshly ground coffee and frothing up the milk for cappuccinos brought a much needed exoticism to the Valleys, while amongst those little tables and chairs and the sawdust on the floor, there was safety, warmth and friendliness. Even walking past and seeing the windows steamed up with condensation gave me a sense of pleasure and I think it did others too. Men had always had pubs and clubs, now women had somewhere. Cafes added a new touch of civilisation. And how convenient it was that the chapels approved of them. Only temperance beverages were served, you see. Although it was a fish-and-chip shop my father was running, it was all part of the same thing. These businesses were popular and so were the people who ran them.

What was I getting up to in those early years? I couldn't pick up a fish. I couldn't hit a ball with a racquet. I couldn't spot an edible mushroom. I was, in Dad's eyes at least, hopeless. As Lily (that's Mam) didn't have another child for some years, I was stuck on my own most of the time. One good thing came from it, though. Simply by osmosis, I learned to read. What I read didn't matter – advertisements, sauce bottles – you name it, I'd have a go and I got good at it. A useful accomplishment, you'd think, and not one you'd expect to cause controversy. You'd be wrong.

Watch. My father is sitting at tea, slowly reading the headline of the *Daily Express* and I'm next to him.

'Look, our Dad. The Queen Mary's crossed the Atlantic.'

'Who told you that?'

'There it is, in the paper.'

A frisson ran through Dad and then Mam. They looked like cartoon characters who'd touched a live wire. What was that all about? I learned soon enough. My father's tennis serve was devastating, he could pot black and score 'One hundred and eighty!' but when it came to reading, he struggled. English was his second language and in Italy he'd been illiterate. I'd accidentally touched a tender spot. His frisson was the shock of realising that I was good at something but worse, it was something he was no good at and he didn't like it. Instead of being an accomplishment to be applauded, reading was a threat. My mother's frisson was quite another matter. She was applauding like mad – inwardly, that is. Something wasn't right between her and Dad. Now, in her bright little boy, she could see a weapon for getting back at her husband. What wasn't right between her and Joe? I didn't know, not yet, anyway.

My cousin Elwyn was completely unaware of any inside-the-family conflict. Aged nine, he was far too busy being an entrepreneur and my ability was a nice little sideline. Holding my hand, he led me out into the street and bet children a halfpenny that I could read. 'He's not in school yet,' they said.

'Ask him,' said Elwyn, having been careful to take their bets first. A child pointed at a shop sign.

'Star Supply Stores,' I said.

'Someone told you,' grumbled the six-year-old punter, anxious not to part with his pocket money. 'What's that?' he said, choosing a test of his own.

'The Ebbw Vale and District Wholesale Cooperative Society.' Collapse of stout party? You might think so, but children are not reasonable.

'And that?'

'Jones's Omnibus Company.'

'No, it's not.'

'Yes, it is.'

'No, it's Joneseses' Omnibus Company.'

Still, as there wasn't much going on in my outside world, I kept on reading. The teachers at the Cwmyrdderch Infants School thought I was so good they put me to work as soon as I started there. While the register was taken, I read to the other children. If I didn't read, I made up stories. That was fine until the others settled down to their own books and then it was all 'Aa, Ba, Ca, Da'. What was the matter with them?

I can't say there was a teacher at Cwmyrdderch who inspired me but there was one who was awe-inspiring – the headmistress, Mrs McBeath. Into the school she swept each morning, her long black dress flowing, her hat pinned firmly to the bun on top of her head and her brolly announcing to the world that she meant business. She was a true Edwardian and looked like Margaret Dumont from the Marx Brothers films. As she worked mostly in her study, she was a distant, magisterial figure. She wasn't daunting, though. She was kind. Mrs McBeath was the first in a long list of characters, big personalities, who were to intrigue and entertain me in the years to come.

Newcombe Terrace was where she lived, up the valley and above the bridge. 'Above the bridge': three simple words, but if you understand their implication, you know how world wars are started.

'You know that Roberts girl?'

'What Roberts girl?'

'You know, the Robertses from Cendl Terrace. She's going out with that Jenkins boy.'

'What? From below the bridge? Never? Oh my God.'

Snobbery, envy, resentment were all in those three words. You see, not only did Mrs McBeath live above the bridge but so did Doctor Sullivan and Mr Thomas the Manse, the Presbyterian Minister. You could also find the police station and the C. of E. church. Authority, in other words, and it was posh. The sun shone more brightly on the houses up there and for longer too, the sunniest spot being the cemetery. But then this was the old village, its main buildings established long before the mines. There was sense in its position. The grid system down in the valley was ruthless practicality. Bosses, wanting their workers near the job and giving not a thought to light, had squashed the greatest number of people into the place with the least amount of sun. My father saw the absurdity of this, so after the shop had been doing well for a while, he rented a house owned by Mrs McBeath and that's where we went to live when I was five. It wasn't only Newcombe Terrace's pleasant position, I have to say, that inspired Dad to make the move. He wanted the family well clear of the business too. A free hand was what he needed and we got in the way. If he wanted to play cards in the back during slack times or nip out to the British Legion for a pint, then he could and nobody'd be watching.

He was doing his best, my father, you can see that. I was always well dressed. There was always food on the table and it was good. When I was two, Dad took Mam to Italy and, while he worked in the fields, she stayed behind at the farm and learned to cook in the style of the north. That's not the tomatoey, garlicky cooking of the Mediterranean, it's subtler. Garlic is used but the flavour is absorbed slowly so the result is gentle. Here was an example of preserving in Wales an Italian tradition that you really wouldn't want to lose. Another was drink. We didn't have beer in the house but wine, Chianti Ruffino, the kind that comes in a flask covered with wicker.

Dad used to put a few drops in water for me. That way, drink was never a problem for me in later life. Obviously, the Chianti was more interesting by itself but that was yet to come.

We even had a car, a Sunbeam Talbot with a dicky seat at the back, and there were only two other cars in the whole village. One belonged to the mayor, the other to the doctor. Dad was doing his best, as I said. Unfortunately, there was this thing between him and Lily that wasn't right.

Caricature Italian, Dad was not. He didn't wave his hands about, chatter irked him and displays of emotion were frowned on. If I wanted something badly, I had to keep it to myself. Show Dad I was keen on something and I wouldn't get it. Work was not to be fun, no jokes, no music. It had to be done in deadly earnest. And that thing between him and Mam? It showed itself in a chill or a silence. I could spot it only too easily but I couldn't explain it and nor could I ask anyone. Mam was so young she was more like a sister than a mother. For her, the effort of standing up to a man who could not or would not communicate his tough upbringing in a far away country was beyond her. I had no ally. This made me keep very quiet, fearful of expressing an opinion. Each morning, I lay curled up in bed with an ache in my stomach that wouldn't go until Dad left the house for work.

Even the car, which should have been fun, became for me an object of hatred. Like any other family, on a sunny day we'd go for a drive but once I'd climbed in, there was to be no mucking about. I had to sit bolt upright and say nothing. Any excitement about cows and sheep was out. Most children look forward to day trips but I didn't.

It was on one of those drives that the good and the bad came together. By then I had a brother, Mario. A little friend for Victor, you might have thought. Not really, he was too little. Between him and me was a gap of five years: what he meant was sticky fingers on my books. Still, he too had to sit up straight in the Hillman Minx, BWO 268, the car we had by then. Mam, fox tippet draped elegantly over her shoulders, the claws hanging down, sat stiffly next to Dad. She loved beautiful clothes but they couldn't break yet another cold silence. Mario and I were sitting in the back. We stopped. At the end of a long dusty drive was a derelict house. I ran up to it. Inside there were no walls and no floors. Instead there was a carpet of pale-green grass and bluebells. I picked as many bluebells as I could and carried them back as a present. Whatever was annoying my father (and still I didn't know what it was) made him snap. He grabbed the bluebells and threw them on the road. 'Get back in the car!' Mario jumped in. I, for once, did not accept what had happened. I'd had it with the power structure imposed by parents. I wouldn't get back into that car until I had picked up every single, and, by then, wilting, bluebell. When I had, I threw them into a stream. The water gushed blue. It was almost as if my childhood was being carried away. This was a desperate gesture but it was a fight for survival and, at least, I had made a decision. I climbed back into the car and, on the journey home, my eyes bored into the backs of my parents' heads. As for Mario, his battle was yet to come. Why those chilly silences? Years would have to pass before I found out.

People give you grief. The countryside round Cwm never did. I loved it, still do. Behind our house was a mountain. That's where I was happiest. Whenever I could, I ran up and across the top, shirt tail flying, past sheep huddled against stone walls, leaping from tussock to tussock like a mountain goat. With tomato sandwiches and a bottle of pop to keep me going, I walked for miles and miles. The idea of inviting someone to come with me never entered my head, I wasn't used to it. There on the top I sat for hours, the wind whipping round my head, looking all the way along to Ebbw Vale and the great, smoking steelworks. A tiny train went up the valley. A little bus snaked round a hill. A Dinky toy car came over the bridge. It was the best train set in the world. Hamleys? Forget it. 'Victor! Victor!' Far, far away, it was Mam and, for a little while, far, far away is where she stayed.

On Saturday nights the shop would get so busy my mother had to help out. I'd be alone in the house then listening to *Saturday Night Theatre* on the radio, my favourite programme. That's not to say I was totally sold on radio. *Children's Hour* meant nothing to me: 'Now come along, is there marmalade yet for tea? Nanny's coming. Oh look, a ginger pussyket!' Those people and their Lord Reith English were from another world. As for *Awr y Plant*, that was even more distant. *Awr y Plant* was *Children's Hour* in Welsh but I didn't speak Welsh and, for that matter, most of Cwm didn't either. So I had a choice of two languages and didn't understand either of them. It was most frustrating.

Saturday Night Theatre was different. You just needed a story that gripped and one evening a play by Emlyn Williams *Trespass,* really did. A medium conjures up a dead person, 'Piccola!' and this dead person comes up the path and knocks on the door, 'Boom, boom, boom'. All the while, the medium is still going, 'Piccolaaa'. I was terrified – and then the light went out. No shilling in the meter! I couldn't open the cupboard to get the shilling because I couldn't move. Worse, the fire was going down and I could not bring myself to go to the back of the scullery to fetch coal. I sat there and sat there in the darkness until Mam and Dad came home. Emlyn Williams, when I told him decades later, regarded this as highly satisfactory.

I didn't always just listen to the radio. Sometimes I *was* it. A cupboard in the kitchen became my studio, a tea strainer my microphone, and the gauze-covered holes that let air in and out of the cupboard my dials. Twiddling away, I broadcast to the world. It had to be the world. There wasn't anyone else.

You might think our little family was a bit isolated, what with Dad having no relatives nearby and Mam being so young and looking on me as little more than a doll. Nevertheless, our Dad was a popular man in the village and Mam at least had plenty of relatives. I wasn't trapped, not quite.

After we made the move above the bridge, the rooms over the Marine Supper Bar were going a-begging. Uncle Bill, a steelworker – either coal or steel, see what I mean – and his wife, Auntie Min, moved in along with their two daughters, Megan and Ceinwyn, and their three sons, Billy, Elwyn and John. That's Elwyn, the entrepreneur. I loved the home they made of the old place and I was always popping in and out. It wasn't posh but it was magical, a 'Peter Pan' house where anything was possible. A family smell came from it and inside there was cosiness and warmth. Every afternoon, as I ran down the road from our house, I anticipated a squeal of happiness and nonsense, jokes and stories – ghost stories. Megan told those. Together, we were a gang. I felt freer there.

It was cousin Megan who created that atmosphere, utterly Welsh but not holy. Actually, to be fair, nobody else in the family bothered much about religion either. I was never filled with fiery Welsh guilt, thank God. On Whit Mondays, the chapels – that's the Presbyterians, the Baptists, the Spiritualists and all the other denominations – would unite and march down Marine Street, one after the other, arms linked, singing, 'Guide Me, Oh Thou Great Redeemer . . .' Behind all this might came a tiny Catholic contingent.

Where was my family? Upstairs, dressed in the smartest Whitsun clothes, waving from the window. We were never in the street marching. However, when our MP, Aneurin Bevan, came to talk, it was another matter. We all went to that. The Workmen's Institute would be so packed, I'd be sitting on a shelf with my legs dangling down. On the stage were the local councillors and there, jammed in together, we'd wait, and wait, an hour, two hours. Nye was invariably late. When he came, everyone cheered of course, and if anyone dared to question him, he'd point a finger and say in his squeaky voice, 'That's Tory thinking!' Thus, any debate was effectively stifled, which allowed him to say five minutes later, 'And I've got to get to Monmouth to talk to those Tory vermin.' 'Yerr!' we'd all shout and he'd be gone.

Did I get the chance to do anything ordinary like other children? Well, Saturday mornings were when, all over the country, children went to the Saturday matinee at the local cinema. Our local was the Coliseum. Ten o'clock the programme started, but where was I? Standing behind my father, waiting, as he trimmed his moustache. It was no use jumping up and down, getting excited. That was fatal. Five minutes would go by: 'Cartoon finished,' I'd think. Another five minutes would crawl past: 'I've probably missed Laurel and Hardy now.' A sound behind me made things worse. Kids were rattling at the door and shouting, 'Victor-o!'

'Sh!' I'd say, 'Go away.'

'What is it?' asked my father.

'Saturday morning pictures, our Dad.'

'Bloody kids,' he'd say. 'At your age I was in the fields working.' Slowly, he'd fish some coins out of his pocket and from them he'd extract the precise number for the cinema ticket and throw them to the floor. I'd pick them up and run as fast as I could to see whatever was left of the programme. As I watched the film stars and the comedians doing their stuff on the screen, I didn't cheer myself up by thinking, 'I'm going to do that,' I just stared and thought, 'I'll know you.'

This money thing was the same at Christmas. It was only at half past five on Christmas Eve that Dad peeled off some notes from a fat wad so that we could buy presents. As the shops closed at six, we had to move fast. Through the snow we slipped and slid, a snow that glistened but was covered in black dust and ran with red oxide from the steelworks when you made a snowball. Come the thaw, the gutters ran red: 'The rape of the Valleys' as Gwyn Thomas said. White snow I didn't see until I was in Connecticut twenty years later.

It was no use any of us planning what presents we were going to buy because we were never sure if we'd get any money at all. I did know when Christmas was coming, though, because in the window of Cammerman's the fruit shop, I could see tangerines, walnuts, little round boxes with slices of preserved lemon and orange in them and dates that came with a wooden fork. When I got to London and saw that you could buy those all the year round, I was astonished.

All we bought were little extras because the basics were already there. We always had good Christmas cooking, *pasta con brodo* to start with, a chicken broth with tiny pasta stars in, *stelle* in Italian, but then with the lids bouncing up and down on the saucepans, Mam would call out: 'Everything's made. Where's yer father?' He was down the Lucania Billiard Hall. The owner was a friend and he'd opened it secretly. It was after all, Dad's day off. I went down and stood outside listening to the click, click of the billiard balls. I knocked.

'Dad, it's Christmas.'

'Wait a minute. No, come on in.' Just the two of them were there, the owner and Dad, under the one light, Dad chalking his cue. I can smell the chalk now. As a bribe, I was given a choc-ice while they carried on playing. Dad knew choc-ice was my favourite but it quite spoiled my Christmas dinner. When that dinner was over and we were sitting around dozing, I opened one eye. Dad wasn't there and nor was the box that contained his personal billiard cue. He was back down the Lucania Billiard Hall.

By saying: 'At your age I was working in the fields.' Dad had, at least, explained himself and again, with the Christmas money, we knew the reason for his behaviour. In Italy for Christmas he'd just got a lump of coal. Most of the time, though, he never explained himself, so whenever anything bad happened to do with that thing between him and Mam it was made worse by it staying a mystery. Take this, for example – I had a cousin, Ivor, a very handsome chap, rather like his namesake Ivor Novello. He came round to stay and help out in the shop. Two days before Christmas, he showed me the present he had bought me. It was a *Film Fun Annual* with Laurel and Hardy cartoons in it, exactly what I wanted. I couldn't wait for the big Day but on the morning of Christmas Eve, when I got up, Ivor wasn't there. No explanation, he was simply not there. On Christmas Day I rummaged around among the parcels and, search as I might, I couldn't find the *Film Fun Annual*. 'He's gone and taken the book with him,' I thought. 'He was so nice too. It doesn't seem like him.' Nor was it. If I'd wanted an answer then and there, I should have asked my father. At that age, though, I'd have only got a cuff round the ear. Still, it would have been a clue.

The days of Mrs McBeath and telling stories to the class came to an end, as they had to. Studying got dryer and dustier. Instead of popping round the corner to the Infants' school, I now had to walk right down to the other end of Marine Street to the big school, Dyffryn. It sat by the river, which stank of the shit-coloured effluence that came from the steelworks. On the other side, piled up as high as you could see, was a huge tip of black, oily slag. It was exactly like Aberfan, where in 1966 a slag heap slid and crushed children in a school. Inside, the place was bare, the teaching basic and bullying started to creep into my daily life. That, however, is part of a new story, nothing to do with fish and chips and mysterious silences.

As kicking a ball around the yard was not my idea of fun and I realised I wasn't much of a joiner anyway, my interests not being the same as the other boys' – boys and girls were separated now – I learned to keep myself to myself. One of the teachers was better than the others, though; D T Davies, known as 'Corky' on account of his funny leg that he had got from the First World War. Here was that teacher who inspires: he taught English and took an interest in me, especially in what I read.

And so I passed the time at Dyffryn, keeping myself amused, one way or another. If it wasn't reading, it was making Christmas cards; drawing the whole school on a giant piece of nicked wrapping paper or making the village of Cwm out of shoeboxes. The paste for that came from the corner shop, another place I loved simply because I could smell reading matter.

Although Dad hardly ever went to church, as I said, some of that 'Do as I say, not what I do,' eventually got to him. He decided I ought to have religious instruction – what a nuisance. The school was even further away than Dyffryn. That meant getting up early, which I hated, and travelling on a bus to Ebbw Vale. The first thing the priest did was give us a lecture on the evils of masturbation. 'If you masturbate, you fling your seed in the face of the Holy Ghost,' he intoned. I burst out laughing, imagining the Holy Ghost going 'Not again!' as all these people ejaculated round the world. The priest heard me, caned me on both hands and sent me home. My mother was blackleading the grate when I got back, or Zeeboing as she would say, after the product she was using. 'You're home early,' she said, looking round.

'Yes, our Mam,' I said, still blowing on my fingers. 'The priest told us if you masturbate, you're flinging your seed in the face of the Holy Ghost.'

'He didn't say that, did he?' said Mam. 'Oh, don't go there no more!' And that was the end of my Catholic upbringing.

So there we were, not particularly Italian, not particularly Welsh, just us. However, 'Bullying' and 'A new story' I said when I was talking about Dyffryn. Now's the time to tell that story, which starts on a nice sunny day in the late 1930s with two people, a young man and a young woman, talking to my father.

2

But am *I* Italian?

The pair were from Cardiff – Welsh, I think. Dad called me in and said, 'These people would like to know, and I'm all for it, if you want to learn Italian.'

'Yes, our Dad,' I said without thinking.

'Good,' he went on. 'Now, Saturday morning up at –' Saturday morning? Ugh! I'd miss the pictures. Too late, I'd let myself in for it. Dad bought me a satchel – real leather, not cardboard, and I can still smell the inside of it – a bottle of ink, and a pen and an exercise book. On to that bus I had to climb, and sit there all the way up to Ebbw Vale again, this time to Carini's Chip Shop. Above the shop, there was a big room with a high ceiling. It was full of that heavy baronial furniture my father hadn't bothered with. I looked around. Children from the other Italian families in the area stared back at me. I hardly knew them. I knew of them but we, my family, hadn't – put it this way – it had never occurred to us that we might occasionally pop round. In any case, each family had its business to run and there was little time to socialise. The lady teacher quietened us down: 'As today is the first day, we won't take the register. We'll get to know each other. We can take the register next Saturday.' Nothing exceptional there, or so I thought. The teacher, beaming round the room, carried on, 'I have some exciting news. The best at their lessons will be taken on a free trip to Italy to meet our beloved Duce.'

Back at home, Dad asked, 'What did you learn?' and I repeated,

'The best at lessons will be taken to Italy to meet our beloved Duce, our Dad.'

'You're not going there again. That's the end of it,' he said. I was so pleased. It didn't mean anything to me about Il Duce. All I knew was that my Saturdays were free again, so it would be back to picking up coins before rushing to the pictures.

At what point in my childhood the following scene took place, I can't tell you. What I can say is that it was vivid and all on its own. I was playing out in the 'backs' behind the chip shop one morning when round the corner came this vision in grey. Up the 'backs' he walked, between the rows of houses – my father's brother Francesco, now Frank. When he went off, leaving my father in Cwm, it wasn't only London he went to. He travelled all over the place doing all sorts of colourful jobs. Handsome, debonair, an entrepreneur and a gambler, his attitude to life was not like his brother's. Work wasn't the be all and end all of everything. It didn't have to be a slog; it could be fun. His appearance alone gave you a clue. It was stylish; that meant impeccable pearl-grey suits, spats, homburgs and silk ties with tiepins. I liked him immensely and was thrilled he'd come. At the time of this visit he had a shop in Treharris, an hour away, and it was from there he'd travelled to see his brother. He went into the back of the shop and sat down. I sat on the step outside and listened.

'There's going to be a war, Joe. You want to get naturalised.'

'Don't be ridiculous,' said Dad.

'I tell you, I'm warning you,' said Uncle Frank. 'There is going to be a war and you should get naturalised.' His voice dropped and all I heard was 'Mussolini'.

'Come on,' said Dad, 'I was born an Italian. I'll die an Italian.'

'No!' said Uncle Frank, 'You get naturalised, I'm warning you,' and off he went to get naturalised. When Italy entered the Second World War, above his shop was a sign: 'Frank Spinetti, British', and painted either side was a Union Jack.

And my father? As I said, I can't place Uncle Frank's visit in time, so before I get on to the war I have to drop in something. Lily's mother, having lost her husband, came to live with us and she wasn't well.

Now the Second World War: I was at Dyffryn when it started, not aware of being Italian, just part of the community. That is until the middle of one night, when I was woken by the sound of scuffling and whispering outside my room. I got up and opened the door in time to see my father's head going down the stairs. With him were two policemen. At the top of the stairs stood Mam.

'What are you doing?' she shouted.

'He's an alien,' answered one of the policemen.

'He's not an alien,' cried Mam, 'He's my husband!' Dad wasn't allowed to take an overcoat or a toothbrush or anything. And to think, a few days before, he'd been out shooting rabbits with one of those policemen. They'd been great friends.

I didn't know what was happening. Mam was crying and she wouldn't stop. I ran into school the next day, 'Derry,' I gasped to the first boy I saw, 'The police took our Dad away last night.'

'Fuck off, you Italian bastard!' he said.

A police inspector from Abertillery came to the house. He sat at the kitchen table. Mam, her mother, Mario and me stood in front of him. It was like that painting, *When did you last see your father?* On the table was a bunch of keys, they were for the shop and the house. The inspector drummed his fingers. 'We can throw you bastards out tomorrow,' he said, ' . . . bombing us.' Lily was not only frightened, she was pregnant again, just about to give birth in fact, and my grandmother had stomach cancer. It seemed to me that life and death was in that house and all of it weighing down on me because, as the eldest, I was going to have to be responsible. By the time the inspector left, he had stripped us of the radio, my father's shotgun and the business. From now on, the fish-and-chip shop was out of bounds. My mother couldn't make a living. A curfew was put on her and she was not to travel more than three miles without police permission. Why had the radio gone? We might be spies adapting it to transmit messages to the enemy.

Overnight, ethnicity was thrust upon us. Stan Amos, one of the teachers at Dyffryn, wouldn't let me in the classroom. I had to sit outside. Boys yelled at me, 'Your father do eat worms.' Women walked out of the Star India and China Supplies Store when Mam went to get her rations, women who had been at school with her. They stood out in the rain until she was served because she'd married an Italian. Mam may have been at home but she was on the front line. Thank goodness Auntie Min and her daughter, Megan, were still living behind Dad's shop. No law prevented them from running the business. They took it over, worked it and, from the back door, slipped Mam potatoes, a bit of fish and some money for the housekeeping. Sometimes I went too and one day, as so often happens while one is fretting about one problem, I began to find the answer to another. Auntie Min's son, Billy, was sitting at the kitchen table reading an annual, a *Film Fun Annual*. 'That's mine,' I said.

'What do you mean?' said Billy.

'Where did you find it?' I asked.

'Behind the safe. Mam moved it to clean.'

'Look,' I said, turning back the pages scalloped now by the nibbling of rats: 'To Victor, From Cousin Ivor. Merry Christmas.' So he hadn't taken it with him and I had a very good idea who'd thrown it behind the safe in one of his rages.

For all Derry, at school, calling me an Italian bastard I felt the need to join things. I tried the Boys' Brigade. They wouldn't have me. I tried the Ambulance Brigade. They wouldn't have me either. The Boy Scouts only took me because they had to. 'Irrespective of creed, colour and religion' was their rule. They were nice enough, I suppose, but when they turned me upside down and used me as a sweeping brush, I knew I'd outstayed my welcome.

After dark one evening, me and my cousin Billy were running through the street when Sergeant Underhill stopped us, 'Young Spinetti, what have you got there?' In my hand was a roll of film. That was enough for the sergeant to take me down to the station. Even though the film was already exposed, I had to wait until it was developed.

Walking down the street in the daytime was hazardous too. Attacks could come either as words or worse. I was drifting past the Drill Hall at the bottom of Newcombe Terrace – sadly remembering the jolly murder mysteries that I and other children had once acted out in the Hall's grand archway entrance – when I heard a neighbour, Mrs Moss, shout to her son, Glenville. He was on the green sward opposite, playing bat and ball. 'Bring that ball into the house!' she went and, without protest, in he ran; the front door slammed. So that's how things were. Next came action. On my way home one afternoon, I was attacked. Two brothers, close neighbours, jumped out from behind a privet hedge. A brick clubbed me on the side of the head. Blood dripped from my ear. I staggered into the house where Mam told me that it was most important to stand up to bullies. 'You go and tell them!' she said. I went and stood in the doorway shaking my fist, which I kept safely behind my back. I'm still deaf in that ear.

When things got really rough, children waited to get me on my way home from school; I had to be inventive. 'Corky' Davies, the English master, was my best hope. 'Wait for me,' he'd say as he scribbled the next day's lesson on the blackboard. Then up the village we'd walk, with me chatting away, usually about my favourite books.

And where was my father? What happened to him after he was bundled out of the house? He was interned on the Isle of Man. Together with Scots Italians and other Welsh Italians, all with Scots and Welsh accents, he was at first taken to the great railway yards at Crewe Station. There, nothing was given out in the way of food, while railway tracks were the only beds. If a bomb had dropped, who'd have cared? These men were aliens and Churchill had made his feelings about those pretty clear. 'Collar the lot,' he ordered and collared they were, under Ruling 18b. That's the one that got Oswald Mosley, the fascist. You can imagine what it must have felt like to be lumped together with him.

The Isle of Man itself was another matter. Internees were billeted in islanders' houses, some of which were rather shabby. In no time, the decorators among them had done them up, moulded the ceilings even – that is, after all, an Italian speciality. Daily activities included swimming and in the evenings there were concerts. The Amadeus Quartet was formed on the Isle of Man. Grub was positively smashing because some of the internees were chefs from London hotels, like the Savoy, the Ritz and Claridges. Out of standard rations they could make the most amazing dishes. The British soldiers guarding the aliens, Home Guard types, had to make do with chips and pint pots of tea.

We didn't know any of this at home and, as life was uncertain not to say gloomy, the idea of a birthday party came up. I'd never had one before, so the prospect was especially exciting. Invitations were sent out and preparations were made. On the day, there I was sitting in the front room surrounded by trifles and cakes covered in hundreds and thousands, waiting. No one came. Actually, I said that because it makes a good picture: one person did turn up, a boy called Gurnos Graydon. At home he never had anything decent to eat because his sister-in-law, who did the cooking, was too busy to do it properly. So, whenever there were any leftovers in our house, say a potato tart Mam had put too much garlic in, Gurnos would eat it up quite happily. At least one boy had a nice time on that birthday afternoon. He must have done because he still drops round today. Gurnos is my oldest friend.

Ten months after his arrest, our Dad came back. 'Corky' Davies and one or two others, like the insurance man, had written letters saying that Joe should be freed. They'd explained that his heart was in Wales, that he hadn't gone back to Italy and that he couldn't now anyway as he hadn't done his national service and would have been shot. Local councillors wrote to the authorities, his papers were looked through and – do you remember the register at my one and only Italian class, the register that wasn't taken? It was taken the following week and, at the outbreak of war, it got looked at and the fathers of the children who were on it were sent to Australia or Canada and had to stay there until the end of hostilities. They were the lucky ones. Some were put on the ship, *Arandora Star*, which sank. The Spinetti name did not appear on the class list and that counted in Joe's favour.

Before Dad's return came the letter. Mam tore at the envelope excitedly and – how she did it I don't know – leapt, 'Wheee . . .!' backwards over the settee. When Dad came in I was amazed. He'd put on weight and had a tan. 'What was it like, our Dad?' I asked.

'Well, I didn't have you bloody kids around me. It was the best bloody holiday I've ever had in my life!'

The house in Newcombe Terrace didn't please Dad anymore, even if it did get the sunshine. That night of being bundled out of it by the police gave the place a bad feeling. Anyway, it was haunted. Something about the passage that went from the front door to the back had always made me run right through and not stop when I got home from school each day. The previous tenant, I found out later, had hanged himself from the banister. In Crosscombe Terrace (back below the bridge, nearer the business but still away from it), two houses were going for the price of one. It made good financial sense, so Dad snapped them up. Now he had a cellar where he could do carpentry and a garden for growing vegetables and flowers, which he adored, particularly carnations and dahlias. He adored them so much he put them in flower boxes as well and, sprinkled them, only too regularly, with liquid manure. It smelt revolting.

Our new neighbours, the Worthings, were both teachers and just as well. Dad's seething and boiling that began all those years before with the *Daily Express* and the Queen Mary erupted into a big row and he burnt my books, saying, 'Only girls read!' His copy of the *Fish Friers' Annual* and my mother's knitting patterns, I noticed, remained intact. So, for that matter, did *Gone with the Wind*, but that was hidden in a drawer anyway because it was a dirty book. I took to going next door.

The Worthings' front room was full of books, George Bernard Shaw I remember in particular. Hours I sat there, so absorbed I heard not a thing, or pretended not to. In fact, there was the muffled sound of Mam and Dad quarrelling.

For all that, nice things did occur and perhaps it's time to tell of one now, even if it happened a few years earlier. This is my favourite because it also has a bearing on my future.

Although Dad took everything he did very seriously, there was a jaunt that even he enjoyed, a trip to London. We made quite a few over the years but this is the important one. Little Mario and I were asleep when Dad came into the room and woke us up. It was pitch dark, early on a Sunday morning. Pestering him with questions or getting excited was no use: if we'd done that, Dad would have called the whole thing off. Meekly we did as we were told and got into the car. Off Dad drove and there we all sat, Mam, Mario and me, as usual, in dead silence. 'I Spy . . .' was out of the question because it would have put Dad off his driving. Anyway, there was nothing to see. I kept myself content with anticipation. Mam had other things on her mind, like her husband's driving. 'Watch that building!' she would squeal or 'Mind that church!' as Dad sped on, imagining himself to be a racing driver, which is what he would have liked to have been if he hadn't had a fish-and-chip shop to run.

We didn't crash. Five and a half hours later – there were no motorways in those days – the car pulled up in Pimlico. We'd come to visit Uncle Bill and Auntie Toni. That's the Uncle Bill who took my father in as a boy. Living with Bill now in Pimlico was his mother who had, all those years before, done our Dad's washing and cooked meals for him. In other words, Bill and his mother were people our Dad was fond of, on the quiet. I liked them too but there was one person in that household I was especially thrilled to see – Bill's father, Harry Watson, my grandfather.

Harry was perhaps the only bookmaker ever who didn't succeed. What happened was, his regular punters evolved a scam. When he wasn't looking, they moved the minute hand of his clock back five minutes, nipped next door to get the results, then nipped back and placed their bets. Not surprisingly, he went bust. Nevertheless, before that he had a carriage and pair, a nanny for the children and the fare to Paris, where he went racing at Longchamps. When not doing that, he brought people back for supper parties, mostly the Edwardian theatre set. Belle Elmore was one of his guests: she was the music–hall singer who got murdered by her husband, Hawley Harvey Crippen.

For a wide-eyed boy, this was all good stuff but I especially liked Harry when he put on his gold pince-nez and read to me. The book didn't matter. The point was, he was the only person in the family to do it.

I'd never been to a theatre in Wales. On that trip to London, Harry took me for the first time. We sat in the gods of the Shepherd's Bush Empire and looked down at Harry Tate Jr topping the bill in a bright, bouncing variety show. He was doing his Car Sketch. 'Twang! Oops! Crash! Tinkle! Oink! Urga, urga!' Back in Pimlico, I was so excited by all that knockabout I could hardly eat the food my grandmother had cooked, even though it was really good. She could make a soup out of a wire coat hanger.

After we'd eaten, my father announced that it was time to drive home. The fairy tale was over. The clock was striking twelve. Still, we'd been expecting that. What we didn't expect was our Dad saying that our Mam, Mario and me could stay on. Wow, that really was the icing on the cake, but then I began to think, 'If all of us stay on, Dad will have to drive home alone.' It was no use. Someone had to keep him company and that someone would have to be me. The odd thing is that after he'd been driving a while and I'd been sitting in silence, a feeling came over me that I was doing the right thing.

Hours later, our Dad stopped the car and got out. I screwed up my eyes to see where we were. Nowhere, by the looks of it. The last town we'd been through was Gloucester and we certainly weren't there anymore. I got out. Dad was standing a few feet away, facing in the direction we'd come. As my eyes grew accustomed to the dark, I made out that we were on the brow of a hill and that it was out across the valley, towards the other hills that Dad was looking. A couple of birds twittered in a friendly but pointless way. There was nothing for them to see. Nevertheless, I was beginning to relish the mystery, and, as it turned out, the birds knew what they were talking about. They were heralding the sunrise. And it became a moment of joy, father and son, on the brow of a hill, waiting. There was a closeness but, I'm afraid, even then, not quite enough for me to take his hand.

As soon as the sun had warmed up the landscape and made it cheerful, we climbed back into the car and Dad drove down the hill to a cafe, where he ordered cups of tea and, for me, a half tin of Jacobs marshmallows, biscuit on the bottom, coconut on top. He knew I loved them and, since I can't resist temptation, I scoffed the lot and before the day was out was sick.

Driving into Cwm, Dad said, 'You'd better stay with your Auntie Min tonight.' Magical news. I loved staying at Auntie Min's. The point was, Dad would be working late in the shop that night and me alone, up above the bridge, was not a good idea. So, after a jolly day re-enacting Harry Tate's Car Sketch for my cousins Megan and Billy, I went up to bed in their room. But I couldn't sleep a wink. The picture of Dad locking the shop in the early hours of the morning and walking by himself up to the cold, dark house above the bridge would not leave my brain. I clambered over my sleeping cousins, tiptoed down the stairs, lifted the latch of the back door and let myself out. When Dad locked the shop in reality, I was standing there outside. He took my hand and we walked, in silence, up over the bridge together.

Obviously that outing to the Shepherd's Bush Empire has stayed with me, otherwise I wouldn't be remembering it now. Less obvious is that, yet again, no little voice said, 'I'll do that.' Nothing so logical. I may have been bursting with excitement but I hadn't a clue what to do with it. A link between Harry Tate's clowning on stage and me clowning in class didn't occur to me. I was brought up to please and make myself useful. Priest, teacher, doctor – those were the jobs I thought I ought to be looking forward to. Fancying myself a rather serious, solemn sort of chap, I even liked the idea. Whether I had any aptitude for any of those jobs didn't really come into it. The picture was good, that was all.

If you showed signs of being reasonably bright in those days, you took what was known as the Local County School Exam and if you passed, you went, rather obviously, to the County School. My name was down for that exam but when the time came for taking it, well . . .

One hot summer afternoon when I was about eleven, my cousins Elwyn, Megan, Billy and I were scrambling up the mountain behind the house. Berries were everywhere, my favourite, wimberries. I fainted. That was odd because I had never fainted before. When I came round, my cousins propped me up between them and together we lurched back to the house. It wasn't the wimberries, not really. If it had been, I would have soon felt better. I didn't and Doctor Sullivan had to be summoned. He diagnosed jaundice, or 'Yellow Jaundice' as people used to call it. That meant I had to lie for days in a darkened room. Mam, thinking she knew best, brought me tripe cooked in milk but I couldn't touch it. Come the day of the exam, I was absent and if you didn't turn up, you didn't get a second chance. That seemed to be that.

It wasn't. Corky Davies came round to the house and spoke to my father, 'You waste Victor here. He must be sent away for further education.' How would Dad react, though? Well it has to be remembered this was shortly after his return from the Isle of Man, a happy event engineered by 'Corky'. Therefore, it was only fair that he should at least listen. Soon after that the insurance man appeared. He too had helped get Dad back and it was he who had set up the penny-a-week health insurance scheme that had paid for me to have my tonsils out. Dad had good reason not only to listen to him but to like him too. 'You really should send Victor away,' said the insurance man, fiddling, as usual, with his bow tie. 'I've heard that Monmouth is a good school.'

A few mornings later Dad told me to get into the car, I didn't know why. We drove down towards Newport and cut across eastwards, travelling on until we reached the rolling hills of the Wye Valley. Their graciousness appealed to me at once. Monmouth, a market town, fitted in nicely, while Monmouth School was old and cloistery. In fact, Mr Elstob, the headmaster, interviewed me in a room that was off a cloister. I looked out of the window and thought, '*Greyfriars Bobby!*' which was odd because I'd never been anywhere near Edinburgh but then books can do that for you. What could all that history tell me? It could tell me that there was an ambiguity about Monmouth. Sometimes it was Welsh and sometimes it was English. That hadn't done it any harm, though. Perhaps I could like it there. Anyway, I was in and, would you believe it, Dad was going to pay.

Back at home, he really got into the spirit of things. A sucker for door-to-door salesmen anyway, he went and bought a complete set of the *Children's Encyclopaedia*. Extraordinary – after all that fuss over books, but I wasn't complaining. They were a real cheer up. As we drove to the school for my first term, and aged thirteen now, my mind started to whir. 'Italian bastard', that had stung. I didn't know Italy. Dad had rarely spoken of it. His accent was Welsh. The feeling of being punished for something I hadn't done had made me resentful. In Monmouth, though, nobody knew anything about me. I didn't need to be this frightened Thing. I could be someone quite new, maybe a new frightened Thing.

3

Contrasts

A confident schoolboy scorns his uniform. His tie is loose, his shirt tail out, his cap either on at the wrong angle or lost altogether. I wish I'd been like that. At Dyffryn, my tie had been done up, my shirt tail tucked in and I'd worn my cap all the time. Anxiety, I suppose. I had to be perfect. It was part of this 'keep your head down, don't give offence' thing, a feeling that went right back to the night when my father was dragged downstairs by the police. In that moment I was suddenly flung to the frontier with my passport not quite in order, and that feeling has remained with me for the rest of my life.

For Monmouth I had a completely new uniform. It was grey from top to toe and had to be ordered specially from Harrods. Cash's name tapes were stitched to every single item. None of it put me off. It was the start of finding the new identity I was seeking.

As another part of the anxiety thing – having to outwit the boys at Dyffryn, fearing a clip round the ear at home – I had formed no opinions and kept shtum. What would happen now? The first stiff days passed, the days when you learn the school, rather than the lesson. Nobody was calling me 'Spaghetti'. The masters hadn't mentioned enemy aliens and the prefects were not the bullying kind. Some of the anxiety eased and when our music master said, 'In my *Oxford Dictionary* it tells me that the spinet was invented by Spinetti. Is that you?' I really cheered up. Although I had to answer 'No,' I was thrilled. At last the name was not a subject for mockery and the Italians, I realised, had done things I could be proud of.

In Cwm, I hadn't had the courage to go to the library because it was in the Miners' Institute and during the war that place represented officialdom, the police in particular. In any case, the downstairs part was gloomy and forbidding, with mayoral chains and a ticking clock. At Monmouth, there were not one but two libraries: the school one, big and formal, full of the classics, and the Bricknell, small and friendly, stuffed with popular fiction like Winifred Holtby's *South Riding* and *The Stars Look Down* by A J Cronin, both of which made a deep impression on me. I cannot tell you the delight of getting lost in a story, while warming yourself up on a tepid radiator.

In class I began to feel drawn in. Mr Shuffrey, our French master, having listened to my Welsh Valley accent said, 'Well, Spinetti, we're going to have to teach you English before we can teach you French.' But I didn't mind because 'Spinet, Spinetti' had already happened, while Mr J F C Dicker, our history master would always insist on 'TRAfalgar, not TraFALgar' and 'HiMALayas, not HIMalayas'. Both teachers were giving me a map to help me find my way around Englishness. Today I would have reservations about that and anyway, no one told me how to read the map. The English way is to leave you on your own but then, it was like learning a new part or adding a string to my bow, an exercise that was both amusing and, as you'll see, useful. Those teachers, according to their own lights admittedly, were helping to put my out-of-order papers into some order, for a while.

The best was Mr Pearson, 'Shinny' Pearson, our English master. His classroom was the Bricknell library, of which he was the librarian, so there was a friendly atmosphere before we even started. He got me to read out loud. It was a speech from Shakespeare's *Macbeth*, very stirring. As I read, I found I wasn't nervous; an ease came over me. Discovering that I could express, through another person's words, all sorts of feelings that I wouldn't dare to in daily life, was a release. 'He has the dramatic instinct,' wrote Mr Shuffrey in a report. Something was definitely happening.

When I witnessed an incident of bullying – nowhere's perfect – I was helped over a hurdle even by that. Again, the 'Spinet, Spinetti' business gave me confidence. A boy was sitting on his bed writing a letter. It was a winter's evening and outside it was snowing. Inside, the blackout was up. Other boys in the dormitory, having nothing better to do, crowded round the letter writer and looked over his shoulder: 'Oh, he's writing to his mother,' sneered one of the bullies, 'Nyah, nyah, nyah-nyah, nyah!' The boy tried to carry on writing but tears, blurring his eyes, made the task impossible. One big tear plopped onto his writing paper at exactly the spot where he had written 'Mummy'. The ink swam about in the salt water. That was it. I'd had enough. Attack, however, was futile. The gang was too big. 'You –' I couldn't say 'bastards' because I didn't swear, not then. Instead, I ran round the dormitory, yanked all the sheets, blankets and mattresses off all the beds, and threw the whole lot, blackout or no blackout, out of the window into the snow. I was in such a rage they couldn't stop me and when it was over, they did nothing, absolutely nothing. Perhaps they thought I was mad. They certainly kept away from me.

And schoolboy sex? I went into the locker room one afternoon to fetch some rugby balls and caught sight of a boy bouncing up and down on another boy but to me, then, it was almost meaningless. I closed the door and went off to the game.

An enlightened, laissez-faire atmosphere doesn't happen all by itself, it has to be made. At Monmouth, three influences did that: Mr Elstob, our headmaster, who'd interviewed me before I came; Captain W R Irving, our housemaster; and the war. Mr Elstob was the kind of eccentric who is the delight of schoolboys. Stomping about in his brown boots, breeches and gold watch chain, he was a country gentleman out of an eighteenth-century novel. All his spare moments were spent in the garden where he could be heard cursing his plants: 'Damned roses, what's the matter with you? Grow!' And yet, there was nothing heavy about him. His benevolent presence spread throughout the school.

Obviously I saw more of Captain Irving and it was he who affected me the most. With his flowing grey hair and bow tie he was handsome but not in a square-cut way. He had about him a touch of the louche. It came from the silk scarf thrown carelessly over the shoulder and the casual way he wore his uniform on Junior Training Corps afternoons. Subtly he was telling us that he was on our side. He wasn't there to judge us. He wanted, if anything, to know what we thought and if he was a stickler for good table manners, it wasn't for their own sake. It was out of consideration for others. At one of our earlier lunches, he joined us juniors. 'Now, let me tell you,' he said, 'When you finish eating, you don't put your knife and fork like this.' Then, imitating some of the boys, he leant his knife and fork on either side of the plate, handles resting on the table. 'A: because it takes up so much room,' he explained, 'B: because gravy runs down them onto the tablecloth and C: because it looks appalling. You put them together like this.' It did look neat and, if I like something, I'm a fast learner. I'm an enthusiastic teacher too, perhaps a little too enthusiastic.

At the end of the first term, I couldn't wait to get home and pass on all this new stuff: 'Oh Dad, you know when you do your knife and fork —' He was furious.

'I taught you how to eat! I was the one who put food into your mouth and now you're telling me how to use a knife and fork! Is that what you've learned?' Uh-oh!

The third influence, the war, I'll come to. It's holiday time now and in Cwm there were things I'd missed: the voices, the mountains, and certain people, the Mazins, for example.

Dr Izzy Mazin wasn't the usual sort of GP. For a start, he looked exactly like Groucho Marx and then, he practised hypnosis. Hardy, grizzled coal miners would go to him, say with a rash caused by their work. 'How about an ointment, doctor?' they'd suggest but when he saw that the problem was not only physical, he'd talk. He talked the rash away. In later years, my sister and my sister-in-law took their children to him. They remembered Dr Mazin using hypnosis on them to relieve the pain of childbirth. Once in his house, I didn't have to be anxious. I could sit and eat Twiglets — Sydney, his wife, was figure conscious — and talk my school nonsense with no fear of being snapped at. Where Dad would say: 'Waste of time,' or 'Here's the one with all the answers,' they simply listened. On one of my Twiglet visits I said to Dr Mazin: 'Why don't you hypnotise me?'

'Raise your arm,' he said. I did. 'Now, you'll find you can't lower it,' I thought, 'I can lower it easily but I won't because he's so nice.' Outside in the hall, Sydney was talking on the phone. As this was distracting, I asked Dr Mazin if he wouldn't mind closing the door. The next second, I could no longer hear Sydney's voice, which was fine, except that the good doctor hadn't moved and the door was still open.

Izzy Mazin, like Monmouth School, dispelled the shame of being Italian, vestiges of which still hung from me like a mouldering old coat. It was there, even when Dad decided to take us on our first proper holiday and we were miles away from home.

We went to Blackpool. I'm not sure why. I think Dad got the idea when he passed through it on his way to the Isle of Man. The drive was long — there were still no motorways in those days — but because of that, Blackpool Tower, seen from the top of a hill, was all the more exciting and so was driving through the town. 'Fleetwood to Pleasure

Beach' said passing trams. Just those words promised delights. On we drove towards the North Shore, the posh end, where Dad had booked us into the Buona Vista hotel because it sounded Italian. All very well, but as the car moved on, we were getting further and further away from Pleasure Beach.

The best thing to do was to get out on the front and as soon as we'd dropped off our luggage, that's where you could find us. As we strolled along, Mario, my little brother, shot ahead. Frightened he was going to disappear into the crowd, I called out but the word that came from my mouth was not 'Mario!' It was 'Mar!' I was ashamed of Mario because that was Italian. Since people around me thought I was calling to my mother, they were only slightly puzzled when a little boy with golden ringlets ran towards me. And now, the name Mario is all over the world because of a Nintendo game, *Mario, the Plumber*. Ringing in my ears, even then, was Derry Price's schoolyard cry of: 'Fuck off, you Italian bastard!' Verdi and Michelangelo I had yet to hear of. Where were you when I needed you?

Golden ringlets – that's just reminded me. Years later, I was visiting my Aunty Nell up the tump, a hill behind the Palace Cinema, near Ebbw Vale, when I met a man in a pub who said: 'Hallo, Mario.'

'Hallo,' I answered, not bothering to correct him.

'Well, you've lost your bloody long ringlets, haven't you?' he said.

'Yeah,' I said, 'Long ago.'

'You're looking well.' he went on, 'How's that miserable sod of a brother of yours, Victor?'

'He's up in London,' I said.

'Best place for him,' he said.

'You couldn't wait to go,' said my mother, remembering the start of any new term, and it's true. At school, I felt at home. And now for the third influence at Monmouth, the war. Because of the bombing, another school, King Edward the Seventh, was evacuated from Birmingham to Monmouth and as this school's lessons were held in the afternoon, we were free then. It had an effect that I see now was beneficial. Surrounded by a wealth of information, the libraries in particular, I now had the responsibility of seeking it out. In this way, the school became a kind of university and I discovered that going where my curiosity led suited me. In any case, the afternoons were hardly empty. As well as games, there were societies: the Photographic

Society, the Music Society, the Poetry Society and the Debating Society. I joined them all and there in the Debating Society I found that thinking on my feet, arguing this way and that, not necessarily as myself, was right up my street. I could get really passionate and, as with the Shakespeare reading, nobody minded. Oh, and when I wasn't doing all that, I went rowing.

It got around that I could imitate people: the teachers, George Formby, Adolf Hitler, characters from *It's That Man Again*, the radio show, 'Can I do you now, sir?' anybody. I'd learned them from listening to Auntie Min's radio, which she kept in the room behind the fish-and-chip shop. I used to run down there on dark nights, our own radio having been confiscated, you'll remember. Hearing of my reputation, P B S Cooper, head boy and A J Stephens, head of house, sent for me and stood me on a table. I did a turn. I even imitated them – Cooper and Stephens – and they still laughed.

Alan Stephens: captain of cricket, boxing, swimming, diving, jumping, you name it, my hero. Blond and handsome, he was the hero of all us young boys. Years later, I had a chance to tell him so when, still tiresomely young looking, even though middle-aged, he came backstage after my one-man show in Brighton. 'Don't be ridiculous,' he said, 'Hero? I couldn't have done what you've just done, holding an audience, being on a stage. Hero? I was only good at games.' With that very remark, modest and unassuming, he proved he was still a hero. At school, before lights out, this kindly young prefect, our dormitory captain, would do his own turn by telling us the latest news – the Eighth Army crossing into Sicily – or singing us the newest hit song:

Mairzy doats
And dozy doats
And liddlamzy divy.

Or, jigging about, he'd dance to:

Ac–cent–uate the positive
E–lim–inate the negative

A good person, a role model, the best. Flashman he wasn't.

Monmouth had school plays and a school chapel choir. The shows, which were Gilbert and Sullivan mostly, with 'Six Little Maids' instead of 'Three' – there being so many keen boys – I didn't take part in. I wasn't asked. Perhaps I had established myself too firmly as an impressionist. The chapel choir I was hardly likely to be in as I wasn't going to chapel in the first place, or the church for that matter. I said I was a Catholic, which I wasn't and that was that. Sundays, I was free. I could go for walks along the Wye Valley. There, if anything, was my religion.

As the impressions made me popular, I found myself recruited for an end-of-term show, which had each house competing with the other to come up with the best. I thought I'd be a magician but not a very good one. I'd break an egg into a hat and appear to make a mess of it and yet not make a mess.

H E R Gill, our maths master, lent me the hat. His wife had borrowed it from the Monmouth Amateur Dramatics Society. I did like Mr Gill. He had the driest of voices and at the end of each term, he would read us *Three Men in a Boat* so wonderfully, we would fall on the floor laughing. If you want to know how he sounded, think of Arthur Lowe as Captain Mainwaring. 'I must give him a present in return,' I used to think, 'I must pass my maths exam. It's my worst subject I know, but I must.' And when it came to it, I did.

Yes, the top hat. There I stood with it, hidden behind specially rigged black drapes in the school library, waiting for my entrance, when the most beautiful thing happened. Toffler, a German-Jewish boy, older than I, who had escaped the Nazis, I think, was playing the piano. The piece was Schubert's Impromptu in A Flat. I was transported. Whenever I hear it today, I'm thirteen years old again, standing behind a curtain, getting goose pimples. My first ever performance was being preceded by this beautiful music. They had nothing to do with each other and yet they had. Even then, I knew I would never forget that moment.

From pathos to bathos, I thought I'd try my hand at the piano myself and off I went for lessons. The teacher was the sweetest woman who lived in the tiniest house where, unmarried and wearing frayed gloves, she lived in genteel poverty, supporting a widowed mother. Her manners were exquisite. Visiting her was like stepping into a Jane Austen novel but there was a problem. The room was very small, only big enough for the piano, an oil stove and her armchair. It was overheated, stuffy and if I raised my elbows too high when I played, I practically poked her in the eye. That wasn't the problem, though. The problem was a nervous condition she suffered from. 'Do, ray, mi, fa, so, la, te, do' – up the keys I went but then, 'Pfluh!' She farted.

'Why've you stopped?' she asked from just behind my back.

'Sorry, Miss,' I started again. 'Do, ray, me fa, so, la, te, do.' 'Pfluh!' She farted again.

'Why have you stopped?'

'Sorry, Miss,' The tension was unbearable. There was no dog to blame and, as far as the teacher with her Jane Austen manners was concerned, the fart hadn't happened anyway. I'd stopped because all my fingers were glued to the keys. They were white with pressing so hard but it was a case of anything to prevent myself from giggling. Would this chronic flatulence pass? I hoped so but it didn't. I began to make excuses for not going: a bad cold, a fall, a knock in the swimming pool. On and on, I spun it out so that at least she would continue receiving her fee. Two or three times a term I went, that's all, but when I couldn't cover up any longer, I had to tell my father that there was no point in going. He was, after all, paying extra for the lessons. And that is why, despite my love of the instrument, I never got further than first grade.

My failed magician, on the other hand, was not a failure. I began to get noticed. Captain Irving's wife, a tiny bird-like creature with an impeccable cut-glass accent took a shine to me. She'd ask every now and again if I wouldn't mind nipping into town for a packet of cigarettes, Players No. 3, very grand because Players No. 3, for me, were posh. Up till then, I'd only heard of Players Weights. 'With the fees I'm paying I'm not surprised she's bloody smoking Players No. 3,' said Dad when I told him.

'We're having a little drinks party,' said the captain's wife on my return from one of these errands, 'If you're free, drop by.'

As the Irvings' quarters were part of my house, New House, not in the least bit new really, all I had to do was push open a green-baize door to arrive in their hallway. I turned to the right and there I found myself in a drawing room filled with bowls of flowers and comfortable furniture covered in chintz. It might have been the set for a country-house play produced by H M Tennent. To me it seemed ineffably glamorous. 'So why then aren't you a practising Catholic?' asked Captain Irving. I suppose that might have frightened me but it didn't because I'd caught the eye of the captain's wife. While pouring me a small sherry, she was giving me the merriest of smiles and so the question became stimulating.

'I don't like the way it's dished up.' I answered.

'Dished up?'

'Yes, those silver salvers and goblets and things, all that clatter and those wafers.' My Deborah Kerr in *Tea and Sympathy,* Mrs Irving, laughed. I was centre stage, being listened to and blooming once more.

Either I'm irrepressible or I never learn my lesson because no sooner was I at home again, than I was pouring out more stories of school and, as usual, they had the same effect on Dad. Instead of looking to the future and seeing how handy all this knowledge would be one day, he remained stuck in the present, frustrated that I knew stuff he didn't. 'Here comes the clever one,' was the best I got. If he didn't want me to know all this stuff, why had he sent me to Monmouth?

Things hadn't improved on the Lily front either. If a man walked into Dad's shop and said, 'I saw your wife up the road the other day. God, she's a good-looking woman,' that would be it. Suddenly, in my father's head, the full Verdi opera would be raging. He'd be convinced she was having an affair. A tight, white-lipped, grim face would come up to the house for the early evening meal and, while he ate, there'd be absolute silence and this could go on for two weeks. A friend, so-called, who helped in the fish-and-chip shop, one Atkinson, only made matters worse. Like Igor to my father's Frankenstein, he crept around in the hope of little favours, a few chips, a piece of fish. In return, he'd take a totally innocent encounter he'd witnessed, like my brother, Mario, talking to a girl and twist it to torture my Dad with the thought of his son getting a girl pregnant.

'Didn't I see Mario over at the bus stop with that girl from Curre Street?'

'No, really?'

'Yes, and . . .' the twist, now, 'You know what that family's like?' Causing trouble was Atkinson's reason for living.

On Sunday evenings, the whole family sat down to eat together: my father, my mother, my two brothers – Mario and I had then been joined by Adrian – and my Auntie Angelina, who'd arrived from Italy having spent the war up in the mountains carrying a gun with 'That-a Tito'. 'Silent supper again,' Mario used to say when my father was in one of his moods and, at one of them, the atmosphere got so bad, Auntie Angelina cried out: 'It's not right. It's-a terrible!' At which point my mother fell from her chair to the floor, where she rolled about screaming hysterically. My brothers looked on, paralysed. In that second, Monmouth School proved its worth. With some healthy distance between myself and the family, I could do something. Books had shown me that there were other people in the world and, as I'd always wanted to teach, now was my chance. 'Excuse me,' I said, 'I'm curious. Do you realise that that woman rolling about on the floor, having a fit like a twelve-year-old girl, is your wife? Why don't you pick her up?' I was that calm. Nevertheless, my father's reaction took me by surprise. He burst into tears and said: 'Nobody loves me.'

The sudden helpless despair from this strong, silent man gave me such a jolt, I shot round the table and put my arm round him. 'We do love you,' I said, 'We do, but you have to give love out. You can't just pluck it like an apple from a tree.'

'Who are you calling a twelve-year-old schoolgirl?' interrupted my mother, having made an amazingly quick recovery from her fit. My father muttered and puffed on his cigarette.

Sometimes, when Dad wasn't speaking, I'd leave little notes round the house. For example, he'd pick up his shaving brush and find a tiny piece of paper, on it written: 'Good morning!' I thought it was shuttle diplomacy. He thought I was trying to drive him nuts. 'You're the clever one, are you?' he said, 'The one with all the answers?' Well, maybe I was. Certainly there were times when I felt I was sent into the world to bring those two up. When I read later on: 'The child is father to the man' I thought, 'Yeah, I bloody know. I was there.'

It didn't stop at that. Dad even suspected Gurnos Gradon of carrying on with my mother. Gurnos, if you remember, was the boy who liked to drop round in the hope of a bite to eat, the food at his own home being so bland. He was only seventeen and if there was anything he wanted, it was to see me and eat. That made no difference. I got a message. 'Your mother wants you.' Up at the house, I found Lily in the kitchen screaming and crying.

'What's the matter?' I asked.

'Yer father!' she answered.

'God, what is it now?'

'He's just been up and he said: "I don't want Gurnos in this house

– he's not allowed to come into this house anymore." I said, "What do you mean, not allowed to come into this house?" and he said, "You and he carrying on."'

I went down the road to the fish–and–chip shop: 'What's this Dad?' I said, 'Gurnos is having an affair with Mam? That's rubbish.'

'What's the matter then?' answered my father, 'Isn't she good enough for him?' Looking over my father's shoulder, smiling, was 'Igor' Atkinson. Even today, I still avoid the play *Othello*. It's too much like home from home and Atkinson had given me enough insight into Iago to last me a lifetime.

All of this didn't mean to say that my brothers and I had nothing to do with girls. Well, in the case of Luigi Antoniazzi's girls, we didn't. Gloomily Luigi, my godfather, would stand next to his delicious ices, the best, a cigarette dangling from the corner of his mouth and say in his Valleys Italian: 'Is–a terrible, see Victor, is–a terrible!' as ash dropped off, narrowly missing the ice cream. 'I can't–a find–a nobody to marry my lovely girls, see Victor.' Five of them he had and by the time he said that, my father had five boys. Paul and Henry were now on the scene. 'I've even–a been as far away as–a Crumlin, as–a Newbridge, as–a Newport.' All of them on the one bus route I noticed, but then, Luigi was never keen on travel. After his death, his body was taken to the Catholic Church in Ebbw Vale to be left there overnight, then taken down to Cardiff the next day to lie in state and was finally driven to the airport to be flown to Italy. My father said, 'He travelled more when he was dead than when he was alive.'

His girls were nice enough but they never left the shop. As strict Catholics, they were carefully protected and if you wanted to get to see them, you almost needed a duenna. My brothers couldn't be bothered. By the time they were teenagers, the war was over and everything was back to normal. The dust had settled and you could see clearly that they belonged. For them, the Miners' Institute wasn't in the least off-putting. They loved to play at darts and billiards there, just like my father had before the war and indeed did after it. Consequently, the girls my brothers were interested in were Welsh village girls.

It was different for me. The only girls I knew were cousins who came to the house with perhaps a friend or two. Playing games was the way we amused ourselves, just as I had years before, only now, they weren't quite the same games. One thing had a habit of leading to another and so, in a pleasurable, doctors and nurses way, I had my first sexual experiences.

My father, during these visits, would be out, usually on a drive with the rest of the family. By then, I was old enough to say: 'No, thank you.' when such trips were mooted. I had other things to do. Mario thought I was still broadcasting from the kitchen, which he thought was extremely funny. If Dad had known that in his own home, a certain childlike, explorative curiosity was being fed, he would not have remained silent for long. He would have exploded. When I was a bit older, merely announcing that I was off to a dance up at Ebbw Vale was enough to have him grumble: 'Bloody dance. I don't know. Girls!' It wasn't as if anything happened at a dance; on the way home, maybe. Since everybody walked everywhere, a boy and a girl, if they were feeling in the mood, only had to find themselves walking down the 'backs' to do what they wanted to do. Those alleys between houses were reassuringly dark.

You could get an unwelcome surprise, though. At night, clanking trains from the steelworks, white with ash, hauling wagons of waste (like those nuclear-waste trains that move through darkened cities), climbed the side of a nearby mountain and tipped their loads back down it. For a few seconds, this molten red liquid, like lava streaming from Vesuvius, gave off a blinding light that lit up the sky for three miles around. Boys attempting a knee-trembler froze in horror as night turned to day.

Once cool, this waste material provided a setting for more innocent games. The jagged mountaintop dusted with a fine, white powder, looked like the moon. Adventurous children, not me, had a lot of fun on it, and less fun when their mothers saw the powder all over their clothes. The actual moon landing when it happened in 1969 held no surprises for me at all. I'd already been there.

I'll just throw this in. The Bessemer process, that of turning pig iron into steel, required vast amounts of coke. This came from a nearby company that gave off the most dismal smell. It wafted over an area known as Garden City. Today, with the coke ovens closed, Garden City is the fragrant spot it was always meant to be.

While the holidays had their ups and downs, Monmouth continued to have mostly ups. The Top Hat act not only led to more gigs at school, it got me out into Monmouth itself. I performed – though I didn't know the term then – fringe shows. The Rolls Hall, named after Charles Rolls who went into business with Henry Royce, was one of our better dates. There, we did a kind of alternative to the school play: magic, ghosts, a cod Sherlock Holmes. What audiences made of it, God knows, but as we were raising money for Old Age Pensioners, we didn't hear a peep from the school. For all this, you still couldn't say that acting was in my ken. I played the fool, impersonated people, made people laugh but it wasn't a career. 'Is it today?' I sometimes wonder. I found out one thing, though. On a stage, I wasn't anxious.

'Your mother's given birth to a daughter,' said Captain Irving, having summoned me to his study one evening. 'And not before time,' I said to myself. Before the war, sons were all Lily had produced. Now with the war well over, a girl was needed to take us on. 'If only I could get home,' I thought and then I remembered the Monmouth Scout Troop's annual outing. It came in July and it was July. They were going on a bus trip south. I wasn't a member and recollections of the Cwm Troop were hardly happy but I wangled an invitation, just for the day. And so, I was able to get back to Cwm and say: 'Surprise, surprise!' Gianina Mariana Spinetti may have looked like a Japanese doll but in no time at all, she did take us on. Come 1953, when all children were re-enacting the Coronation, she announced: 'I'll be the Queen and you,' she said, pointing at Paul and Henry, 'Can be the crowd.' No mention was made of anyone being the Duke of Edinburgh.

As for my school work at Monmouth, every term I came top of the form. Every year I won prizes and every time, there to see me collect them, were Mum and Dad. This was a mixed blessing. It was good that Dad took an interest in me but as I walked up between the parents, all smelling of the sweet peas they wore as buttonholes, I became self-conscious. This did not happen when I was performing on stage. Now, I was inwardly yelling, 'It's not me they're staring at at. It's the black-heads in my nose!' Even when I walked into a room and heard people laughing, I was convinced those people were laughing at me. A cure did come but not for a while.

One year, the whole top-of-the-form prizewinner thing didn't happen. I didn't work much, I didn't do anything much. I came bottom in everything and I didn't care. However, it wasn't negative what was happening. A change was coming over me; I didn't know it then but I can see it now. I was less anxious, I didn't worry so much about being good. I wanted to freewheel and so, when it came to exam time, that's what I did. Twenty minutes before 'Stop writing,' I noticed that there was this other question. It was about Shakespeare. So I wrote about Shakespeare. Out poured this stream of words about words, how, on the ski slopes down the mountain, there was only one trail and that was Shakespeare's. His was the first mark, the first glorious discovery of language and of phrases like 'Into thin air'. I exploded all over the page and I got nought. It was overblown, overexcited, not thought out, not reasoned and yet it was the first essay I wrote that wasn't saying 'Yes sir, no sir, I'm doing what I'm told, sir.' It was original and it flowed and it was all because of this great poet who discovered language for us.

My father opened the report. I knew what was coming but I was past caring. Bottom. Bottom. Nothing. Bottom. But then, underneath, in – was it purple? – ink, 'This is his most interesting report so far. W R Irving.' And, as far as my father was concerned, what Captain Irving said mattered. What he'd written was good enough for him. It was at last the beginning – of what? My future? Yes, I think so.

Captain Irving had not only saved my life but, without realising it, had also pointed me in the right direction. Unfortunately he left, as did the headmaster, Mr Elstob. From that moment on, things changed. Into a gentle, leisured, freewheeling, perform-in-town, discuss-anything, glowing, lazing-on-the-river world, came this 'Muscular Christian' in a dog collar who stopped the lot. Not only was he our new headmaster, he was my new housemaster. Under him, glasses of sherry and bowls of flowers were right out. It was a hard-edged, collar-studded, sit-up-straight, 'the devil finds work for idle hands' world he created, a world in which we ran to the bell.

At night, the Muscular Christian padded along corridors, darted into dormitories and flicked his torch over the beds. 'What are you doing?' he snapped, convinced that some boy somewhere had to be playing with himself.

'Nothing sir,' answered a dazzled boy who until then had been sound asleep. This new housemaster was like a missionary denouncing an African tribe's perfectly civilised way of life. We were sinful. The result? Decadence and disease – the tribe, not us. At the school we simply became unhappy.

I was in the Bricknell library reading out my latest essay to a full class when Muscular Christian entered. He stood at the back and listened. Shinny Pearson had already discussed the subject with us, Henry the Eighth's syphilis, so I knew I was on solid ground. However, I also knew it was daring of me to use the word 'syphilis' as I wasn't a sixth former yet. I did not expect the reaction I got, though.

'Syphilis? Spinetti,' he said, emphasising my name, 'Are you a Catholic?'

'What sir?'

'I suppose as a Catholic, Spi–nett–i, you've been reading a Catholic historian.' I waited for another 'Spi–nett–i'. It didn't come. A silence filled my mind. I was trying to grasp the fact that a history book could be written from a Catholic point of view. In my naivety, I thought history was fact. Now he was teaching me that it was nothing more than propaganda. A chill came into the air. A barrier clanged down. Bigotry was back. I might have been in Northern Ireland.

Decades later, when I was directing Fiona Richmond in *Let's Get Laid* over in Norwich, a brown envelope, containing a flyleaf for the show was delivered to the theatre. It had been torn down in the foyer. I turned it over. 'Disgusting. A good Christian boy from a good Christian school with this filth.' The word 'filth' was underlined twice. Whether Muscular Christian had actually seen the show, he didn't say.

At the school, his influence soured the atmosphere, for me anyway. Fortunately, I'd passed the Oxford and Cambridge School Certificate Exams, in some subjects, with distinction. This left me with a choice. I could either do my national service right away or defer it by taking the Oxford and Cambridge Exam and go to university first. I decided to do my national service and think about university afterwards. In the meanwhile, there was a gap.

While I'd been away, Cwm had had a severe winter with lots of snow. When I got back, I heard of something that had cheered the place up. First, you have to know that rationing was still on the go, despite the war being over. Food was not only limited but dull.

One night a lorry, having set off from Ebbw Vale, was driving down through the village, down the hill, when, reaching some flattened snow, it skidded, knocked into a bridge and toppled over. Hundreds of sides of bacon fell out. Whispering, sliding and slipping, the village came with bags, boxes and sledges. The bacon, in no time, was gone.

Early next morning a pall of smoke hung over the village, not to mention a delicious smell of frying. The police went round, knocking on doors: 'You've got to give it back,' they said, rather pointlessly, as most of it had already been eaten, not quite all, though. I found a side in the cellar. It was my brothers who had nipped out to get it.

When the snow was flat like that, it was fun to slide down the streets deliberately, on sledges. I was doing that, once, when I felt two icy cold hands placed on my neck. I can still feel them now. They belonged to the local undertaker, Mr Coombs.

You could call Mr Coombs a pillar of Cwm society and by now, you could say the same of my two brothers, Mario and Adrian. They didn't have to think about it. They didn't have to be particularly good at rugby or football. They simply had to do it and they did. But then, nobody had attacked them for being Italian. That was over. Me, I still found the Miners' Institute daunting. I still had the memory of the local village policeman petitioning to have me taken away from my mother. Wounds like that don't heal quickly. My mother, even at ninety-three, on seeing policemen, says: 'They were the worst, the bastards!' My brothers playing their billiards at the Miners' Institute, they didn't give it a second thought.

Since I was no good at rugby, football or billiards anyway, I had to find something else, so round the village I went, doing my turns. As usual, I imitated other people and it was this that led to what happened next.

The Ebbw Vale Playgoers' Society was short of men who could speak with an English accent. All the other players performed in their natural Welsh Valleys voice, even when doing the plays of Noël Coward. At Monmouth, I had absorbed this English sound, merely by being there. I could even remember to drop the H from hotel: 'I'm staying at an 'otel,' so the Playgoers asked me to join them. As well as the accent, I had a different bearing. I'd got it from the school's Junior Training Corps, a public-school throwback to the First World War. A few hours a week of marching up and down and you're hurried through to lieutenant when you join the real army. You see what I mean by a map of Englishness?

The one who spotted the accent and the bearing was Heulwyn Richards. She was the director of the Playgoers' Society and it was she who cast me in a sophisticated part. Dinner-jacketed and dicky-fronted, I found myself on the stage in *Claudia* by Rose Franken, saying, 'I hate milk. It's so damned hoo-wite,' which had the audience falling about.

Just so you know, I wasn't merely a gentleman of leisure during this time. Work came from my father. As his business was doing well, and had been since 1926 actually, he needed the extra help. A wage didn't come into it but he still resented me escaping to rehearsals.

Heulwyn was not just a director. She was a mentor. When we weren't actually working, she would quiz me. There was a General Election coming up. 'It is most important to make a choice,' she insisted, ringlets a-quiver. She, herself, was a socialist. 'One can only vote Labour,' she said, 'If you care about humanity you can't possibly be a Tory.' I, by this time, had read Jeremy Bentham and was able to come back with: 'I'm for the greatest good for the greatest number.'

And now I remember. It was Heulwyn who gave me the cure for my self-consciousness. 'Staring at the blackheads in your nose? People laughing when you come into a room?' she said, 'How conceited you are. Those people have more important things to laugh at.'

An amateur dramatic company was to be found in every Welsh valley and its productions were taken very seriously. Performed in Miners' Institutes, churches and village halls, they were invariably sold out weeks in advance. The plays chosen were good too: 'No rubbish here, Vic,' said one of the chairmen and rubbish they weren't. Ibsen, Strindberg and Chekhov, that's what you got and during the performances, you could hear a pin drop. What's more, these plays were entered into a competition and the director of the winning company was chaired through the streets almost like a god. Those shows were good to be part of and only television signalled their end.

I was cast in a competition play, Strindberg's *The Father*. The Doctor, that was me. Maerdy was the venue, a town where mostly Welsh was spoken. When the performance was over, the adjudicator who, with his cape and flowing white hair, looked like Lloyd George, rose from the audience like a prophet rising from the sea to review the production in the language of the country of my birth. I didn't understand a word of it. However, I could tell from the rise and fall of his inflections, as each member of the cast was considered and evaluated, what he thought. 'The Captain. James Evans.' and then a great roar of upward-spiralling Welsh before a huge round of applause.

'The Nurse. Audrey Williams.' His Welsh became gentle, soothing, almost feminine. More applause. 'The Doctor, Victor Spinetti.' He stopped speaking for the first time and gazed at his notes. 'Well,' he said, his first word in English, and then, sighing: 'Well, well,' Three words in English. A thin, flat sentence in Welsh came out. No applause. I turned to the stagehand.

'What did he say?' I asked.

'About you?' he said, 'He said you were bloody wooden.'

Still, the adjudicator voted us the best production and it was Heulwyn's turn to be chaired through the streets. I'd filled my gap. It was time for national service.

4

Private Spinetti

Until I was 21, everything I did was on the same bus route, either going north or south. To join the army I had to go north. I took the Western Welsh. Their buses were posh with comfortable seats, red and green and upholstered. It was a line we very rarely travelled on and, because of that, I always looked forward to it.

The day I joined up was 20 November 1947, the day that Princess Elizabeth married the Duke of Edinburgh. That's why I remember the date. Whilst everyone was celebrating the wedding, I was setting off for freezing-cold barracks in Brecon. There was snow on the ground when I arrived but then there always seemed to be snow on the ground in Brecon.

Basic Training came first: drilling, lectures, taking a rifle to pieces blindfolded, that sort of thing, but as I'd made sergeant in the Junior Training Corps at Monmouth, I was told: 'You'll probably be down for a Wosby,' That's the War Office Selection Board. It meant that, before too long, I had a good chance of becoming an officer. Things didn't look so bad, really no worse than going to another school. After all, I was used to being away from home, used to sleeping in a dormitory and used to getting up first thing in the morning. Even a breakfast of liver and bacon covered with a thick, thick gravy that had a skin on it and drinking pint pots of tea held no fears for me. I didn't sit there weeping on my bed. Anyway, civilian life was only round the corner. After work, if we wanted to, we could go to the local pub, have a drink and chat to the barmaid, not that in the first six weeks we did much of that. We were too busy, Blancoing belts, Brassoing buttons and polishing boots.

The boys who suffered were those who'd never been away from home, like the one who used to read his bible aloud sitting up in bed. He looked like Arthur Askey. In fact, that was his name, Arthur. He was bound to get some stick and he did. One of the biggest, burliest guys in the platoon, Ginger Flynn, to show what he thought of this bible-thumping freak, came in one night and pissed all over him. Arthur got up from his bed, his blankets soaked in Ginger's piss and said. 'This is what I have to go through for Jesus,' so he was fine. Luckily, Ginger Flynn, being Irish/Welsh, quite liked me. 'You're all right,' he said.

The regiment was one of the toughest in the army but I've always said that the rougher the regiment, the gentler its officers. Our platoon commander, with his insouciant air, was a true-born aristocrat and he was so nice, so kind. I was almost in tears he was so nice. We'd be standing on parade, the wind from the Atlantic blowing snow and ice all down one side of us, the rifle side, while leaving the other side untouched, when his little Volkswagen would come puttering onto the parade ground and stop. After a long pause, for hat adjustments probably, the door would open and out would step this immaculately shod foot, this beautifully pressed uniform, this greatcoat flung over shoulders and a hanky. It was the first time I'd ever smelt aftershave on anybody. Until then it had only been Palmolive Soap on a boy called Dennis at Dyffryn and even Palmolive was a bit dicey in those days. The rest of us washed with carbolic.

In a cloud of 'Irish Heather' by Creed, our platoon commander walked along the line, flicking his hanky at any miscreant soldier.

'You beastly man. What are you?'

'Beastly, sir.'

'Your boots, look at them. Sergeant, take his name.'

'And you, you're frightfully naughty. What are you?'

'Frightfully naughty, sir,'

'Your cap badge is absolutely filthy. Sergeant, take his name.'

Then he'd come to me and go: 'Hallo, Spinetti,' flicking at me with his hanky, not because I was naughty but because I'd been to a good rugby-playing school. The downside to this was finding myself in front of a blackboard with a piece of chalk in my hand, teaching rugby to what I can only describe as, to a man, football-playing thugs. And, to add insult to injury, at Monmouth I'd been the worst rugby player they'd ever had. Why? Because whenever the ball came near me, I closed my eyes. They were so tightly closed, my eyes, it was a wonder I didn't fall over.

As I said in the last chapter, homosexuality, contrary to popular opinion, did not run rampant at my old school. Apart from some mutual masturbation, there was nothing out of the ordinary for any crowd of young men living together. In the army, where the men had girlfriends or were married, it was quite another matter. My being an ex-public schoolboy made them think, erroneously, that I was going to be the platoon slut. A sergeant, for example, started by asking me why I went home for weekends. 'It's just a bus ride away.' I answered.

'But we show blue movies,' he said, 'And get together.' Another time, I was room orderly, a cushy job. All you had to do was sit by the stove, stoke it and read a book. Anyway, that's what I did but then a corporal came in and said: 'Would you like to see my tattoos?'

'Yeah, all right Corps,' I said. In a trice he was totally naked with an erection. I looked at the tattoos: 'Great Corps,' I said and went back to my book. I was never room orderly again.

Next, a sergeant said, 'Go up to my room – here's the key – give the place a tidy. When you've finished, sit there and wait. I'll be along soon. When I knock on the door, let me in.' Upstairs I went, tidied his room, sat there until he knocked, let him in, said, 'Good night, Sergeant' and left. It was an assignation but I didn't know. If I had, I might have quite easily become the platoon slut. In fact, if it meant tidying rooms and sitting by a roaring fire all day while the others were outside marching, I would have become the slut of the hut. Why did no one tell me?

The first time I was kissed by a man was not in the theatre but in a rugby scrum there in the army. Afterwards, the man who'd kissed me chased me, and anyone else he could find, round the shower. His dick was huge. 'Oh, put it away,' I said and then: 'What the hell were you before you came into the army?'

'An actor.'

'No, really?'

'Yes. Do you want to see my press cuttings?'

'Oh, all right.'

'I was in a play by Emlyn Williams.'

'No?'

'Yeah.'

And years later, I said to Emlyn Williams: 'Do you know, the first time I was ever kissed by a man was in a rugby scrum in the army. He was in a play of yours.'

'Oh, really?' said Emlyn.

'Yes,' I said, 'He had a cock like a gnarled oak.'

'Oh, yes, I remember him,' said Emlyn.

Even though army life was rough and ready, I felt at home. Hadn't I been through the war, rationing and public school? So, if conditions had been merely Spartan, I would have been all right. Trouble came because conditions in those very old barracks were unhealthy. My bed was at the end of the hut next to the wall and, apart from it being cold anyway, condensation dripped down that wall. We had no sheets, no pillowcases, only, as I think Rupert Brooke says, 'The rough male kiss of the blanket' and each night these blankets were invariably damp. Soon I was having night sweats and fits of shivering, but as they were gone by morning, I thought there was no problem. When the sweats became high fevers and I lost weight, I still took no notice and carried on with basic training.

Drill brought its own problem, nothing to do with night sweats. The sergeant would yell an order and I would turn and march off in the wrong direction. I was doing a Norman Wisdom and I didn't know it. My trouble was, I'd heard the order but I wasn't sure where it was coming from. Something from years before had come back to haunt me.

At Monmouth, as a matter of course, I'd had a medical, part of which had been a hearing test. There I sat, my mother and father opposite, while the doctor put a big clock on my right ear. 'Brrr,' it went. 'What is your name?' asked the doctor.

'Victor,'

'Where do you live?'

'Cwm,'

'Fine.'

He put the clock on my left ear and again I waited for him to speak. And waited. I looked over at my parents. Their jaws had dropped open. Their eyes were popping out. It was like a film. I looked round. The doctor was red in the face with shouting.

'You're deaf in that ear! Did you know that?'

'No, I didn't know.'

But I did realise what had caused it, the brick clubbing me over the head in Cwm at the beginning of the war. At Monmouth, the loss of hearing hadn't mattered. Now, in the army, it did. An examination was ordered. I was sent to Chester. At the station I couldn't keep my eyes off the food on the refreshment stall. Why was I always so hungry? Not that I could do anything about it. Payday was Thursday and this was Wednesday. I had nothing. They'd bloody sent me on a Wednesday when I hadn't a penny. The woman running the stall saw this young man in uniform, so thin by now he looked like a drinking straw in a dog collar and said: 'Nick something. Go on, I won't look.' She turned away. I took a ham roll. At the hospital, when I arrived, no one was expecting me. I sat in a chair all night in a corridor and waited.

Next day, the specialist confirmed I was deaf in one ear but listed me as A1. Why? Because that's how I'd been listed when I joined up. I'd told them about the deafness but they hadn't believed me because the eardrum was intact. The nerve was dislodged but the nerve wasn't visible. However, for the specialist to go back on that listing would have left the army in the wrong. So A1 I remained. To all intents and purposes, though, I had been lying. Unpleasant as this was at the time, it's an ill wind, etc. If I want some sleep in a noisy city, all I have to do is turn on to my left ear.

Back at the barracks, still losing weight, I came to the conclusion I'd better report sick. This was easier said than done. Before you can report sick in the army, you have to pack everything up, roll your blankets up so tightly and neatly they can be measured with a stick, and then arrange all your things, your spoon, your cup, your cap. This was quite an effort and I was feeling dreadful.

When I reported to the Medical Officer it was first thing in the morning but there was a suspiciously strong aroma of whisky in the room. The MO was Scots. 'Drop yer trews,' he said, having first tapped my chest. I did. He put his hands under my balls: 'Cough,' he said. I coughed. 'No venereal disease?' he said.

'No, sir,' I said.

'Well, yer all right,' he said, 'Medicine and Duty. Here you are, a couple of aspirins. You've got a cold on the chest.'

But I wasn't all right. At night, I lay there, wheezing and steaming like an old kettle. It was little better during the daytime. I could hardly breathe and if the MO couldn't see it, my fellow soldiers certainly could. They took to helping me out. They packed up for me, polished my boots for parade, even cleaned my rifle. They were wonderful and that includes Ginger Flynn. If you messed with me you messed with him. Perhaps it was because I could make him laugh.

We were moved from Brecon barracks – they must have been there since the Napoleonic Wars – to barracks at Derring Lines. Despite being brand new, with much better facilities, they were still very cold. Try as I might, I couldn't get warm. Out on a march, it was pouring with rain – we came to a ploughed field. 'Right,' said the corporal, maybe the one I'd spurned without realising it, 'Go and camouflage yourself.'

'Where?' I asked.

'In that ploughed field,' he said. I walked over and fell into the mud. It felt wonderfully warm with the rain running in rivulets down the furrows, and as I lay there I went to sleep. The next thing I knew was a voice saying, 'He's asleep. Get up!' A boot prodded me none too gently. There was a great glurp sound as I got to my feet covered in mud. I didn't care. I'd had forty winks.

We were marched off and halted next to a tree by a river. The sergeant – was he the one whose room I hadn't really tidied and whose door I hadn't locked? By then, I was too tired to care. Anyway, this sergeant stepped up to the tree and said: 'Right, climb that rope.' It was hanging from the tree and the idea was you climbed it, transferred your hands to a pulley and slid, with your kitbag on, down a wire over the river. 'I can't,' I said.

'What?' said the sergeant.

'I can't climb that rope. I'm sorry.'

'Sorry? You'll be bloody sorry if you don't.' but it was no use. I hadn't the strength. 'Right, come on you.' And off the sergeant marched me to the platoon commander, muttering: 'You've 'ad it now, son,' as I trudged on covered in mud. 'You've bloody 'ad it now.' This was it. I'd disobeyed an order. 'Jankers for you, my boy, jankers.' It was the end of my life. I didn't care. All I wanted was sleep.

Our platoon commander sat there, looking at me. 'Oh Spinetti,' he said, 'You're really naughty. You're a naughty, naughty boy, aren't you? A real beast. This morning your boots were filthy. Your rifle was quite shocking. I ignored that but now, look at you, refusing to climb a rope. Is that right, Sergeant?

'Yes, sir!'

'What am I going to do with you?'

The sergeant stood up straighter. A gleam came into his eyes and a half smile played about his lips. The platoon commander thought a bit more and then said, 'We've got a rugby match on Tuesday.' You'll remember I was the team instructor. 'So, I'll tell you what I'll do, I'll give you a little weekend leave.' A long, slow, hissing sound escaped from the clenched teeth of the sergeant. 'Go home,' said the platoon commander, 'See your family. Come back for the rugby match on Tuesday, all right?' By now, the sergeant was spitting tacks whereas I was practically in tears and our platoon commander had, unknowingly, saved my life.

I went to clean up, longing for the warmth of a hot shower. The new gleaming barracks had not only showers but radiators, unfortunately, not for us. Some of the platoon members had come in drunk one night, swung on the showerheads, pulled off the taps and smashed the basins. They'd wrecked the place. The next day, our platoon commander announced at parade: 'Those amenities were put there for your use. From now on, you will wash in cold water. There will be no repairs.' I had never seen him so angry. To this intelligent young officer, the mindless destruction of our own showers was inexplicable.

I went home on the bus, the Western Welsh again, changing at Abergavenny. Doctor Mazin, who'd been seeing one of my brothers, was just leaving the house. 'You look terrible,' he said. And I did. By now I was a drinking straw in a horse collar. 'I feel terrible,' I said. The doctor tapped my chest, left and right.

'Go to bed,' he ordered. Now that very morning, our Medical Officer at the barracks had done exactly the same thing and again said, 'You've got nothing but a cold, a cold on the chest. Medicine and Duty.'

I went upstairs and sank into bed. All I wanted to do was sleep. Within a few hours, a specialist arrived summoned by Doctor Mazin. He inserted a big needle between my ribs and drew out a basin full of Fairy Liquid, or at least, that's what it looked like, green with froth on top. This liquid, once out of me, meant I could rest. Up until then, I'd been drowning in my own fluid. My left lung had collapsed and the fluid was building up around my heart. My playing rugby on Tuesday would have been the answer to the army's prayers. I'd have died of a heart attack.

In the meanwhile, Doctor Mazin had rung the barracks, only to be disbelieved. 'We looked at his medical report. He was examined this morning. There's nothing wrong with him.'

The next thing I was aware of was a banging at the front door and a policeman saying, 'Mrs Spinetti, your boy's deserted from the army.'

'Deserted?' said my mother, 'He's upstairs bloody dying!' That was the first time I realised how ill I'd become.

Within a few hours, a brigadier, RAMC (Royal Army Medical Corps), bristling with red tabs, was marching up the stairs into my bedroom: 'Lie at attention when I'm talking to you,' he snapped, but I couldn't because I was propped up on pillows at an angle that kept the liquid draining. 'Lie at attention!!'

'Oh, go away,' I said. He leant across the bed, his well-scrubbed pink face, medals and white moustache all calculated to frighten me and said, 'Now look here. If you sign this form to say you have no complaints about your medical treatment in the army, we will send you to a hospital near here, so that your family will be able to visit you. If you do not sign this form, we will send you as far away as possible and your family will never be able to visit. It's up to you.' This face that said nothing but 'I'm protecting my pension,' got to me. I wrote: 'Illness due to medical incompetence and negligence' and handed the form back.

Next morning, an ambulance came and I was driven up to North Wales and onwards, to the top of a mountain, where the wind blew night and day, a place called Llangwyfan. There I was put into the Tuberculosis (TB) ward of the military wing of the North Wales Sanatorium but I didn't have TB.

To my astonishment, the other patients wolf-whistled as I was wheeled in. Well, most of them were sailors. Had my reputation as a possible platoon slut preceded me? Some of these sailors had TB of the hip and were up on platforms that held them at 45 degrees, head down, feet up. They couldn't move. Their arms were free but everything else was encased in plaster. All had to have bedpans and catheters. Of those from the other services, two were RAF and two, army. The rest were farmers, some who'd been kicked by their animals and had TB of the spine. They, after a long treatment, sort of got better. Those with TB of the lungs didn't, to whit, the man I was put next to. He, in fact, had miliary tuberculosis, that is, TB in every part of his body. Although TB was not what I had, I did have a pleural effusion and that leaves you wide open to infection. The army seemed to be making a determined effort to get rid of me. It's a pity for them MRSA wasn't on the go.

At night, with a gale howling round the ward, trees soughing and distant doors going 'rat-a-tat-tat', I tried to sleep but through the soughing and the rattling a voice croaked out of the darkness: 'You're going to get better but I'm going to die and I'm going to take you with me. All I have to do, when you're sleeping, is spit in your mouth. Or, I'll use your thermometer and nobody'll know, not even you, and you'll die and I'll take you with me, ergh.' Every night he said this, the man in the next bed. Well, from then on I was awake like an owl, terrified to sleep at all until, one night, my radio earphones were suddenly pulled off. I looked across. This man who was going to take me with him sat bolt upright and coughed a rasping cough. His lungs shot out of his mouth onto the bed and he died.

'Nurse! Nurse! Nurse!!' I shouted. There was nobody about. Then, the clip-clop of heels. The duty nurse had arrived. In the dim blue light that suffused the ward at night, screens were put round the bed. Then, the clip-clop, clip-clop of heels back to the end of the ward. By this time, most of the people who had been sleeping, having heard the screens being wheeled in, were awake, so, with the largest audience possible, the duty nurse picked up the phone and in a loud voice said: 'Griffiths has just died.' She made no attempt to whisper or hide it. She just said it, matter of fact. By now we were all owls, wide-awake. The bed was wheeled out and next morning, somebody else was there, a cheery sailor who kept lifting his bedclothes, displaying an enormous erection and saying: 'Eh Vic, give us a wank.' Obviously somebody from the barracks had been in touch with him.

The men opposite were equally life affirming. 'Never mind about a wank,' they said, 'We're going to fuck you, you wait and see.' It wasn't as if I were wearing lipstick or bangles or anything. I was simply the one they picked on. It must have been the public-school accent. I probably sounded like a BBC announcer. Anyway, all of them were up for fucking me, including the male nurse: 'Am I going to give you a bed bath you won't forget. You just wait.' The ward was a hotbed of predatory sexuality but I was quite safe because none of these randy types could move. The torrent of words that swirled around my bed, the sexual banter from all quarters, it was just the high sex-drive of their illness speaking. In their way, they were typical of those romantic, consumptive lovers of the nineteenth century. It was quite different, though, when their families came to visit. They'd sit there as nice as pie and introduce me very correctly: 'All right, Vic? This is the missus. This is my mother.' As soon as the families left, the banter picked up again. 'You're going to get it, mate.'

My treatment proper was simple and primitive. It was called a phrenic crush. They don't do it anymore. First, you're given a local anaesthetic. Then an incision is made in the left-hand side of the neck, so various nerves can be got at. One after the other, each is pressed – the leg jerks, the eye twitches – until the one that's like a great grasping hand on your chest is found. This is then crushed to give the collapsed lung a chance to reflate. It can only happen gradually, though. From then onwards, it's simply a matter of rest, bed rest.

My arrival at the hospital coincided with the birth of the National Health Service. To mark the occasion, local MPs came to visit. They stood at the end of the ward, made speeches and left. They did not come in and shake hands. Also, flags were put out and patients made rugs. The latter were meant to be part of a display but as soon as a patient had finished a rug, he gave it to his wife or another member of the family to be sold. Failing that, he sold it himself to a visitor in the hospital. There was one left, half made. I tried my best and it was the simplest pattern, a green and white swirl, but I couldn't get the hang of it. Wool got everywhere, into my pyjamas, into my groin – the others took pity on me and passed the rug from one to the next, each doing two lines. Twenty minutes later, it was finished and there it hung on the end of my bed, the one and only display to celebrate the birth of the NHS. I won a prize for it, a trophy. It was in my mother's front room for years.

When I was allowed to get up and walk round the ward – the hospital word was 'ambulatory' – I tried to make myself more useful by offering to assist the nurses. What I could do was help those patients who weren't able to move because they were stuck in plaster, take food to them, that sort of thing. Those of us who were able to move were lucky in a specific way. It wasn't just that we had the use of our legs. We could also maintain contact with anyone in the ward we got on with. Others were not so fortunate. The matron had a policy, I'd say a whim, that was designed to do good but to me seemed cruel. If you're in hospital for a long time, you make friends with the patient in the bed next to you and if you can't move, that relationship becomes the most important one you have. There isn't anybody else. Every so often, though, the matron would come in and say: 'Right, all the beds to be moved.' She thought she was giving the patients a new horizon, a fresh view of the world. She may even have been breaking up relationships she thought were getting too special. I didn't see it that way. Those relationships gave security at a time when there seemed to be so little. You could tell from the calls across the ward at night between friends who'd been separated. They were quite touching, like the calls of soldiers across the trenches in the First World War.

'Good night, Fred!'

'Good night, Jim.'

'You all right?'

'Cough, cough, cough, yeah, I'm all right.' It wasn't as if any thought was given to where the beds went. It was arbitrary. As for visitors, they didn't know what to expect. Sometimes, they'd come to a bed, find no one there: 'Where's –' and for a moment think that their nearest and dearest had died. 'Oh, hallo! There you are.'

It was while walking around clearing stuff away that I discovered something I'd always considered a joke: North Wales versus South Wales. 'Oh, come on, it can't be true,' I'd said, but it was. This is how it went. Most of the patients were North Waleans. A few, myself amongst them, were South Waleans. The North Waleans spoke in Welsh the entire time. Nobody else understood it. That's to start with. Then, there were the food boxes. North Walean families, not having far to come, paid frequent visits to their loved ones and every time they came, they brought boxes containing eggs, apples, fresh stuff like that. Sometimes, pieces of this food were left untouched. Instead of giving them to someone else, though, the North Waleans let them go off and rot. When I say someone else, I mean specifically the South Waleans who only had infrequent visits, transport between South and North Wales being virtually non-existent. This untouched food is what I had to throw out, mushy apples, black bananas, oranges with mildew on, even farm butter beautifully wrapped in greaseproof paper but rancid. This, when the rest of us were making do with margarine because we still had rationing. There was no question of 'Would you like an apple?' or 'Would you like an orange?' 'Above the Bridge, Below the Bridge', it was the same thing all over again.

My father, having wangled the petrol (rationing again), was able to visit more often than I'd expected and naturally, my mother came too.

The cakes and tins of food she brought, I was able to share with all and sundry but when she came – well, here's what happened.

The big doors of the ward swung open and there in the centre of the doorway, my father behind her laden with boxes, stood my mother. 'Victor!' she shouted because she didn't know where I'd be. And off she set. No sooner had she reached the first bed than she froze and stared in horror. 'Oh my God,' A little further she went but – 'Oooh! My God! You all right, love?'

'Yes,' croaked 'Give us a wank' who was so concave he could make a bottle of beer vanish in his chest. A few more steps she took, trying to fix her eyes on the end of the ward but the rasping cough of a desperately ill patient turned her head again.

'Oh! OH! OOH!' Weeping by now, she stumbled forward, tears blinding her eyes while I shouted: 'I'm down here!' until finally she got to me.

'Don't – ' I said. 'Stop looking, Mam!'

'I can't help it,' she wailed, 'Look at him. His arms are like strips of cotton on the bed.' Her voice dropped tactfully to a whisper only to rise on the words: ' . . . looks as if he's dying!' Lily couldn't hide her thoughts, that was the trouble. She had to show them and, to be fair, she never told a lie. Well, she couldn't. After she left, came the clip-clop of heels down to my bed. This time it was the matron.

'When's your mother coming next?' she asked.

'I'm not sure,' I said.

'Well,' she said, 'When she does, please will you let me know and we'll put you elsewhere because she's depressed the entire ward.' Elsewhere turned out to be the sluice, so, the next time my mother visited, she was greeted by me with the door shut and surrounded by bedpans.

Apart from wheeling the beds around, whoever was in charge had another surprise for us. We were shown a film. Patients who were able to, walked but most were wheeled – feverish, sweating, shaking – along the corridor, bed after bed after bed, into a large dining room that had been turned into a makeshift cinema. This was before television, so it was quite a treat. The film, *Green for Danger* starring Alastair Sim, was about a lunatic anaesthetist killing people on the operating table. The music menaced. Eyes above a mask looked through the round window of an operating theatre. A hand went to a canister of gas. 'Tsss.' Another put a rubber mask down over the face of the patient and the screen went blank. He was a goner. Going in to the cinema, there'd been a lot of excited chatter. Coming out, dead silence. Who organised such a film? Some of us were due to have an operation the next day. One chap was to have one and three-quarters of his lungs out. He did not lose his sense of humour. As he was pushed back into the ward, he sang to us: 'All of Me, Why not Take All of Me?' Naturally, he was one of the sailors, an erstwhile lover, you could say. That kind of humour always amazed me. In that ward, there was a tremendous amount of laughter.

People died but I lived. I began to get better, so much better in fact, that I wasn't only helping the nurses, I was taking an interest in them, one in particular. Round the back of the recreation hut, which I'd never been in, during a quick fumble, reminiscent of the back streets in Cwm, I was caught and sent to the registrar. He leaned back in his chair and put his feet up on the table: 'Now look here, Spinetti,' he said, 'Your behaviour is appalling. If you continue this kind of carry-on, we will throw you out. Good heavens, if you're like this in hospital, God help you when you get out. God help us all when you get out.'

Back to books I went, of which there was no shortage, thank goodness, and to an attachment with a bit more romance about it. At the film I'd met a patient from the ladies wing. I wrote her letters. Answers, brought by nurses, came with drawings of flowers on the envelopes, so I scribbled SWALK back on mine (that's Sealed With A Loving Kiss). Another chap in the ward was up to the same thing except that his girlfriend was in a village somewhere. We took to reading our letters out to each other, the ones we'd received, that is. It brought us together. With the other patients I rubbed along in a rough, bantering sort of way. With this chap, I could talk properly and, if you've got that, time whizzes by and your heart is light. A good habit was formed by this correspondence. We've exchanged Christmas cards ever since.

I got better, even though I'm convinced the army would have preferred me to catch TB and die. There'd have been no bother about negligence and incompetence then. Instead, I got fat. The day I left hospital, I weighed almost as much as my years, eighteen stone. It wasn't just the food, it was the Guinness. A bottle a day, we were given, as part of our rations. This was the standard method for building people up. I was also – would you believe – given cigarettes. TB or no TB, they too were part of a soldier's rations, so I received mine. As I didn't smoke, I gave them away. Maybe that is why I was so popular.

Ten weeks in the army, a year in hospital, all in all, so what had I gained from national service? Well, I received more offers of sex than I ever, ever would have in show business. What else? I look back now and it's not a bad list: the basic goodness and cheeriness in the hut, where rough men, or so they seemed, cleaned my kit because I couldn't; our platoon commander saving my life with his kindness; the banter in the hospital ward that no, didn't save lives, but lightened the load, enabled us to cope; and, finally, the resilience in the face of death.

During my stay in Llangwyfan, matters concerning my illness hadn't stood still, not that I had a clue, being so isolated. Soon after I was sent to my mountain fastness, our platoon commander wrote to Monmouth School, saying that he was so sorry, that I was a promising 'blah, blah, blah' and that I'd been taken ill. Monmouth didn't leave it there. My records were looked at and the ear test was found. You won't believe this. I even received a sympathetic letter from the Muscular Christian signed 'With Love'. My father found it and said, 'What's this? Who's this man sending you love?' but then, he still wouldn't have liked it if it had been a woman. What happened to the army Medical Officer, I don't know. I had to say 'Medical incompetence and negligence' firstly, because I was angry and secondly, because he shouldn't have been in charge of a row of dominoes, let alone a platoon of soldiers. He was an idiot and a drunk.

Next, Monmouth informed its local MP, Peter Thorneycroft, who asked a question in the House about army medical treatment. The upshot was extraordinary. I was invalided out of the army with a full disability pension, £2 10s a week. This, while soldiers who had lost limbs in the war or had their eyesight impaired, were obliged to fight for any kind of recompense.

When I first met Sean Connery – yes, Sean Connery – in the early 1950s, I discovered that he too had a full disability pension. He'd been invalided out of the navy with a stomach ulcer. It was not only a handy sum of money, this pension, but it also became a sort of link between us.

One has to be careful to whom one tells these army experiences, though. For example, I was on a cruise quite recently when a very upright, pleasant sort of chap joined me in conversation. All was going fine: 'I've always wanted to be an actor. What's it like in the theatre?' the usual, but then we got onto the subject of the army, 'One thing about the army,' he said, 'It does look after its own. It takes great care of its men.'

'Well,' I said, 'Here's my story.' I shouldn't have started because, when I got to the brigadier bristling with red tabs protecting his pension, this chap said in a very tight voice: 'I'm sorry you feel like that. I am, in fact, a brigadier,' at which point he turned on his heel and walked away, never to speak to me again.

Back to 1948. I returned home better but not at ease. There was something missing. I felt wretched, I had no interests. Usually I loved reading but when I picked up a book, I couldn't finish it. At the cinema I just stared at the screen and saw nothing. I didn't know what it was. It was nothing to do with TB or pleural effusions. It would turn out to be a totally unexpected discovery.

5

Cafe Society

After those gales whistling round the sanatorium, that summer back at home in 1948 should have been glorious, particularly as the doctor, before I left, had recommended a short rest every afternoon with no sunbathing and no swimming. Perfect. I've always hated sunbathing. On the beach, I'm the one under the umbrella. And I can't swim. I've tried but it's useless. Even putting my head under a shower has me spluttering, while siestas, I love those. Ten minutes, as long as I can find somewhere to stretch out. But what was wrong? I couldn't eat or sleep. I couldn't concentrate. I simply moped about, all eighteen stone of me, interested in nothing and still feeling ill. 'That's because he's been in hospital,' said the family, 'He'll be fine.' I wasn't. There was something I didn't realise and until I did, the wretchedness was going to stay.

I couldn't even work out whether it was physical or mental, the problem was so confusing. Then, in a rush, the solution came. I was in love. How obvious. I was displaying all the classic signs of lovesickness but then who did I love? That's what I didn't understand. Around me, there was no one. My thoughts spread outwards and that's when the penny dropped, but what a shock. It was a man. I was missing and moping for a man. Impossible. It couldn't be but it was. I had fallen in love, deeply in love with a fellow patient from the sanatorium, a patient who, of course, had no idea of my love for him. Him? I can barely write it even now because it was so unexpected. The rumba-ing kid at the Miners' Institute, the tango-ing terror from the Ebbw Vale Drill Hall, the one who could pull any of the girls with his virtuoso dancing now had to face this fact. He was in love with a man. I was appalled. Was this the 'coming in the face of the Holy Ghost' the priest had warned me of all those years ago? I was even more of an outsider than I had realised.

Having to be careful of expressing this love that had suddenly arisen. 'The love that dare not speak its name,' seems so silly now but that's how it was. And that is why today, as my heart sings for young men holding hands, my mind returns to the moment in 1997 when Graham, my life's companion, was told he was terminally ill. I could see a vein pulsating violently in his neck but I was not able to reach out and take his hand, even though no law forbade it. In any case, his reaction would have been one of embarrassment at so public a display of affection, such had been the awful power of repression expressed by society and its living and loving God – but I digress.

Back at home that momentous summer, the weight fell off and I started moving around again. That meant work but what work? Priest, doctor, something useful, something to help, that's what I'd been considering. Not anymore. The thought of blood had finished the idea of doctoring and as for being a priest, well, since God had set his face against the newly realised part of me, it was bye-bye Deity. Two can play at that game.

Performing or acting, making a living out of that, had still not occurred to me, not for a moment and that, despite the amateur dramatics and taking an act round Cwm. In fact, if it weren't for a God Almighty clash which was soon to come, the career that I did have might never have happened.

Next door to the fish-and-chip shop had been Doctor Mazin's surgery. My father bought it in 1946 and turned the space into a cafe. Even before going to the army, I was running that cafe. I went back to it. My idea of how to run it, though, was not the same as my father's. A farewell party before I left for the army was a taste of things to come. Not only did I invite my friends but also the people who worked at the visiting fair. They lived in caravans and had never been asked into anyone's home before. It was great fun. I put out bales of straw and turned the cafe into a hootenanny parlour.

Parties I was always good at and after the army, I wanted to keep that up, but first I wanted to make an attempt at getting my father's business affairs into some sort of order. Out at the back he had built a dairy where he was always planning to make ice cream. He never did because the two big confectioners, Lyons and Walls, steamrollered all the little ones out of existence. First they lobbied the government, insisting that, for hygiene's sake, ice cream had to be made with prohibitively costly equipment. Then they offered fridges to all confectioners who wanted one, on condition, of course, that they sold only Walls or Lyons ice cream. Their basic ingredient thought by many to be whale blubber meant that their 'ice cream' had no appeal to my Italian father whatsoever, so he didn't get a fridge. But then again, he didn't buy the machinery either. It was too expensive.

The dairy was, literally, a waste of space. I cleared it out, scrubbed it out, put in shelves and made an office. My most useful contribution, I thought, was swapping Dad's accounting system – dusty bills on a wire hook – for a stock book. He had never had one before. A traveller would turn up trying to sell things and Dad would sit at a table with him, drink coffee, smoke a cigarette and talk, politics usually, or sport and then buy tons of sugar or tea, which as like as not we didn't need. He would always buy something, taking up a table while he was at it, where a customer could be sitting. Now, with the new stock book and the office, it was quite simple: take the traveller out to the back, give him a coffee, take down the stock book and say, 'We've got plenty of sugar and tea but we do need salt and vinegar.' But no, Dad never once set foot in that office. Glancing at it he said: 'That's clever but what do you expect from the clever one?' and went back to his table, where he blew the dust off his bits of bills and continued doing his deals.

As for the cafe itself, my main aim was fun and with that in mind, I set to work. At the start we had nothing, so my mother baked. She baked sponge cakes, apple tarts and scones. On the counter they sat and on the counter they stayed. For all the business we did, they could have been glued there. Apple tarts were for homes, not shops thought the customers, who simply stared at them. Next we tried meals. My mother cooked those too but this time the result was quite different. Her signature dishes were roast Welsh lamb, roast beef and steamed fish. If anyone asked for fish and chips, that was no problem either. We only had to pop next door. Lunches and dinners we did, basic food but it worked. We became very popular. Commercial travellers from miles around made a beeline for us because they knew that whatever they ate would be home cooked.

It was even better when we were able to serve chicken. Over the way was the pig man and to him went all our potato peelings and scraps to feed his pigs. In return, we got chickens and eggs. When there weren't enough scraps, we topped up with cash but really, it was never much. This meant that on Saturday nights we could, for a very small outlay or often none at all, do chicken dinners at 5s a head. Actually, 5s was the top price for any meal in any restaurant, even the Ritz. It was part of rationing which was still going on. How the Ritz coped, I couldn't tell you.

When we weren't serving meals, it was over to the counter where we sold coffees, teas, pop, orange juice, biscuits, sweets and cigarettes. I loved the cafe and kept it open till late at night, only to unlock the door, first thing in the morning, seven o'clock. Those very miners that I'd heard walking up the street in the dark, when I was a child, would now put their heads round and ask: 'Are you open?' But this time their faces were no longer black. Pithead baths had been installed. In they came, bought cigarettes, drank coffees and were quite unable to believe that anything could be open at that time.

I'd always loved detail and at the cafe I discovered it could pay off. It was possible to draw customers simply with an attractive table. One customer, a woman who lived in a permanent mess, had a table at home covered with newspaper but as she entered the cafe, it was always: 'Hallo, a pot of tea and a cloth please,' her untidy house, not to mention her brood of children, entirely forgotten.

Other regulars during the week, after doing their shopping, were the women of Manmoel, a tiny mountain-top village where, the joke went, everyone was inter-related. They'd be very disappointed though, if I wasn't there, so first, they made sure I was. The lesson you learn from running a business is not only that you have to be there but that you have to be there all the time.

Sundays were flat. All day, right along the mile that was the main street, nothing stirred. The cinema stayed shut and no pub opened. In the playground, the swings were chained up – they had been since midnight on Saturday – and the slide was blocked off with a bar. It was that flat. I wanted to do something that attracted my friends. So, having collected together some records, I picked up the gramophone and sneaked it down to the cafe. Sneaked because I didn't want my father to know. 'Where are you going with that?' he was asking as I closed the door behind me. I was going to make my pleasure-dome, a place of lights, warmth and music, that's where I was going. The gramophone was to be, possibly, the first jukebox in Wales. My party at last, there it was. The place was packed and my friends, before leaving, even did the washing-up. Fun and economy all at once. The cafe was my theatre and, for the show, I never, like my father, wore a white coat but always a dark jacket. I was quite presentable.

Monday evenings were quiet, so I let the local bridge club use the dining room upstairs. My father thought I ought to charge. 'It's a new business, Dad,' I said, 'You've got to get them to open the door. Anyway, they order teas and coffees, don't they?'

'Yes, and they mark the walls too, with their chairs.' grumbled Dad.

When I had the idea of making crisps, he didn't mind so much. After all, between half past two and six o'clock, his fish-and-chip shop next door was shut. 'Why don't we use the fryer to make crisps?' I suggested. 'We've got the potato peeler. We've got the oil. We can sell them locally.' As the two girls who waited in the cafe had nothing to do then, the only extra staff was Uncle Bill, who came in to do the frying. We set to it, one and a half scoops per packet, a twist of salt, a special machine to zip the whole lot up and biscuit tins already there to put them in. At 1½d per packet they were cheaper than Smiths Crisps, so the local pubs were only too happy to buy them and, what's more, our crisps were fresh.

Who got out of his fish-and-chip shop for once and drove round in a special van delivering them? My father. He enjoyed that because at each pub and club, he could talk, sell and occasionally have a drink.

We expanded. Outside catering was the next step, weddings mainly. Clients sat in my little office poring over menus and doing their sums. Occasionally there'd be a function for Ebbw Vale Urban District Council. The Duke of Edinburgh came to lunch there once.

Ice-cold drinks on hot days advertised in white letters dripping down the shop window; a surprise sale of cream buns, more cream buns than you've ever seen in your life, all going at a penny each; I'd try anything to keep the place buzzing. The Saturday night dinners were a special hit. Even the doctor and his wife came, unheard of in those days. Cardiff was where they usually went. So busy was it on Saturdays, that Uncle Bill put on a black tie and white jacket and became the head waiter. In fact, the place was that full, we had to bring in extra tables and chairs. 'You'll want your bloody bed down here next,' said Dad.

'If it's busy,' I said, 'I'll sleep under the counter.'

Of course – and I didn't realise this at the time – I was encroaching on his territory. The crisps may have got him out and about but the rest of my activities he watched with growing, not to say, growling disapproval. In his book, work and fun were not happy companions.

Wednesday afternoons was half-closing. I'd look forward to some free time, the amateur dramatics perhaps, but: 'Come on, let's do the safe and *your* books,' Dad'd say. No half-day off for me then and certainly no amateur dramatics.

Money burst out of the safe when Dad opened it, crumpled up notes, half-crowns, florins, threepenny bits, pennies, halfpennies, farthings, all mixed up together. As I sorted and counted, Dad watched and made sure every last farthing was bagged. It made me feel uncomfortable, as though I could have been a thief, rather than his son. Hours I sat there before he gathered those bags together and took them to the bank.

After a particularly successful Saturday night chicken dinner with my mother, Uncle Bill and I having worked away like Pavlov's dogs to the ring of the cash register, we were sitting drinking cups of tea, Bill enjoying a cigarette and all of us falling about at the antics of the customers, when Dad walked in. He looked around, took the cigarette from the corner of his mouth, blew out the smoke, picked up a chicken bone from which hung a tiny bit of meat and said: 'What's this? Throwing this out, are you?' We should have laughed but the atmosphere he'd created was too oppressive.

One New Year's Eve, we closed early. 'You go home,' I said to the waitresses, 'I'll finish off here.' And as soon as I had, I rushed up to the house, changed into my demob suit and ran to the local dance, where all the people I knew were going to be, upstairs at the Miners' Institute. When I got there, almost at once a different feeling came over me. 'It'll soon be twelve o'clock,' I thought, 'I'd rather be at home.' Down from the dance hall I ran, down the 'backs', up the steps at the back of the house and slammed into the kitchen. There sat my father and mother. It was striking twelve. 'Happy new year!' I shouted.

'Oh,' said Dad, looking up, 'Here comes the playboy.' I'd left the cafe barely half an hour before and I'd been there all day.

'Happy new year,' I said again and went back to the dance.

As the crisp packing was very much a routine, I thought it would be a good idea to liven things up with some music. I brought a radio in. There we were, packing away when in walked Dad. Again, he took the cigarette from his mouth and blew out the smoke. It was getting to be like Clint Eastwood, only this was a Spinetti Western. 'What's this?' he said, pointing at the radio.

'Music while you work,' I answered. He picked up the radio and smashed it against the wall. The waitresses stared in disbelief. My authority was gone. There was no longer any place for me in that cafe. The landscape was entirely Joe's. Yes, I knew nothing of his tough childhood in Italy and yes, my mother had been working for me and not for him but that's hindsight. At that moment, I couldn't have cared less. All joy, strength and love drained out of me.

I went up to the house where I found my mother screaming and crying like Anna Magnani. It might have made more sense if she'd been Italian. Dad had been there complaining about the girls, the music, the laughter, the dancing, as if the cafe was being run by Busby Berkeley. And, in a way, to him it probably was. It all looked too easy and he couldn't bear work to look easy. The tale of the eldest son and the father all over again. 'There's nothing here for you,' said my mother, 'You should go.' I agreed.

Up in Falcon Terrace, above the bridge, lived Joby Cool, a County Councillor, strict chapel, honest. I went to seek his advice. Perhaps I could be a teacher? 'What would you like to teach?' he asked. I told him an idea I'd had.

'The sun doesn't rise and set. We do the moving, this planet we're on. That's what I'd like to teach.' Children would then understand that we're all together on the one thing.

'Too radical for us,' said Joby and, of course, it was. If we were to become aware that we are one family, our power structures would crumble, and flag waving and nationalism would come to an end.

'There's only one spaceship, Victor,' said Richard Buckminster Fuller, 'Spaceship Earth. The trouble is, it's got four hundred Absolute Admirals.' Thrilled as I was by that remark, decades were going to have to pass before I actually heard 'Bucky' make it.

'Aren't you with the Ebbw Vale Playgoers?' asked Joby.

'Yes,' I answered.

'Well,' he went on, 'They've just opened a college of music and drama in Cardiff. You could go there and be an actor. Monmouth County Council will give you a grant. You already have your Oxford and Cambridge School Certificate.' Joby knew that it was a matter of pride for each county – Glamorgan, Carmarthen, all of them – to send a student to this new college. The timing was perfect. Going to Cardiff would solve all my problems. I needed to get away. I needed to be independent and I needed some money to live. The grant came through and I went to Cardiff.

When I'd gone, Dad gave the cafe, lock stock and barrel, to my brother Mario who didn't want it. What he and his wife, Eira, did want was a proper home where they could entertain. The stock room was turned into a bedroom. The front half of the dining room upstairs was turned into a sitting room and the back half became a tiny corner where a few customers, peering out of a small window at the mountain behind, could have something to eat. The crisp making was stopped and the whole place closed at six o'clock. Soon after that, Mario got a job at the steelworks down in Llanwern and My Uncle Dick and Auntie Vi came down from London to take over the business.

Sausage and chips, fish and chips, pie and chips they served. No chicken dinners. The business dwindled into a little shop where Uncle Dick smoked Wills Whiffs and began to paint. Women were his main subject – well, only one really, his wife Vi – but he didn't know that and nor did anyone else, unless they were prepared to look through a smearing of black that went right across the canvas. Still, his reputation as a *primitif* spread, and even if every 5 November the family joke that they're going to burn the lot, they all have pictures painted by Uncle Dick, me included. Two Richard Watsons are in a museum in Cardiff.

Any refreshment-seeking customer, on the other hand, having the cheek to enter this atmosphere of turpentine and Whiffs, got short shrift from Auntie Vi. 'Tea?' she'd retort, 'Go home and make your own. Coming in here . . .' Dick, her husband, Whiff in hand, would stand there, a distant look in his eyes, possibly thinking of his first wife, Rene, who'd been all glamour, furs, scent and a distant promise of something naughty. Later on, John Lennon told me almost the same thing about an auntie who used to visit him. She too was all silks, satins and exotic scents. He sat on her lap, wanting sex with her, to marry her even. When he was older, he found out that this exotic lady was his mother. Who knows? Some people have always been perplexed as to why he was besotted with Yoko Ono but then, what chord had been struck from the music of his childhood?

By putting Uncle Dick and Auntie Vi into the cafe, Dad sealed its fate and, to think, if he had come into it that Saturday night, joined in, sung *Avanti Populi*, kissed the girls and said, 'Isn't this wonderful,' I'd probably still be there, married with ten children and the mayor of Cwm.

Despite the row and despite leaving for Cardiff, I didn't lose touch but then, I never close doors. Over the years, there was a gradual opening up. I finally uncovered that thing between my mother and father, for instance. Lily told me. 'He was never certain I loved him. Was I thinking he'd only married me for the big family and the job? That's what worried him and the trouble is, I was never sure.' That was devastating but they didn't part. In due course, I taught Dad to hug, my brothers too. We got so good at it that every time there was some kind of reunion, we looked like the mafia. When my father died in 1985 and my mother was given his wallet to open, she found press cuttings of shows I'd been in, a drawing I'd done of him and a poem I'd written. I had never felt he was proud of anything I had ever done.

6

Escape to Cardiff

The College of Music and Drama was in Cardiff Castle itself, so we sat in all the splendour that the Bute family had left to the Corporation. That's nineteenth-century Gothic outside, Pre-Raphaelite murals inside and a big bathroom with a giant bath, round which ran a mosaic of marble and gold designed by Sir Edward Burne-Jones. The gold pieces were fish that glinted among the other colours. It must have taken hours to fill. Elegant surroundings but, as with any stately home or cathedral, it's hard not to think of the people who actually made them happen. Artisans living in hovels built cathedrals. Men, mining coal for a pittance, financed Cardiff Castle. The thought of living there never appealed to me. Where I did live was digs in Cathedral Road with Mrs Bangey who would say of her husband: 'He has a bad heart. One of these days he's going to go just like that,' and then attempt to click her fingers but fail. They were too fat to click. Why, I couldn't make out because her food was terrible. Everywhere lingered the smell of cabbage. She, however, was kindness itself.

In the castle, swearing was frowned on. We weren't allowed to smoke and we definitely weren't allowed to be critical of anybody. But how could I resist? Some of the girls, when they got up to recite a poem on the podium, would lean backwards on the right foot, sway forward on the left foot, go, '*The Highwayman,*' and by the time they got to

> . . . And the highwayman came riding –
> Riding – riding –
> The highwayman came riding, up to the old inn door.

I'd be falling about. 'He's laughing at us,' the girls would complain. 'We're not reciting in front of him,' and I'd be thrown out of the class.

'*The purple bullfinch in a lilac tree,*' droned the Welsh voice, reading a pamphlet on T S Eliot. I dozed at the back, while from the walls, knights in bright armour and women with masses of red hair looked down at me.

When it came to standing up and actually doing something, in plays, that is, I was chosen to be an Italian conductor, The Great Musoni. Immediate typecasting and I hadn't even left drama school! I did win the prize for comedy, though.

'If you're very good and behave yourselves,' said our teacher, Winifred Darby, 'We can get you an audition for the Cardiff Little Theatre.' But it was an amateur group. 'I've already done that,' I thought, 'And I've been in the army, run a business and been kissed in a rugby scrum.' I must emphasise here that the college had only just opened and was still finding its feet. In any case there was Cardiff, my first metropolis. When you're in a city that big, you can get out, hop on public transport – in this case, trolleybuses skimming through the rain – and do what most of us do, educate yourself.

At The Gwendolyn Davies Bequest, there were French Impressionist paintings and at the cinema, films from Europe. They were shown with subtitles something I hadn't seen before: Rossellini's *Rome, Open City,* de Sica's *Bicycle Thieves*, Jean Cocteau's *Les Enfants Terribles,* a feast of films. After *Old Mother Riley*, they came as quite a surprise.

Certain individuals, as I've gone through life, have taken me by the hand, opened doors and shown me a new view. 'Corky' Davies and Heulwyn Richards were the first and now, in Cardiff, came Henry Davies, a fellow student. He, like me, lodged at Mrs Bangey's and he was adorable. Together we could be seen walking round town, talking away, nineteen to the dozen. The other students called us Oscar Wilde and Bosie.

His most wonderful present was classical music. 'We must go to a concert,' he said, and as I'd never heard a symphony orchestra live before, I went along. However, when it finished, I was slightly disappointed: 'Is that it?' I thought, 'Is that all that happens?' I was so used to the cinema. But now I realise everything was happening. You sit there and it's true. Music transports you. Delius was one of Henry's favourite composers, so the first time I heard *The Walk to the Paradise Garden* was when he played it to me. Vaughan Williams, on the other hand, made me impatient. 'He's always doing variations on someone else's air,' I complained.

'But listen to this,' said Henry and then played me something that wasn't a variation and which, of course, I had never heard before.

Henry's greatest passion was theatre. That summer he took himself off to Stratford-upon-Avon and as soon as he got back, described the great performances he'd seen. I was agog. In Cardiff, we went to the theatre together. The Prince of Wales was the one that hosted the big tours in those days. John Gielgud and Sybil Thorndike turned up and so did Donald Wolfit.

In all, where the college really succeeded was in bringing together a group of young people who were mad about the same things and had minds that wanted to explore. If most of our explorations into theatre, poetry and music took place in cafes, isn't that what goes on at any university? Friendships were formed. It was a beginning for all of us and my first stepping stone into theatre and for that I'm very grateful.

I needed to top up my grant, though. At home I'd gone round Cwm doing an act. Old Age Pensioners had rather liked it. I brushed it off and set out to make it earn me some money. What I'd done before was mime to Danny Kaye singing the Lobby Number: 'Manic Depressive Pictures presents . . . from the film *Up in Arms'* To me, his comedy was an inspiration, unlike British radio comedy which was always one class laughing at another. 'You? you'll be lucky, mate.' I couldn't bear the 'know your place-ness' of it. In Cardiff, I built on Danny Kaye's high-speed nuttiness and worked up another act. It was still mime – even now I hadn't found my own voice – and it still used a tape recorder but this time the tape would deliberately misbehave. Either it would slow down, speed up or produce a sound that was totally unexpected and I'd be forced to go along with it. It's possible the idea came from that moment when Laurel and Hardy sing *In the Blue Ridge Mountains of Virginia* and a woman's voice comes out of Stan's mouth. I'm not sure. I do remember sitting in my digs surrounded by all these bits of tape, trying to stick them together.

Gigs came my way and a local critic, Roy Brewer of the *South Wales Echo*, gave me my first review: 'This six-foot shock-headed fellow, with an electric personality,' it started and then went on into a rave.

A few days later, a woman came up to me and said, 'I'm a local agent. I can get you some more work.' She did too. Betty Kellond was her name, International Artistes Representative, her office, a basement in Churchill Way. I became the only student at college to have an agent.

Ta-da! On I went, performing in all sorts of places, a couple of halls, a couple of chapels, The Royal hotel, the Angel hotel and the Park hotel, posh hotels that did dinners. I could earn £20, sometimes £30 a night.

During the daytime I was still turning up at the college. Also there and lodging with Mrs Bangey was Gurnos Gradon, my old friend from childhood. He was studying music and at the same time, going to French classes. After one of them, he said, 'There's somebody in my class you ought to meet,' and the next day he took me into the old part of the castle, where, sitting on the green sward outside the keep was Graham Curnow. Gurnos introduced us. I sat down on the grass.

'Those your own teeth?' Graham asked.

'What?'

'Your teeth, are they all your own?'

'Yeah, except these two. They're on a plate.'

'Oh, what happened?'

'I was in the army and I had to go to the dentist for a check-up and he said, "Good God, call yourself educated? You've got two bad teeth there." And he yanked them out. He didn't try to save them at all. Why do you want to know?'

'I was going to say, whatever you do, don't have a mouth full of fillings.' And on he went asking me even more questions about teeth. The odd thing is, I didn't stop answering. Graham's directness was entrancing me.

No big explosion took place, no big thing. We simply got on well. The grilling on the subject of teeth, by the way, came from his training to be a dental mechanic. Reluctant training, as he really wanted to be an actor. To make ends meet while he was doing this training, he was working in a shoe shop.

At weekends and during holidays, either he'd come and stay with my family in Cwm or I'd go and stay with his family in Efail-Isaf. That was rare, though. His house was so cold, you could let it out as the deep freeze of Wales. The fire in the grate was tiny and his mother, to keep the sheets from getting damp, put newspapers between them. It wasn't that the family was poor but they did live very carefully. His father, seated by the tiny fire, was treated by his mother as if he was hanging on the back door from a peg, while she, the strong one and I suppose, a romantic (though I never saw any signs of it), lived for the cinema. As a consequence, Graham knew about Bette Davis, James Cagney, Humphrey Bogart and Judy Garland long before I did. During the five years at Monmouth I'd only seen three films: *My Friend Flicka*, *Mutiny on the Bounty* and *The Song of Bernadette*. That was it.

At eight, Graham knew he was gay. 'I used to sit in the bedroom window just to watch one of the boys go by because he was so good looking.' Later, when he got a bit worried about it, he went for treatment. 'I think I'm a homosexual,' he said.

'Do you realise that's against the law,' said the psychiatrist.

'Fuck you,' said Graham and left. That was him. It was great, that attitude.

He was into all the things I wasn't. Consequently, he and my father got on fine. While I helped out in the shop, he and Dad played tennis together, after which he'd go to the shop's fridge and help himself to a Britvic orange juice. 'Lovely, I'll have one of those.' And a Kunzle cake. 'Aren't they delicious?' Which took my breath away. Normally, we sold the orange juice at 7d and the cakes at 1s 6d each but Dad didn't mind at all. It should be explained that Graham's mother ran a small shop where he was accustomed to going and cutting off a slice of cheese, so he was only carrying on as usual. 'The reason I came,' he said in later years, 'was because I fancied your dad.' And to be fair, Dad, with his well-proportioned physique and Northern Italian colouring, was certainly the Stanley Kowalski in our house.

When Graham and I weren't together, we'd phone each other, always at a certain time, he from a phone box in his village, me from the shop or the house. Long conversations we held which ended with: 'You put the phone down first.'

'No you put it down.'

'No, you say 'goodbye' and I'll put it down.' It was the real thing.

While doing what he had to do during the day, Graham didn't give up the idea of becoming an actor. He read books and dreamed of winning a scholarship to the Bristol Old Vic Drama School. That's how I first got to find out about Stanislavski's book, *An Actor Prepares* and heard Shakespeare's sonnet, 'Shall I compare thee to a summer's day?' Graham recited it to me. Before that, I knew nothing about them at all.

On a day off from the shop, he came along with Gurnos and myself – we two were just skiving from college – to Porthcawl, a seaside resort. Walking along the front, we found ourselves by the Porthcawl Pavilion where a Spiritualist meeting was being held. 'Let's go in,' said Gurnos and Graham. 'And don't you laugh,' they said, turning on me.

'I won't,' I promised.

No sooner were we inside than a man stood up, spoke the words of the Lord's Prayer and, sure enough – I could feel it coming – pointed at me. 'Brother!' he called out. I didn't know what to do. A woman turned round and said:

'It's all right. Say, "Yes, brother."'

So I said,

'Yes, brother.'

The man said,

'Ah. Ah. You have the gift of healing in your hands – no, a gift of laughter. You must go on with what you're doing. I can hear applause.' And then, turning to an invisible someone, said, 'Yes, I'm telling him as quickly as I can.' Turning back to me, he said, 'This person's looking after you. He's telling you, you must go on with what you're doing.' He listened again. 'All right. Does the name Wedgwood – no, Derby mean anything to you?' I went quite quiet because the name did mean something to me but before I could get the story straight in my head, the man turned to Gurnos and said, 'There is only one string left on your violin. You would do better to throw away your books and get out into the fresh air.' As I've said, Gurnos was studying music at the time. Finally, the man looked at Graham and told him that he'd recently received a bump on the head while swimming. It was true. He had.

Afterwards, I went backstage and found the man sitting next to a big tea urn. I was about to sit down, when its lid shot up in the air and clattered to the ground. 'Don't worry,' said the man, 'These things are always happening.' I was terrified. 'Yes,' he went on, 'The person looking after you is your grandfather.' I went away in a daze. Firstly, there was no way he could have known I was a drama student and secondly, the grandfather/Derby thing was a family story. It really was. My aunt Nell used to tell it by the fireside.

Harry Watson, my grandfather, the Pimlico one, left London, came to Cwm and made himself quite a local character. In a village that was a hotbed of communism, he founded the Cwm Conservative Club. 'Don't go out there with that on!' said my grandmother to him as he pinned a blue rosette to his lapel. 'They'll lynch you.' But round the village he walked wearing it and, because he was unusual, he was extremely popular. He played cards. He gambled on the horses. He was quite the swell. How did he live, though, we wondered. Every month, my grandmother would go to the post office and collect £5, a shilling of which she would give to Harry. The rest she kept for running the house and the children. The money was his but where did it come from? When he died, we found out that it had come from the estate of Lord Derby. 'And that's why he was interested in horses,' I thought to myself. I liked the idea of him being my guardian angel but, good fun and encouraging as all this was for me, it wasn't for Gurnos. He failed his music exams and cracked up. He's still alive, well and thriving, don't worry, and so, for that matter, is the Cwm Conservative Club.

As for the spiritualist hearing laughter, there were soon to be some times when I wished *I* had heard it.

7

Betty Kellond Tours

From time to time, Betty Kellond would ask me to stand in for her at the office and it was out of making myself useful there that I found myself, that summer, as we came out of the 1940's, looking after the great pianist Solomon, at the Llanrwst Eisteddfod. Betty had a tent there and my job was to meet guest artistes at the station and see that they were all right. Eisteddfodau, if you weren't sure, are festivals of music, poetry and drama, usually in the form of a competition.

Solomon took one look at his hotel bedroom and said: 'I can't sleep here. It's too small.' I pointed out that it was only for the one night but no, that was no good. In the end, the hotel manager had to give up his quarters. When we'd sorted that out, I took Solomon to the rehearsal place, a tent. 'I can't rehearse in a tent,' he said.

'But the whole Eisteddfod's in a tent,' I said. He looked over at the piano.

'Upright?'

'Just for rehearsal,' I said. Next thing, I was running round Llanrwst on the cadge. I found a baby grand. Solomon banged away on it, not in a village hall or a practice room but in the local schoolmaster's house. When he saw the piano for the actual performance, he froze.

'It's a Bechstein. I only play Steinways.' I rang the Liverpool Philharmonic. A truck arrived bearing a Steinway. Tuning was still going on as the audience was entering. Solomon himself was backstage refusing to play a note until he was paid. 'The Welsh are barbarians,' he said, 'I shall never play in Wales again.' He then, in that tent in Llanrwst, sat down and gave the most wonderful performance.

The tent next door to Betty Kellond's was a ladies lavatory. Outside, it was blazing hot, so you can imagine what it was like inside, much worse, stuffy as well as hot. Sat in there in all that heat-retaining canvas, was a woman whose job was to take money and give out tickets. Next to her was a pale-faced girl of whom she would say: 'I like to bring her out to give her some fresh air!'

There were jobs in those days that don't exist today, like performing between films in cinemas. When those jobs dried up, survivors used what they knew to get into television. Jess Yates was a good example. In a Cardiff cinema, he assembled a bunch of us students, mounted a pageant and just like on his TV show, *Stars on Sunday,* played the organ. Come to think of it, a job for him it may have been. It wasn't for us. We got nothing.

Back with Betty, I was given my first job on radio, quite a big thing in those days when absolutely everyone listened to it. Television hadn't got a grip yet. The show was called *Welshmen All.* On it was another Welshman, so to speak, Shirley Bassey, who was also one of Betty's artistes. We broadcast from Corey Hall in Cardiff. I performed something I'd written. Shirley sang a popular song of the early 1950s, *Burn My Candle At Both Ends.* It was her first broadcast too.

Sometimes Betty sent us out of Cardiff, us being a little troupe consisting of two girls who played the piano accordion and myself. Round Wales we went, performing in hotels. Usually Betty drove us but on one occasion she didn't. If she had, what happened that night in Llandovery wouldn't have. It started well enough. The two girls did their act, finishing as usual with Katchaturian's *Sabre Dance.* They wore headbands with feathers in and nodded as they played, so I called them 'The Pit Ponies'. At the end, the audience, men eating dinner, clapped enthusiastically. Confident, I walked onto the stage. Moments later all confidence had drained away. The men were just staring at me. I was getting no reaction at all. Nervous and sweating I walked off to dead silence. 'What was that?' I asked a waiter.

'They don't speak a word of English,' he answered. 'They're Poles.'
'They're what?' I said.

'Poles, working for the government, building a dam up here or something.' Then I remembered they hadn't booed. Now it made sense. They'd paid attention to the act. They just hadn't understood it.

The manager invited me and the two girls to his room for drinks. What he gave us, God knows. In ten minutes the Pit Ponies were legless. With me pushing them up the North face of the Eiger, or so it seemed, they climbed, stumbling and giggling to their bedroom. No sooner there, one of them said: 'You're not leaving here tonight, kid,' locked the door and dropped the key into her bra.

'Fine,' I thought, 'They're pleasant enough. I'll stay here.' Both girls started to take their clothes off. The one with the key took off her bra and, as she did, a pair of rolled-up silk stockings tumbled from the cups and fell to the floor with a clatter – the key in the middle. A hammering at the door started up.

'Quick, hide in the cupboard,' said the other girl.

'Don't be ridiculous,' I said and opened the door. 'Yes?' Standing there was the manager.

'I knew it!' he said, 'You bloody theatricals, you're all alike. This is a family hotel. We have a reputation in this part of Wales. You should be ashamed of yourself, a young man like you. Go to your room!'

The next morning, I went down to breakfast where I found the two girls, so trembling and white, they looked like poached eggs on tripe. Not only that, their make-up was smudged and their eyes shielded by dark glasses. 'Where were you?' they groaned. 'What do you mean?' I asked.

'That man, he wouldn't leave our room.'

'What!'

'We've been running round our beds, locking ourselves in the bathroom. It didn't make any difference. We couldn't get rid of him.' Welsh hypocrisy, then, at its most strident but I'd fallen for it.

As I grew more involved with work at Betty's office, it became obvious that she fancied me. At first I thought: 'I'm in my early twenties and she's over forty,' but she was thoughtful, she was kind and for that I was grateful. Anyway, it was clear her feelings were not going to go away, so I suggested an evening together. 'Wonderful,' she said and invited me up to her house in Roath Park which is quite posh. I found her serving drinks when I arrived and got the impression, since she was stumbling about a bit, that she'd already had a few by herself. 'Excuse me kid,' she said because that's the way she talked, 'I'm going upstairs to change into something more comfortable.'

So there I was on the settee, a drink in my hand and music playing, when down the stairs she came, making this entrance, wearing a frilly black negligée and big hoop earrings. For all the world she looked, God bless her, like Olive Oyl. I took her in my arms – it could have been my hand, she was so thin – and embraced her. Thinking it was best to stay where we were and wanting to take my clothes off, I started to lay her back on the settee when she whispered in my ear, 'Listen kid, I hope you don't mind if I keep my stockings on.'

'No,' I said, beginning, out of warmth for this sweet woman, to feel quite aroused.

'Only, you see, I've got athlete's foot.' Crash! Arousal over. Fortunately Betty, by that time, had drunk so much, she passed out. I made her comfortable on the settee and, after a little while, let myself out. The next day at the office, she fluttered gooey eyes at me as if we'd had the most amazing night of love and romance. 'Where's the harm?' I thought and after all, telling me that she had athlete's foot was very considerate of her.

Unfortunately it was the beginning of Betty growing possessive. Ah Betty, Betty the Keck, I called her, after her terrible smoker's cough. We kept in touch until the day she died but at the end of that year in Cardiff, things were getting tricky. 'Beep, beep, beep!' would go her car horn as I came out of the Castle in the evening, chatting to the girls. 'Oh, hallo, Bet,' I'd call, 'Excuse me.' And over to the car I'd go.

'I'll give you a lift to Cathedral Road,' she'd say, 'You are going to your digs, aren't you?' but then, as we drove along, it would be, 'Who was that girl you were you talking to?' The feeling that Betty was taking me away from something I was enjoying to a place where she knew I would be unhappy was getting on my nerves. I needed to get away again.

Graham won a scholarship to the Bristol Old Vic Drama School. It was great. Out of the whole country, only five people won scholarships and he was one of them. At last, things were moving for him but it meant he would no longer be in Cardiff.

Betty and I went to the pictures. The film was *Sunset Boulevard*. 'Must you chew gum? Why are you wearing that tie?' said Norma Desmond to Joe Gillis. It might have been Betty talking to me. 'What am I doing here?' I thought and that did it, that moment in the cinema. I had £20 in my pocket. I was rich. The next day, I caught the train to London.

8

London: There's No Business Like No Business

If you catch a train from Cardiff to London, you arrive at Paddington Station, and not far from there is Notting Hill Gate where at 35 Colville Terrace, I found a room: breakfast and full evening meal, £3 10s a week, sharing.

Through a London of bomb sites and pea-soupers, I walked each day to make myself known to agents who always asked the same question: 'What have you done?' and weren't very impressed when I told them. 'In any case, you'll have to change your name,' they usually added. 'There aren't that many parts for crooks and waiters.' Neil Kinnock, curiously, said pretty much the same thing not so long ago:

'You should have changed your name, Vic. You'd have had lots more parts on television.' Maybe it was advice I should have listened to but then why should I be obliged to deny the efforts of my father and grandfather?

It would have to be on yet another disappointing day that I got caught while going home in one of those pea-soupers. Dirty, yellowish fogs, they were, so thick that your hand, if you stretched it out in front of you, disappeared. By the time I got to the Bayswater Road, I was forced to hold on to the Hyde Park railings to prevent myself from getting lost. For all the traffic there was though, I could have walked down the middle of the road. There was not a single car about.

It was paradoxical because although I was in a fog, I was learning, learning about London, even if it was just where to eat. Schmidts, a large German restaurant in Charlotte Street did Wiener Schnitzels, which were new for me and rather exotic. As often as not, though, it was The Lyons Corner House in the Strand where they had an area called 'The Salad Bowl'. There, for a fixed price, you could eat as much as you liked, though of course it was mainly salad. The top price for any meal, just like in Cwm, was 5s as rationing had still not come to an end.

Now that I was admitting to myself that I could be attracted to men as well as women, I found walking round the centre of London peculiarly exciting. Men's glances gave me a frisson – two, in fact: there was the knowledge that anything we got up to would be illegal but also there was the realisation that it was both available and possible when it hadn't been before. But one visit to the 22 Club in Soho, put paid to all that. The 22 was a bar that had been opened by Ivor Novello. 'A Welshman,' I thought, 'I'll go there,' and in I went. Men, and only men, sat around drinking but before I had time to make head or tail of the place or even order a drink, the door burst open and in charged a bunch of policemen. 'Up against the wall, Mary!' 'Come on, Gladys!' they shouted, and pushed the drinkers roughly against the wall. Once they'd thoroughly frightened everyone, they started to take down names and addresses. The policeman who spoke to me had a very familiar accent.

'Where are you from?' I asked.

'Tredegar,' he answered.

'No?' I said, 'I'm from Cwm.'

'Never?' he said, 'What are you doing in a place like this? Quick, scarper, before they take you in.'

After that I stuck to more ordinary pubs. Even so, things happened in them that don't today. I was at one near the Globe Theatre when in walked a man who said, 'You looking for work?'

'Yes,' I answered.

'Come on then,' he said and took me into the Globe.

'Right,' he whispered and pointed to a ladder. 'You go up there and when the light comes on you pull that rope and the curtain comes down. When the light comes on again, you pull and the curtain goes up. Got that?'

'Yes.'

'Are you in the union?'

'No.'

'Well, don't tell anybody,' and up the ladder I climbed. At the top, I looked down. Far below me and quite small was a golden rectangle of light, the stage, and on it was Sybil Thorndike.

At Banham's the Locksmith in Kensington High Street worked a character called Arthur who, by night, was The Incredible Krama, hypnotist. Having seen my act, he invited me to join him and his little troupe. Performances were mainly at American Air-Force bases. It was in a rather rowdy sergeant's mess, a large, hangar-like building in Norfolk, that things did not go as usual. The Incredible Krama was onstage attempting to start his act. He had a marvellous, grand, somewhat affected English voice and wore a dinner jacket or 'jecket' as he would have said. Speaking softly, he began: 'Ladies and gentlemen,' but the audience carried on talking. 'I would like now to demonstrate some hypnotism for you. Will you all, please, place your hands on your heads,' and despite the hubbub everybody did. 'By the time I have counted to three, you will be unable to remove your hands. One, two, three!'

'Whumpf!' You could actually hear the sound of hands coming down but then a woman shouted: 'I keeyant. I keeyant.' Beads of sweat broke out on the back of Arthur's neck.

'Oh, come – madam – come – please – up onto the stage,' he stammered.

'I keeyant, really, I keeyant,' the woman continued to wail as she made her way through the audience.

'Aw, c'mon,' said the sergeants, 'It's a plant.'

'No, no,' she insisted.

'Please, madam,' said Arthur when she'd arrived on the stage, 'I want you to listen very carefully to me. I will count to three again and this time, when I get to three, you will be able to take your hands down. One, two, three!' and she took her hands down. The audience clapped. Arthur, relieved and emboldened, carried on. 'Madam, who is your favourite movie star?'

'Van Johnson,' answered the woman.

'Well you're very lucky,' said Arthur, 'Because tonight madam – one, two, three – Van Johnson has just come into the room,' and with a flourish he pointed at a chair over which was draped a coat. The woman turned, looked and said,

'That's a coat.' A roar of laughter went up.

'Sit down madam, thank you.' Arthur hurried on, 'Could I have a gentleman from the audience, please.' A squashed-faced Ernest Borgnine type with lots of stripes on his arm lumbered up and sat down. 'Hold your hand out in front of you,' Arthur instructed, 'Keep it rigid, rigid, absolutely rigid.' Taking out a cigarette lighter he flicked it on and, with the audience quite silent now, put the flame under the sergeant's fingers.

'Jesus Christ!' yelled the sergeant snatching his hand back, 'You stupid, fuckin' bastard!'

Beer cans, some empty, some half full, flew through the air and clattered onto the stage. The Incredible Krama, trying to fend off this barrage, ran to the wings where the tour manager, grabbing hold of me, shouted, 'You're next!' and gave me a shove.

Out I went tripping, falling and sliding amongst the cans. My act, in the face of continued hooting and yelling for the previous act, went down, shall we say, well enough. As I came off, a member of staff approached me. 'Ah yes,' I thought, 'The one who asks us to join him in the bar for a drink and a bite to eat.' Not so.

'Get out,' he said, 'Now, while you can.' All of us crammed into the car which made a beeline for the gate.

'Who goes there?' demanded the sentry. I wound the window down.

'Floor show escaping!' And off we drove, laughing all the way back to London.

The Incredible Krama offered me a tour. I took it. Top of the bill was a South African tenor who was putting up the money. His fellow performers included a cousin, Reg Darnley, who played the harmonica, Arthur, The Incredible Krama, a couple of dancing girls and me with the misbehaving sound effects.

The tenor had what he thought was a good idea for his act but achieving it meant first rushing round the local furniture stores at each date in order to put a set on the stage. This comprised a three-piece suite, a standard lamp, a cocktail cabinet and a carpet. So when the curtains parted, the tenor, wearing a smoking jacket and a bow tie, was able to say in his strangulated tenor voice: 'Good evening. As we are now invited into your homes on television, tonight I would like to invite you into my home.' This would have been more convincing had not each item of furniture been clearly labelled 'Dane's Furniture Store' or whatever shop it had come from, there being no time to print it in the programme.

Reg Darnley played the harmonica very well. However, that's not all he did. To fill out the second half and save his cousin some money, he also performed a comedy and piano act. It started with a tiny figure being discovered alone on the stage, though, all you could actually see was a sombrero, a newspaper and a pair of Little Tich boots. 'English weather! Outlook black!' came a voice from behind the paper, whereupon it was cast aside, revealing a little man in a plastic mac with a black face. The man picked up a hand mirror from the stage looked in it, yelled, 'Outlook black? Ugh!' and tumbled over in horror. He, Reg, then stood up, rising to his proper height, while discarding the plastic mac, the big boots and the black face, which was a mask. That was his opening gag. After it, he went over and sat at the piano to play renditions of popular melodies. 'Come on, all together now, let's have a sing-song!' he called out but the audience – as often as not, four or five people who were only there to get out of the rain – sat in silence, staring. 'Now, for my big finish,' said Reg, 'I'm going to play *On Top of Old Smokey* with my nose,' and rather slowly, he went 'Dang-dang-dang-dang, dang, dang,' with his nose before saying, 'Come on all together now!' and carrying on, 'dang-dang-dang, dang, dang,' but no one joined in. Being next on, I was standing in the wings waiting for my entrance and as the act ended, I heard something I'd never heard before and indeed haven't since – the closing of the curtains. They came together in a dusty 'fwooo'. Total silence. There was no applause whatsoever. As for the Incredible Krama, it was the same as usual. His hypnotism never, ever worked. Apart from myself, who was paid a wage, all the other performers were on a percentage. It's not hard to work out who was the only one to have any money.

There were lots of tours in those days, television having yet to knock a dent in theatre and kill off variety. Travel day was Sunday and this had its moment of fun when actors, singers, dancers, comics, musicians, magicians and acrobats converged at Crewe station, which they always did. As they changed trains, they swapped news. You'd get: 'We're transferring to the West End. We've just heard,' and 'Lucky you, it's Glasgow for us,' which was name dropping, really. Glasgow, Birmingham and Manchester were very good dates, so the speaker was probably on a number one tour of a big musical. Of course, the trains eventually had to draw away and at that moment the platform went from bustle and chatter to emptiness and silence because nobody actually got off at Crewe. Nobody, except me. Worcester, Attercliffe, Chesterfield, Crewe, I was on a number ten tour. At least I had the price of a train ticket. The others hadn't and that's why I was alone.

Lugging my tape recorder, props and change of costume, I walked down Crewe's main street in the pouring rain. Through it loomed a semi-nude woman on a large, garish poster. She was advertising last week's show, a nude revue. With her skimpy bikini and piled-up hair, she seemed to be mocking me because even before television, variety was dying and it was nude revues that were killing it. Behind the poster, rain had found a gap and was trickling down to collect up at the V of the semi-nude's groin. So big and bulging by now was her mound of Venus, that the paper had split and through a tiny hole, a thin stream of water was curving out and hitting the pavement. She was, for all the world, pissing on variety, pissing on Crewe and pissing on me. There was more truth to this than I had bargained for.

I went into a pub. 'Do you have any digs?' I asked the landlord.

'No,' he said, 'But I've got a caravan out at the back. Five bob, the week. You can have it for that.'

'Oh,' I thought, 'How wonderful.' So I went out into the back yard. The caravan was oval, like an egg, with windows that were oval too and it was up on bricks. I doubt if it had been out on the road since the thirties. I went in. It stank. I cleaned it, scrubbed it and having found a lantern, lit the gas in the hope of warming the place up and making it habitable. After the show that night at the Grand Theatre, I had a quick drink at the pub's bar, went out the back and got into my little caravan. I was lying there in bed when suddenly, though the weather had been fine a few minutes before, it began to rain rather heavily, drumming on the roof of the caravan. As suddenly as it started, it stopped. I went to sleep. The next night, I came through the pub and got into bed. About an hour later, it started to rain again. Thud, thud, thud and then it stopped. On the third night, when yet again it started to rain, I opened the little curtains of one of the oval windows. A line of men was standing there, peeing over the caravan. The game was to bypass the Gents and see who could, after all that beer, piss over this tiny caravan. The winner obviously bought the others another round of drinks. I tapped the window: 'Hey,' I called out, 'I'm in here!'

'Oh, sorry mate,' they said and stumbled away laughing into the night. So you see, I have really stayed in a toilet!

At the Hippodrome, Chesterfield, after the first house on Monday, the manager, Vic, came round. 'You've got no bloody show,' he said and pointing at the star, the South African tenor, went on: 'You're bloody 'opeless, you are. You,' He was now talking to me, 'You've got a bit of life in you. You can top the bill. And you,' he said, looking back at the cringing tenor, the man who, after all, had financed the tour, 'Can close the first half. Oh and, by the way, get yourself some girls, some nudes. That's what we need now, nudes.'

Even though we were preparing for the second house, Arthur managed to nip down to the local Woolworths and find a couple of girls. So that evening, Reg Darnley, standing in the wings, was able to announce: 'And now, we have England!' as a girl posed naked onstage holding up a Union Jack. 'And now we have Wales!' meant another nude but with a Welsh flag. 'And now we have Ireland!' brought back the first girl, holding up an Irish flag.

'Hurray!' we were all urged to shout.

When I came on I didn't know what to expect. Up until that point, the coal miners of Chesterfeld had just been looking at us. I marched out in a big floppy bow tie and a pair of white gloves, all set to do an impersonation of Al Jolson, apparently. The film, *The Jolson Story,* was popular at the time and as I looked a bit like Larry Parks who played him, it seemed logical. 'I would like to pay tribute to that great artiste, Al Jolson,' I began but the audience groaned. Everybody was doing Jolson and they'd had enough. That, however, is what I wanted. The introduction to *Swanee* started: 'Yatatata-da-da-da-da, bam, bam, bam,' 'I've been away from you a long time –' and nothing. That's all they got. A ghastly silence followed. I shuffled over to the wings, apparently to ask the stage manager to put the record back on but no sooner had I reached the wings than out came *We'll Gather Lilacs*. I threw up my hands in horror but tried to keep going and would have done if church bells hadn't started to ring: 'Dang, dang, dang, dang!' requiring me to pull ropes. Then all hell broke loose: a train, 'Djer-djer-djer-djer-djer!', a World Cup goal, The Last Night of the Proms, everything, and I had to keep up with the lot. When we reached The Last Night of the Proms, the finale, I had to be the conductor, the orchestra, the audience and Constance Shacklock singing *Land of Hope and Glory*. It was a very busy act and Chesterfield responded to it. So, years later, did the *Sunday Times* theatre critic, Harold Hobson. 'The joy of this man trying to catch up with all these things,' he wrote, after seeing me at the Edinburgh Festival, but he gave the wrong name, another performer. I wrote to him and he wrote back suggesting I let him know when I was next doing the act. He would come and see me again.

Back in town, I got my first London gig. It was at the Masonic Temple, the Freemasons' HQ behind Drury Lane. I was to take part in an evening's entertainment for the showbiz lodge. The best bit came after I'd finished. Bud Flanagan of the double act, Flanagan and Allen, came up to me and said: 'You've got it, son. You don't know what the bloody hell to do with it but you've got it. Let me give you some advice. Go on with what you're doing. There's plenty of room at the top and no room at the bottom. Keep going.' It was the first piece of advice I'd been given to do with any kind of career.

9

London: the Early 1950s

I said that I was sharing at Colville Terrace. The guy who had the other bed was a young man called David who worked in advertising. What he actually liked, though, was Noël Coward. 'Poor Little Rich Girl' was never off the gramophone and, with his golf clubs and tennis racquets, he looked as if he'd stepped out of one of Noël Coward's plays. I think he'd have been happier as a critic.

'You must come and meet my girlfriend,' he said one Saturday and off we drove to her flat near Oxford Street. The door was opened by a very attractive young woman who was wearing nothing but a pink bath towel. 'Dulling,' she said to David speaking in a French accent, 'You never told me Victor was so good looking. Go and get some milk and bananas.' Then, turning to me, added, 'I'm on a milk and bananas diet.' When David closed the door, she let the towel drop. This time, there was no sign of athlete's foot and, next thing, we were in bed, soon to be drinking champagne and eating black grapes with David banging at the door.

'What are we going to do about him?' I asked.

'Dulling, he'll love it,' she answered, 'He's a masochist.' So, in the space of one hour, I had a mistress and a friend who was a masochist, not that I had a clue what the word meant.

As cabaret was the way she earned her living, singing 'in five languages by candlelight,' she was my Sally Bowles. She was daring, she was witty, she was beautiful, and though it was London in the 1950s, with her it could have been Berlin in the 1930s.

She amused me in tiny ways. 'Let's go for a walk, dulling,' she suggested and up Oxford Street we went, crossed past Marble Arch and walked into Hyde Park. 'Oh, dulling, I can't bear this,' she said, 'I'm homesick for London.'

Flowers and chocolates arrived at her flat all the time, along with tickets for shows, which meant I no longer had to rent a stool to sit in

Before the war. A day out. Mam, Dad, and little Mario are in the middle. Cousin Derek, tough, relaxed and assertive is on the right. I, cold wet and whingeing, am on the left. With such a son, why did my parents bother with more children? They did, though, four, after the war.

From the left, saintly aunt Matilda who, for all her devoutness, had her handbag stolen in church, a small Conti, and signora Spinetti, my grandmother or 'nona' as they say in Italy. What a relief, after the disaster in Ischia, to arrive at their farm, a converted convent overlooking the river Po.

Emlyn Williams. Actor, playwright and Taffia godfather. Emlyn looked out for lost Welsh actors in London. 'Still keeping your head just below water?' he asked one day. The next morning, I received a cheque for £1000. 'I intended to leave this to you in my will,' said his note, 'But as I also intend to live longer than Hayley Mills, here it is now.'

In the garden at Crosscombe Terrace, surrounded by Dad's dahlias, are me, Dad and Mario. By now, my little brother is golden curl-less. I, though dressed in regulation street urchin outfit, am wearing a clean white shirt. That's why I'm able to look at the camera.

Outside the Cort Theatre. New York. 1960. A friend took this intending to give it to me as a present. Little did he know that the figure on the left in the pale jacket is Brendan who'd just fallen off the wagon. The guy with him is turning him away from his own play. For all that, Brendan still got onstage, where he held the audience in the palm of his hand.

Winston's Nightclub. I'd just changed and nipped round to join Joan Littlewood, my university. At this time, the early 60s, she was dreaming of her own university, the Fun Palace and there, with her, is its architect, the brilliant Cedric Price. Contrary to the image people had of Joan, she is not swilling beer.

On holiday with Peter Shaffer in Morocco where I learned to think less conventionally. Travelling between Casablanca and Marrakech, I became convinced my wallet had been stolen. Deeply suspicious, I turned back to the hotel, only to find the owner standing at the door waving the missing object. He'd found it under my pillow, exactly where I'd left it.

On the morning of this day, I drilled trainees at Sandhurst. Now I'm drilling actors, Griffith Davies, Larry Dann and Murray Melvin from the *Oh What a Lovely War!* company. The whole day was devoted to charity. For the real thing, see the next page.

Oh What a Lovely War! Wyndhams Theatre, 1963. Me, Murray Melvin and Griffith Davies, all of us dressed slightly differently. The point was, each of us had to have our individual characters. That was Joan's way. The gibberish I'm speaking was based on real drill, so at least I knew what I was doing, even if nobody else did.

The play I didn't go to Paris with, *Every Man in His Humour*, at Stratford E.15, 1960. The servant, Brainworm, that's me, gulls the merchant, Kitely, that's Bob Grant - and it was only four nights off I wanted.

Three cabaret artistes share a joke over a glass of champagne: Ronnie Corbett, very boyish, myself and Anne Hart. Anne became Mrs Corbett and is still Mrs. Corbett today.

At the Irving Strip Club off Leicester Square. This Al Jolson impersonation caught the eye of *Sunday Times* theatre critic, Harold Hobson. If only he'd put the right name in his review.

With Roy Kinnear in the grounds of the Bahamas hotel, the one with the cool bungalows. 'I've looked like this all my life and I always will,' said Roy, 'But everyone else will change, including you.' He was right, as you will see.

During the filming of *Help!* in 1965, bachelor, Paul McCartney, world's heart-throb, out with captain of the bodyguards.

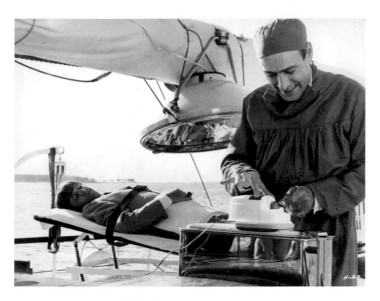

The Bahamas. The first shot of the film, *Help!*, Strapped to the table is Ringo. Dressed in scrubs is me. 'Sand in the generator!'

With another heart-throb. He's the one on the left. This could also be called George Harrison with Victor Spinetti's mother. 'You've got an incredible karma.' George once said to me. 'Thanks,' I replied before going to look it up.

With Miriam Karlin at the time of *Fings Ain't Wot They Used T'Be*. Elegant and tasteful, Miriam, in real life, could not have been further away from her *Rag Trade* image.

With Diana Dors in the 70s. Her friend in the middle, I'm sorry, I cannot identify. As Emlyn Williams was a godfather, so Diana was a godmother, a wise and kind one.

the gallery. A spectacular musical from New York opened at the Casino Theatre. *Wish You Were Here* it was called, its star, a body-builder. Since one of my Sally's admirers had sent a couple of tickets, we went. Down to the front of the stalls she strolled, wearing leopard-skin slacks and a tight black sweater. From her wrist hung, not a purse, but a little gold birdcage in which was suspended a red handkerchief. In her other hand was a long cigarette holder. I followed her whispering: 'Whatever you do, don't ask for the souvenir programme. I've only got a shilling.'

'Souvenir programmes!' chanted the usher, 'Buy your souvenir programme!'

'No thank you, dulling,' said my Sally. 'I want everything to be a big surprise.' Ten minutes into the show came a bathing scene with a real pool. I felt sorry for the performers. It was the middle of January. 'Oh look, my God!' said my Sally, pointing at a girl on the stage, 'I've not seen her since we had an affair at school!' She had the attention of the entire front row, so much so, that a man behind us tapped me on the shoulder and asked if the two of us would like to join him in the interval at the champagne bar. We did, and drank rather a lot of champagne, after which, the new admirer invited us to dine with him at the Mirabelle in Curzon Street. All through dinner he sat, hooked, staring at this chattering, amusing, beautiful woman.

But then my Sally could always handle men well. The clever thing was, she could also keep them at a distance, one way or another. Here's a way: 'Oh my God, what day's it today?' she asked, as she woke up one morning.

'Monday,' I told her.

'Find a champagne bottle.'

'What?'

'A champagne bottle, quickly.' I went out into the street and rummaged through the bins until I found one. I took it back. She washed it out and disappeared. When she returned, she put the bottle in the fridge. A little while later, the owner of the flats, a charming man with a villainous background, appeared and went off with the bottle.

'What was in it?' I asked.

'The rent.'

'The rent?'

'Yes, he likes to drink urine and he happens to like mine, so that's the rent, dulling.'

My education was coming on apace but some lessons were less pleasant than others. Late one afternoon, my Sally came in looking quite pale.

'Get me a drink.'

'What's the matter?' I asked.

'I've just had an abortion.'

'Why didn't you tell me?'

'Did you want it?'

'No.'

'Well, neither did I. Now where's the champagne?'

It was business as usual when, another day, she said: 'Dulling, I must go out. I have a little job. Eva and I —' Eva was a cabaret star, famous for singing: '*Ne me touche pas. Laisse moi tranquille*,' despite being Hungarian. 'Eva and I have to beat —' She then named the grandson of a celebrated nineteenth-century poet. 'It's too boring,' she explained, 'We tie him to a radiator and beat him not very hard at all.'

'Well, if that's how people are,' I thought, 'That's how they are.' Anyway, I was learning.

The idyll lasted six months and then it was: 'By the way, darling, I'm afraid our romance is over.' This, in a perfect English accent. As we weren't in love, I wasn't too hurt. 'You see,' she continued, 'I've met a man who has twelve inches.'

'When you've finished with him, let me know,' I said, and although we parted, we still keep in touch.

The champagne and black grapes were a delightful interlude. They were not typical of what I was getting up to during those early days in London. I was still the young performer trying to find work. I auditioned at the Celebrity Club in Clifford Street, taking my Ferrograph tape recorder with me as usual. The owner fell about. The waiters who were cleaning fell about. 'Right,' said the owner, 'We'll put you on tonight.' It was a Sunday. 'If you do well, you've got a week.' I thought: 'Gosh, the West End, a nightclub.' That night, the owner introduced me: 'Ladies and gentlemen, this evening, we have a surprise guest . . . Blah-blah-blah . . . Victor Spinetti!' I switched on the Ferrograph and went on stage. The lights dimmed. The spotlight came on and what happened? The Ferrograph had been plugged into the dimmer. It went s-l-o-w-e-r and s-l-o-o-w-e-r and the sounds got d-e-e-p-e-r and d-e-e-e-p-e-r. The audience threw pennies at me. Knowing it was the only money I was going to get that night, I was careful to pick up every single coin. Not that it was enough to get me home. Lugging the Ferrograph, I walked ten paces, stopped, sat on it, got up again, walked another ten paces and so, that way, eventually made it back. There were times when tying the Ferrograph to my neck and throwing myself in the Thames seemed easier.

All this while, Graham was still studying at Bristol but during the week, as like as not, a letter card would arrive. 'I'm so looking forward to coming up to London and seeing you,' it would say, 'By the way, can you get tickets for *Oklahoma!* and Olivier?' which meant come Friday evening, off the train he'd jump and off we had to run – he had no sense of time – so that we wouldn't be late for the show. The next day, we went not only to an evening performance but a matinee as well. I was exhausted. In this way, though, I got to see all the shows, serious plays, big musicals, everything from *Tamburlaine* to *The King and I*. Were it not for Graham, I'd never have gone. More likely I'd have daydreamed in the park or lain on my bed and written a poem. Actually, I did that anyway. A dramatic thunderstorm inspired me to write some gloomy lines about Wales.

It was odd this. There was my Sally going to the theatre to be seen, fine, and there was Graham going to the theatre to watch actors and acting, fine. But then there was me. When I wasn't actually up there performing, I was perfectly content to sit at home reading rather serious writers like Koestler and Sartre, imagining a career in research of some kind.

People didn't stop introducing me to their passions though, and I'll always be grateful for that. David, my room sharer, with his enthusiasm for theatre, introduced me to the actor and writer, Hugh Hastings, who wrote *Seagulls Over Sorrento*. Hugh, charming and witty until just before midnight, when he would ask his guests to leave because he was haunted, introduced me to his neighbour, Diana Dors. That's how it went. 'Where are you from?' she asked. I told her.

'Listen, I know what it's like when you've come up and you're trying to get established,' she said, 'The important thing is, don't go without food. This house, the door is always open. I have a cook. If ever you turn up and I'm not here or Dennis isn't here,' – Dennis was

Dennis Hamilton, her husband – 'it doesn't matter. She will fix you a meal, OK?' It was very OK. I was already amused enough just by being there. A television picture projected onto a wall was intriguing me. I'd never seen that before. On the floor was a tiger-skin rug and the projector was inside the head of the tiger.

Sometime later, when I was in the neighbourhood, I thought I'd drop in for a cup of tea. As I approached the house, a tiny object in the gutter caught my eye. It was a ring. The actual band had been crushed quite badly but the stone was perfect. It was light blue like Diana Dors' eyes. She was in when I knocked and when I showed her the stone she said: 'Darling, what a wonderful colour, how sweet,' but better than that, she had it set in a new ring and wore it for the rest of her life.

Diana, in turn, introduced me to the film director, Brian Desmond Hurst, best known for *Dangerous Moonlight*: 'Darling, you must meet him,' she insisted, 'He'll love you.' How he would love me, I didn't quite realise. Brian, Irish, tall, with a shock of white hair, gregarious and full of the joys of life, didn't beat about the bush.

'Ah, come and live with me,' he said. I, a bit buttoned up at the time, explained that not only did I already have a home but also a friend who would be coming up for the weekend. 'Bring him over,' said Brian and in due course, Graham and I did turn up at his place in Kinnerton Street where, sitting in a high-backed chair, he contemplated the two of us. 'I don't know whether you're any good at acting,' he said, 'But you both look as if you need a good overcoat for the comin' winter. I start a new film next week. There'll be a day's work for the both of you. Then you can buy those coats.' The film *Behind the Mask* had Michael Redgrave in some kind of hospital set-up, so I played a porter and Graham was a patient. I even had a line: 'This way, mate,' and the money we earned was enough to buy warm overcoats for the winter. That job was extraordinary but what about ordinary work?

A useful gig was singing at The Rifle pub in Hammersmith, run by a boxer called Alf Mancini. Whatever other work I might have got, the £3 he paid covered the rent at 16 Stanley Gardens, where I'd moved and had my own bedsit. At the Rifle, I was able to sing Al Jolson songs such as 'There's a Rainbow on my Shoulder' and 'Swanee, how I Love you!' all the way through, because those old ones worked there. In any case, I added the latest hit:

If ever the devil was born
Without a pair of horns,
It was you, Jezebel,
It was you.

Frankie Laine was singing that at the London Palladium and the ladies sitting in the snug loved it.

Even so, by Christmas I was desperate. In a few days' time, I was due back in Wales and had no money for presents, but then a regular at the Rifle, a young man about my age, sent a drink up for me. 'What do you do?' I asked.

'I'm in the army,' he answered.

'But you have a car,' I said, 'You're very well dressed. When I was in the army I got 15s 6d a week. How can you afford all those things?'

'I'm a hustler,' he said. Or, rather, he may have been, because I'm not sure he used that particular word but it's certainly what he did. He was in the Guards and he had sex with people for money.

'Oh,' I said, 'Well, find me somebody. I need some money. Christmas is on the way and I'm the first person in our family to leave and come up to London, so there's a houseful of people in Wales all expecting to be impressed with presents and I don't know what I'm going to do.'

'What will you do?' he asked.

'Anything,' I said, 'Just find me something. I'll work it out.'

'All right,' he said, 'I'll let you know.'

A few days later, he rang: 'Meet me in the Colony Room. Muriel's. Wear your demob suit and pretend you've just been demobbed from the Welsh Guards. And, for Christ's sake, you're not an actor, OK? And drink beer.'

I couldn't bear beer but I agreed.

The Colony Room was a drinking club in Soho. It's where people drank when the pubs were shut. Up a narrow flight of stairs you climbed and there it was, on the first floor. As you looked through the doorway you immediately saw the boss, Muriel Belcher, sitting by the bar, smoking her fag. From her you'd get a raspy, drawly, abusive greeting. If you got past that, you found yourself in one dimly lit room, which in proportion to its reputation, was surprisingly small. Francis Bacon, Tom Driberg MP and Dan Farson, the journalist, were members. It's been written about, it's been painted – Michael Andrews has done a good picture – and it's been in a film. Arty with a hint of sleaze, it was the essence of Soho, disreputable but with reputable people in it, usually looking for something or someone disreputable to do.

'Hallo dahling!' This was Muriel as usual, with her fag. I looked to my right. The hustler wasn't there. However, there was a couple on their own, middle-aged. I went over. For a while, neither said anything. I looked at the woman's hands. They were like parrot's claws with dozens of rings on each talon. Wrapped around one was a tiny cigarette holder of the kind Gloria Swanson wore in *Sunset Boulevard*. After a while the woman spoke: 'Would you like a drink?' Her accent was faintly Viennese.

'Beer – pint of beer,' I said.

'Pints?' barked Muriel, 'We don't sell pints in here, dahling.'

'Oh, I said, 'Well then . . .' and on a low shelf I saw a bottle of Worthington Pale Ale, 'I'll have one of those.' Ugh, it was horrid.

After a bit, the woman said to the man, 'It's all right. We can trust him.' I could have been in *The Third Man* – 'Dang, derrang, derrang-derrang'.

'Come tomorrow night at half past seven,' said the man.

'OK, thank you,' I said and got up to go.

'What would you like to eat?' asked the woman. My mind raced. I had to get this right. I had to think of butch pub food.

'Beef. Hard-boiled eggs. Tomatoes. Celery. Pickled onions.' I hoped that 'eat' really meant a meal and held no strange sexual connotation.

'Good night,' said the man and off I went.

Of course, I was awake all night. I could not sleep. 'What have I done?' I thought, 'I'm not going to go,' and then, 'You'd better go. Christmas is looming.'

The address was a big block of flats in Abbey Road near the EMI studios. I rang the bell. The man opened the door and started to speak but such a screeching and squawking was there coming from inside the flat, I couldn't hear. It sounded like the parrot house at the zoo. He beckoned me in. I followed, noticing that he wore nothing but a dressing gown and, considering the stifling heat in the place, I was not surprised. The first thing I made out in the dimly lit living room explained the screeching, the squawking and the excessive heat immediately. Round the walls, tropical birds in cages, hopped up and down flapping their wings. The high back of an armchair caught my eye. In it, wearing a brightly coloured peignoir, her legs crossed, sat the woman. She was smoking her cigarette in its Gloria Swanson holder and looked for all the world like a bird of paradise.

To one side was a card table, on it, beef, hard boiled eggs, tomatoes, celery and pickled onions, the pub food and, horror of horrors, a bottle of Worthington Pale Ale. In that stiflingly hot room, amid the birds' twitterings, with the woman quietly smoking and watching, I sat and tried to force the food down. So nervous was I, my throat so dry, I could hardly swallow a thing and, to get at least something down, I had to keep sipping that revolting ale. The beef wasn't too bad but the pickled onions would keep rolling around and when one fell on the floor for the third time, I decided that I'd had enough. 'Thank you. Thank you very much,' I said.

The man, who until then had remained silent, spoke: 'Now, I do not want to have sex with you,' he said, 'I want you to whip me.'

Inside my head a gun went off and a flock of birds rose up from the branches of a tree, 'k-k-k-k', leaving it bare. I'd never heard of this in my life. 'He's crazy,' I thought and then something flashed through my mind. 'Dulling, Eva and I have to beat —' I *had* heard of it before. What's more, my Sally didn't seem to have been too put out by it.

'Please, go next door into the bedroom. You will find a uniform. Put it on,' said the man. I went through and it was quite a relief because the bedroom was cooler. There on the bed, as if laid out by a valet, was a full SS uniform. Inside the jacket was a label: 'Berman's Theatrical Costumiers'. I pulled on the breeches. They weren't a bad fit. The boots were a bit of a struggle, though. Finally, I put on the peaked cap and peered in the mirror. I looked rather good but then, glancing sideways, I caught sight of a long, leather thong with little knots in the end still lying on the bed. 'Victor, what are you going to do?' I thought, 'You've never hit anyone in your life,' and then, 'You're meant to be an actor. Now's the time to start. Go and act.'

Into the next room I burst, snarling. It was a great entrance, the best bit really, because in striding across the room, my shiny soled boots slipped on a pickled onion and sent me flying, the thong too. Scrambling to pick it up, I took in the scene. It had slightly changed since I left the room. The card table had been folded away and in its place was a narrow divan on which lay the man, totally naked. At his head sat the woman, still smoking. Around us, the birds continued twittering. 'Come on,' I said to myself, 'Think of Christmas. Think of Christmas.' and flicked the thong across the man's bottom.

'Ow!'

'Sorry, I mean – *Schwein!*'

Was I to carry on? Since the man said nothing, I thought I'd better. 'But I won't do it there where I've just whipped him,' I thought, 'That wouldn't be very kind. I'll do it here,' and I flicked again. 'And now I'll do one over there, I think.' It was a performance I was giving, all right. I'd become a painter, the thong little more than a brush. Even then, I was hardly Francis Bacon. He was much more violent. The way I was dabbing, I'd be lucky to end up with a genteel watercolour.

'That's enough,' said the woman quietly. I gave another snarl, for good measure, threw down the whip and marched out. In the bedroom, I looked in the mirror as I took off the cap. 'Who was that?' I asked my reflection. 'That was you, you became someone else.'

I changed and returned, almost apologetically, to the living room, where the man had got dressed. 'Thank you so much. That was wonderful,' he said and gave me fifty guineas. Well, in those days, that was like £500.

'Really?' I said. I couldn't believe it.

'Yes, yes,' he insisted, 'And please, let me have your address.' As soon as I'd scribbled it out, I bounded down the stairs of the flats and raced along Praed Street. Earrings for my mother, cigars for my father, a football for my brother, I bought the lot and climbed onto the train. At home, I staggered in, laden with presents and, having put them round the tree, went up to the club, the British Legion, to buy Dad a pint.

'How you doin' boy?' he asked.

'Not too bad,' I said, 'I had this part as a German officer.'

'Oh yes? That's good,' he said.

It was a fine Christmas and it didn't finish there. On my return, I found at the bedsit in London a parcel from Harrods containing a suit, a beautiful suit, with a waistcoat, embroidered. In those days, an embroidered waistcoat under a black suit was quite the thing. Now they're in again. I rang to say thank you. 'Please, come round,' said the man, 'Come for dinner.'

This was both nice and disappointing. A proper invitation to a proper occasion, I was to discover, shattered any prospect of this new job becoming a regular thing. Or, as John Lennon would put it years later at the EMI Studios when, pointing at the flats, I told him this story: 'What a pity. I thought you were set up for life.'

I went for the dinner and the couple couldn't have been more charming. After we'd finished eating, they told me their story. It was like Somerset Maugham. During the war, the man was in a concentration camp and afterwards, his fantasy was to be beaten by a total stranger in front of his wife. They were then able to have wonderful sex. Well of course, I was no longer a stranger. So that was that. Perhaps I never really had been. 'We knew you weren't an ex-Guardsman,' they said, 'We realised you must be an out-of-work actor.'

'Yes,' I was forced to agree but, afterwards, for many years, they sent first-night telegrams and came to see me in shows. For *Oh What a Lovely War* they came down to Stratford East and they always sent little things, lovely people.

There's a coda. Ten years later, I was in New York spending an evening with Tennessee Williams. We were talking away, he about sexual fantasies and things, and that made me think of my story. 'Let me tell you it,' I said, and I did. I told him about the squawking birds, the uniform, the long leather thong, the money, the presents and my family.

'Victor, that is the most beautiful Christmas story I ever heard,' he said, 'Because, you see, everyone was happy.'

Graham, when he found out, wasn't. He was appalled. 'You send that suit back at once!' he said, 'That's disgusting.' And on he went to berate me some more. I didn't send the suit back. Instead, I put it to work. Not only was it good for auditions, it got me jobs modelling. At least it was earning its keep. Only once did it have a wobble. I heard about a Bloomsbury pub where Dylan Thomas and Augustus John used to drink and decided to have a look. In I went wearing the suit. The pub was rowdy, sailors and drunks mostly, but the landlord, on getting a flash of the red embroidered waistcoat, was over like a shot. 'Push off. We don't want people like you hanging around here.' Had he heard about the Nazi uniform and the whip? For one sickening second I thought he might have done. The moment I realised he had me down as a common or garden pouf, I felt almost relieved.

So, Graham was shocked about what I'd been up to. Well, I was too. I was shocked to realise I was capable of such a thing. He was shocked because somebody he knew 'Could do that?' I didn't believe I could have done it either, not at all, but, in a funny sort of way, I quite enjoyed myself.

When I went round those agents who kept asking: 'What have you done?' I was never so depressed that I forgot to leave my telephone number. I always managed to do that. The number I gave, though, wouldn't be Stanley Gardens. I didn't have my own phone there. It would be my place of work, whatever that was, something non-showbiz if my act wasn't booked, something I could leave quickly, like the Sterling Light Company. This was a factory in Westbourne Grove where I dipped things in paint. It wasn't that bad. The girls who worked there were very jolly, especially the one on the switchboard; she was smashing. Whenever a call came for me, she'd avoid saying: 'Sterling Light Company,' Instead, she'd say: 'One moment, please,' as if she was putting the caller through to my office.

The tannoy was playing 'Some Enchanted Evening' as I was dipping away one morning, when I was called to the phone. It was a casting director I'd left my number with, Robert Lennard. 'Can you get down to Drury Lane?' Of course I could. That was the virtue of The Sterling Light Company. We were paid by the hour. If I took an hour off, I wouldn't get paid for it but then again nobody would object. 'It's the second year tour of *South Pacific*,' Robert went on, 'They've got a non-singing role they need to cast.'

'Isn't that funny,' I said, 'Can you hear? They're playing 'Some Enchanted Evening' right now.'

'Yes, yes, fine,' said Robert, 'Just get down to Drury Lane. Now.' With no time for a wash and brush up, I set off.

10

Here We Go?

At the stage door of the Theatre Royal Drury Lane, I gave my name and waited my turn. Against the walls, other actors in smart suits, holding bowler hats and furled umbrellas, leaned nonchalantly. I could have been in the shop window of a Fifty-Shilling tailor. If only I'd had the time to put on that new suit I had. In those days a good audition suit was de rigueur. Jeans and T-shirt splattered with paint were not amusing. They were simply out of place and a crew cut I'd recently had was beginning to worry me too.

My call came and I found myself walking from the back of a stage that's as deep as its auditorium and it's an auditorium that holds over two thousand people. It's a very deep stage, in other words, and I felt very small. When I reached the front, an American guy in the stalls, burping and stirring a glass of fizzing bismuth, called out: 'Who are you?'

'Victor Spinetti,' I answered.

'What? You're an actor?'

'Yes.'

'What have you been doing?' He seemed to be in a state of shock but I carried on, picking out the best jobs I'd done, making them sound more important than they were and leaving out the bad bits, like getting the sack.

'Where are you working now?'

'A factory.' The guy fell about laughing. 'Jesus Christ, you're the first Englishman I've ever met that fucking works. OK, read that.'

The stage manager handed me a script. 'You're a CB,' he muttered. I hadn't seen the show, so I didn't have a clue what a CB was but I read the scene. It was clear enough. A sailor tries to explain to his commanding officer why he was on the island of Bali H'ai when he knew it was off-limits: 'I just happened to be by the hatch, sir, and I kinda got sucked out.' Or words to that effect.

'All right,' said the guy in the stalls, 'You're in the American Navy now. Join the show tonight. It's in Coventry,' then, nodding towards the stage manager added, 'He'll sort you out. Thank you everybody! That's it!' The actors in suits put on their bowler hats and made for the street. I walked with the stage manager while he told me about trains and fares.

'Who was that in the stalls?' I asked.

'Oh, that's Jerry White. He supervises all Rodgers and Hammerstein's shows over here.' Six years later, I described this day to Richard Rodgers over dinner at his place in New York.

There was actually only one train I could catch if I wanted to make Coventry on time and it was leaving soon. I dashed back to the factory, gave my notice, went up to Stanley Gardens, packed up my bits, came back down to the factory to say goodbye and, as the cab wheeled round and headed for Euston Station, out everybody ran to wave. It was a scene from an Ealing Comedy!

On the train, I found myself surrounded by the actors in suits. They didn't say a word to me. All they did was look. When I got off, they were still there, a whole phalanx of them and, when we reached the stage door, in they came too, hurrying past. They seemed to be late. A man, on his way out, bumped into me. 'Good, I'm glad you've arrived,' he said, 'Because I'm leaving this tour.' It was the understudy I was due to replace, Rick Shaw. 'I'm going back to my first love,' he announced, 'Cinema!' and went out of the door, closing it behind him. I've never seen him since.

As the orchestra started to tune up – I could hear it on the tannoy – the men in suits, except they weren't anymore, re-emerged. In oil-splattered jeans and T-shirts, they were now dressed exactly like me at the audition. I had turned up at Drury Lane, looking as if I was ready for that evening's performance, a CB and I didn't know it. What's CB? It's short for Construction Battalion, a branch of the American Marines that constructs airstrips and, if you go to *South Pacific,* you'll see that they are the backbone of the show. So the men who were now on their way to the stage had, that morning, put on their best suits and caught the train for London in the hope of getting a better-paid job in a show they were already in. No wonder they weren't very talkative.

From the tannoy came the first notes of 'Some Enchanted Evening', my lucky song. 'You're in that dressing room over there,' the stage doorkeeper said indicating.

As I walked towards it, I thought: 'My first ever job in a big show. I don't have to lug the Ferrograph or my costume or my props.

I don't have to sort out my entrance music with the Musical Director. Here, they do all that for you.' I went into the dressing room. A man, totally naked, was peeing into the sink. He turned round and, extending a hand, said, 'Hallo, I'm Sean Connery.'

I was so startled, I didn't know what I was shaking.

I have to make it clear, this sink business was not some habit exclusive to Sean. Everybody did it. I simply hadn't seen it before. Nineteenth-century theatre architects didn't care about the actors. They always put lavatories miles away from the dressing rooms. One on one floor for the girls and another, up yet another flight of stairs, for the boys. In girls' dressing rooms across the land, you could still find signs saying: 'Please refrain from sitting on the basin as cracking can occur.' What am I saying, nineteenth century? Architects still do it today. Try finding a lavatory mid-performance at the RSC's Swan Theatre!

It was Sean's first job in theatre and he'd been on the tour since it started. He'd stayed on partly to work his way up the ranks and partly because he was studying acting with Robert Henderson, who was also in the show, playing the Captain. Robert had given him lots of books to read, like *An Actor Prepares*. It was here on *South Pacific* that Sean told me about the pension he received from the navy, the one like mine from the army. As I said, it seemed to bring us together.

In the company too was a South African. Unpleasant to people in the show, boastful about his achievements in South Africa and appalling about 'the Blecks', he was torture to listen to. I had to say something, so I spoke to Sean. 'Stop blathering,' he said, 'If you don't like him, go and hit him.'

Upstairs I flew, walked into this guy's dressing room, said, 'Listen, I've had enough of you,' knocked him to the ground, came back downstairs and said, 'I've done it.' Sean fell to the floor laughing.

'I was trying to shut you up. I didn't mean it.' Feeling rather foolish, I wondered what would happen. What happened was, the South African became amazingly polite and didn't mention 'the Blecks' again.

When I joined *South Pacific*, I was playing a character called Stewpot and understudying another character, Luther Billis, the comedy lead.

Luther was in his fifties. I was in my twenties. In Coventry we had two understudy calls and then moved to the Opera House in Manchester. On the opening night, Eddie Leslie, who was playing Luther, came on to dance 'Honeybun' in the well-known costume of raffia wig, bra made of coconuts, grass skirt and gold high-heeled sandals, when he slipped, fell and shattered his kneecap. He'd hit it on one of those old microphones that stuck up out of the stage. I was in the wings, not believing what I was seeing. Where was Rick Shaw when you needed him? As Nelly Forbush continued singing, 'A hundred and one pounds of fun, that's my little Honeybun,' two sailors picked Eddie up and helped him to the wings. Simultaneously Sean, standing next to me, said, 'You're on,' and pushed me, still wearing my Stewpot costume, out onto the stage where I finished the dance.

The entire action could have been on a conveyor belt and looked like part of the show. No sooner was I off than Robert Henderson whispered, 'In the next scene you —' It was just the help I needed. The lines, I sort of knew. The flow of the story I was less familiar with. These little headings got me to the end of the performance.

Sean was marvellous. We were sharing digs in Moss Side. It was a hot summer night; the window was open. On my little portable radiogram, a blue Pye, Eddie Calvert, the Man with the Golden Trumpet was playing my only record, 'Cherry Pink and Apple Blossom White'. We drank cups of black coffee, one after the other. 'Again, again, again,' said Sean as he took me through every scene. 'Tonight, you got through on nerves,' he said, 'Tomorrow, you've got to give a performance.'

The next night, unbeknown to me, Jerry White was in the audience. He'd come up from London specially. After the show, he came backstage. 'The part's yours,' he said. The name of Eddie Leslie was not mentioned again. A few days later, I went to see him in hospital. He'd been paid off with two weeks wages. As he described his accident, I realised that only a couple of nights before, the same thing had nearly happened to me. In the stage was a revolve and at its edge was a piece of lino that had worn right down, leaving a gap. In Luther's 'Honeybun' get-up, particularly those high-heeled sandals, it was only too easy to trap a heel in the gap and indeed, I had nearly fallen over.

'Will you say that to the management?' asked Eddie.

'Of course, I will,' I said.

'Because,' said Eddie, 'I'm going to sue. I have to. I've been playing this part for two years and what have I got to show for it? Two weeks' wages.' When I mentioned this to the management, I was told that if I persisted, I would never work for them again. I did persist. I didn't work for them again. Eddie got his compensation.

All that took a lot longer than it took me to say it. In the meantime, there was the show to get on with. For a start, I was moved into a posher dressing room down at stage level and paid a posher wage, £100 a week which then was enormous. West End actors playing leads were only getting £85, some of them. I had a dresser too and in Manchester I was able to live the life of Riley, stay at a hotel and eat out. I developed such a taste for this that I'm still living like that today, in funds or out.

I found some scent, Tweed, in my dressing room. It belonged to Eddie. 'Use it and good luck,' he said. So each night, as a ritual before going on, 'Pssst,' I went. Then both I and a cloud of Tweed sailed onto the stage where sailors around me sang, 'There is nothing like a dame'. Actually they sang, 'There is nothing like a dame-ma.' They'd been taught that to give the number punch. Still in a haze of Tweed, I lay on a box apparently dozing but in fact looking up at the ceiling where the shadow of the Musical Director's hands were conducting the music of 'Bali H'ai'. When the music stopped, I'd have to speak, I knew that, but I wasn't nervous. On the contrary. 'This is it.' I thought. I loved it and today I can still smell the Tweed. It's my madeleine. When I opened a cab door outside the Palladium not so long ago, I was hit by it again and who stepped out but Ken Dodd. 'A comic, like Eddie,' I thought. 'It must be a tradition.'

In the show, everybody was bumped up one, which meant that Sean got out of the chorus to play Lieutenant Buzz Adams. Just as he intended, he was making progress, all the while keeping up the acting lessons, not to mention the weight training which had got him the job in the first place. To get to and from our digs, he rode on a little scooter with his girlfriend Carol on the back. She was in the show playing Liat and, along with her at the digs was Mary, the show's wardrobe mistress. She was my friend. The theatre wardrobe is where the washing and ironing is done and I loved to go there because it was warm and comfortable. The smell of ironing reminded me of home.

Sean, Carol, Mary and I became close friends. That's how you make a tour pleasant. You find friends in the company because, in the towns you go to, you rarely have any.

Sean's relationship with Carol was not a casual 'just for the tour' fling. He was madly in love with her and in fact asked her to marry him. Her parents came up to look him over 'He's just a chorus boy. He's a nothing, a nobody,' they said, 'We've got a nice doctor lined up for you in New York, a good Jewish boy. That boy in the show is a nothing. In New York, you'll be well looked after.' Carol turned Sean down. We were in Dublin by then, not only sharing digs but also a bed. It was cheaper.

'You're South Pole. I'm North Pole, OK?' Sean would say. We were round the corner from Mountjoy gaol, where Brendan Behan got the idea for *The Quare Fellow*. I'd be getting to know him in a few years' time.

When the landlady answered the door, she said, 'Ah, a couple of Kerry men,' obviously because we were both tall and dark. But of course, Sean was grieving. He was devastated. He'd get up and walk through the night. I walked with him, silently, through the snow. It settled on our faces. I thought he was going to kill himself and so, on we walked beside the Liffey and I stayed around through the nights until, one day, he woke up and he was OK again. Carol was still in the show and he was still in the show but that was it. It was all over.

Years later, I was in *Fings Ain't Wot They Used T'Be* at the Garrick Theatre when the stage-doorkeeper said: 'There's a young lady called Carol to see you.'

'No?' I said, 'I wonder how she is. Send her in.' It was just before we were about to go onstage. She walked in wearing a full-length mink coat, looking marvellous.

'I'll do anything to get to Sean,' she said.

'Darling,' I said, 'You know he's married to Diane Cilento now. They have a house together in Acton, in the park there.'

'I'd do anything to get back to him,' she repeated, 'Anything,' and she dropped the coat. She was bollock naked and it was winter.

'I've got to go onstage.' I said, 'Stay here. Make yourself comfortable. I won't be long.' I managed to contact her mother.

'Oh my God,' she said. Carol had got out from a place where she was under supervision. The mother came and collected her.

Carol, after *South Pacific*, had gone to America and married that 'nice Jewish doctor' who'd turned out to be an absolute rotter, a sadist. She'd returned to England where Sean had already made a name for himself. Among other things, he'd done *Requiem For A Heavyweight* on television, so she couldn't help but be aware of him.

Some time after the dropping of the mink at the Garrick, I was walking down Marylebone High Street and there, coming towards me, was Sean's mother, Effie. She was a wonderful looking woman with dark hair and dark eyes. 'What are you doing in London?' I asked.

'I've come down to see Carol.' She'd received a letter from her saying that she was dying of cancer in St George's Hospital. So serious had Sean been about marrying Carol that he had introduced her to his parents. They knew everything, which is why Effie had come down, on an overnight train, sitting up all night, to see this girl. Marylebone High Street was where I'd found her because that was where she thought she'd find all the hospitals.

'And tonight, where are you staying?' I asked.

'I'm not. I'm catching the train back home.'

'You can't. Come and stay with us.' She accepted.

'But don't tell Sean,' she said, 'He'd be very upset.'

Together we went to St George's Hospital which was not in Marylebone but at Hyde Park Corner. It's a hotel now. When we got to Carol's bed, she wasn't there. She was off somewhere, talking to someone else. She wasn't dying of cancer. She was around the wards, most likely telling people about this lovely man she was going to marry, Sean. She even went round to his house and threw stones at his window. The police had to be called.

Years and years later, I was at the Hippodrome Theatre, Bristol, when I got a message saying that Carol was living nearby. I went to see her. She was in a house with a shrine in the garden set with stones stuck in a wall and pictures of Sean everywhere. He was by then a big international star and she, quietly and dottily still in love with him.

In Plymouth, back on the tour, it was just Sean and I. We found digs run by a Scots-Italian called Tony Moreno. 'Oh yeah, great. Come in,' he said and everything was laid on, food, booze, the lot. It was amazing, very busy though. People went up and down the stairs all the time. 'Come down one night and have a drink with me,' said

Tony and I did, down in the basement. It was full of marines, all drunk, dancing together and singing. After Sean and I had left, we heard that the place had been raided. It was a brothel. The theatrical digs were just a cover and that's why Tony Moreno was so pleased we were there and why the booze ran so freely and the food was so plentiful. He didn't care whether we paid him or not.

I got good reviews for *South Pacific*. The critic of the *Birmingham Post*, J C Trewin, wrote: 'This is the third tour that has come to Birmingham but there's a good reason to see it and that is Victor Spinetti as Luther Billis. This young man brings vitality (and so on and so on) to the part.' It gave me tremendous hope. We were nearing the end of the tour and I could see that, when I got back to London, I would have something to show those agents at last. Strictly speaking, I'd been lucky. I hadn't been right for the part at all. In fact, ages later, I had to ask Jerry White: 'Why did you give me it? I was too young.'

'You seemed like a typically American showbiz kid.' he said, 'You looked as if you could do it and if you look as if you can do it, we can make you do it.' That's American thinking and pretty much the way they choose their presidents.

Back in town, clutching my bundle of reviews I went round the agents. 'Very impressive,' they said, flicking through the sheaf of cuttings, 'But what have you done in London?'

I felt as if I were back at square one. Graham wasn't. He and I had been exchanging letter cards and spending weekends together for three years but now his course had ended. Very quickly he found a bedsit in Sussex Gardens and together we moved in. Simultaneously, a top agent, Al Parker, snapped him up and sent him out on number one tours playing juvenile leads. He was doing everything I hadn't. I mean, his understudies were Harold Pinter and Anthony Hopkins.

When not at work, Graham was homemaking and a good thing too because I was hopeless at it. The bedsit had two single beds, a gas ring and a tiny corner cupboard where you could wash dishes. That was it, so he scoured markets and antique shops for objects that would make the place feel like a proper home. My contribution came about in a different way. I got a tour of a popular 1950s comedy, *All For Mary*, but trouble struck in Harrogate. The producers ran out of money and fled with the takings, telling the company it could take the set. We divided it up and so the actors, instead of taking home a wage, could be seen staggering to the station carrying chairs and bedsteads. I took the bedding, which went straight to Sussex Gardens.

Actors try to be at home on Sundays and Graham, when we were both able to make it back, kept up the Welsh tradition of roast lamb and mint sauce. The gas ring couldn't cope with all that, so downstairs he went to Mr and Mrs Seeley, our landlord and landlady, where they invited him to put the joint in their oven. We were often short of things but at least it was a time when people helped each other out. As there was no table in the bedsit, we ate sitting on our beds with plates on our knees. This, however, was not going to stand in the way of Graham inviting guests. He loved entertaining and so, for one of our Sunday lunches, we were joined by Dennis Price. Highly amusing he found it but he was touched too. It reminded him of his own early days in London.

He and Graham were on a tour together, a number one tour, of course. I, for the first and only time, was in rep, High Wycombe. It meant handling a gun. A Canadian guy I was playing snatched it up and pointed it at a woman saying, 'You'd better be careful. I'm rough and clumsy.' After that, the audience found everything I said a hoot.

'You're fired,' said a man in the wings when I got off.

'I got a reaction, didn't I?'

'Not the reaction we wanted.'

'But you're doing *All For Mary* next week and I've got the clothes,' and indeed, they too had been my wage. The clothes appeared in *All For Mary*. I didn't.

In Irving Street off Leicester Square, there was a club called the Irving Theatre. It's a pancake house now. In my mind's eye, it was a cosy but smart little revue bar where actors dropped by for a late-night drink and a witty show. My compatriot, the fiery Rachel Roberts, and her husband, Alan Dobie, went there and in the bar, Eric Maschwitz, who wrote 'These Foolish Things', played the piano. I knew also that Danny La Rue, appearing as a model on the cover of *Harper's Bazaar*, had made his London debut there. Perhaps they'd give me a break too.

As I turned the corner into Irving Street, I saw on the front of the theatre a large sign garishly picked out in lightbulbs: 'Irving Strip Club. The only theatre in London where the nudes can move.' This was not what I'd remembered at all. It sounded more like the Windmill, which was the other side of Leicester Square, only this place had evidently got one up on it. The nudes at the Windmill had to stand absolutely still. God, I was wet behind the ears. I always thought the word that described them was 'Statyoosk'. Here, at the Irving, the management must have found a loophole to evade the Lord Chamberlain. But who was the management? I went down the stairs where I found an Indian gentleman, Mr D P Chaudhuri; he was the management. Stepping through the loophole, he'd discovered that customers could join a club and twenty-four hours later, became full members. This meant they could watch a naked girl go, 'bu-bu-bu-bul', to the rhythm of a drum roll, with her breasts and hips this way and that, then respond by going 'bu-bu-bul' back, stretching to its limits, occasionally, the meaning of the words 'full membership'. The bar, run by Mr Chaudhuri's mistress, was now mostly frequented by bowler-hatted business men on long lunch breaks. Five shows a day were given, four on Sunday.

'I'm looking for an actor to play with my lovely girls,' said Mr Chaudhuri, 'Do these revue sketches.' Revue sketches, that sounded more like it.

'What about me?' I said and showed him my sheaf of cuttings. He responded by handing over a pile of songs and sketches.

'Start Monday.' It was Friday.

For the next forty-eight hours I learned material by Herbert Farjeon, Ronnie Cass, David Climie and Alec Graham, all contributors to shows you could see in theatres up and down Shaftesbury Avenue, no membership required. Intimate revues they were called. Obviously Mr Chaudhuri wanted to preserve a touch of class.

On the Monday, I was all set to go. Squeezed into a space the size of a bathmat, the wings, I stood there wearing my bow tie and dinner jacket, running through the words of my opening number, 'So this is London where the Sophisticates Meet'. 'Ready everybody?' I asked. 'Yes,' said our three soubrettes, poised to go into their dance. 'Yes,' said Lindsay, our nude, stood on a box at the back. All I had to do now was cue the orchestra – well OK, piano and drums. Spotting a gap under the curtains, I leant down to take a look. All was well, so I stamped my foot twice. They do something similar at the Comédie-Française.

The curtains, like two pocket handkerchieves, parted. At last, the West End. I opened my mouth: 'So this is London where the sophisticates –' The entire audience was composed of four Chinese sailors playing with themselves. 'Sophisticates – ha, ha, ha,' I tried to carry on but I could not stop laughing. Behind me, the soubrettes fell about too, while Lindsay fell off altogether, her unrehearsed move rousing the sailors to even greater frenzy. It was mayhem on the stage. What made it worse was the stage manager standing in the wings, shouting, 'Control yourselves! You're supposed to be professionals!'

'Oh God,' I thought, 'Vic, you've had it. This is it.' But I still had all these other songs to sing and, right away, a quick change. On I had to charge, dressed as John Osborne. The curtains parted again and out I went singing, 'I'm an Angry Young Man with a Bank Roll'. The Chinese sailors were still at it and this time there was only me on the stage. Full marks to the Chinese for stamina, though.

As I left the stage, I thought: 'You've really, really had it, Vic. That was your West End debut and your swan song, rolled into one.' It wasn't. We carried on and did the rest of our shows for that day and, as the weeks went by, it was not only Chinese sailors we had for an audience. From the stage, I recognised Kingsley Amis, accompanied by his friend, Philip Larkin, and Alec Waugh, Evelyn's brother, who wrote *Island in the Sun*. The sketches were what they came for. The actors Jimmy Villiers and Ronnie Fraser were there for the girls and the bar.

'You shouldn't be working in a place like this,' they'd say from time to time, Sean Connery, in particular, but then they'd also say: 'I've brought a friend. Is that all right?'

My reaction was, 'I'm in the West End, aren't I?' and it wasn't a prison. We had lots of laughs. The point is, you always make the most of everything, and backstage there was a terrific camaraderie. The dressing room might have been tiny. I might find myself chatting to a girl who was shaving her legs in the basin but I got used to it and those girls were not predictable anyway. If anything, the soubrettes were the ones who acted to type, keeping themselves covered up at all times, reading *Woman's Own* and crying on the phone to their boyfriends. The strippers were much more open. If their dressing gowns didn't quite close, it wasn't provocative. It was more 'So what? That's what I do,' and when they weren't onstage, they read proper books like Caitlin Thomas's *Leftover Life* or plays like Genet's *Le Balcon*. We could actually talk about them. Some married poshly; one or two married millionaires and most live very comfortably. We still exchange Christmas cards.

Out front, an audience member displayed erudition too. 'The way you delivered that witty revue material,' he chirruped at me in the bar, 'It was wonderful, so stylish.'

But then Mr Chaudhuri appeared:

'Hallo-ho, the last time you were in here, you were a naughty boy-hoy!' Mr Witty and Stylish had been thrown out for flashing.

A way punters tried to avoid being caught at this was to rig up a piece of string that went from their cocks up to a spot behind their ears which would, of course, be remarkably itchy. The girls, however, could always detect it: 'Row two, third in. He's got a string.'

When I came on, it was quite another matter – up would go the newspapers. I didn't ignore them, though. I used them. I read the backs of the newspapers out loud and made something of that.

Word got round that a young man of some talent was playing at the Irving and one day I got a message to say that the Grades were in, Lew and Leslie, the top variety agents. 'This is it,' I thought. They came to the 7.30 show. The packed one was at 6.00 when commuters left the office. The 7.30 was quiet, with only a handful of people in the audience, apart from the Grades. No sooner had I started than someone started barracking.

'Call yourself a comic? Is that supposed to be funny? Whoever wrote that should have been shot!' and right through the show, it was the same thing. There wasn't a sketch the man didn't have something to say about. He was a white-collar drunk – in Lenny Bruce's opinion, the worst kind. Blue-collar drunks you can answer back but white-collar drunks just go on regardless. With more experience I might have handled things better but at that 7.30 show the man destroyed me. After it was over, I ran round to find him stumbling out into the street.

'And what's your job?' I asked as I grabbed him by the collar and shook him like a rat.

'Surgeon,' he managed to get out.

'Good,' I said, 'Next time you operate, I'll be standing there and every time you pick up a scalpel, I'll jog your elbow and spoil *your* timing.'

I never heard from the Grades. Today, it amuses me to think what might have happened if there'd been no drunk and I'd done my stuff properly. I'd have been on the bucket-and-spade circuit, summer seasons at the ends of piers and, if that had worked, television would have followed and now I'd be a quiz-show host. I know, because other bucket-and-spade entertainers have done just that, so there we are, a whole different career.

In spite of this disappointment I was, at the Irving, moving towards the career I did wind up with.

Mr Chaudhuri, not a typical nude-show boss, as I'd suspected, decided to send the revue side of our show to the Edinburgh Festival. We needed some slightly different material for that, so I dug out the mime act, the one where everything went wrong and I had to keep up, the one I'd done on The Incredible Krama's terrible tour. It still worked and it was at that point, up in Edinburgh, that Harold Hobson the theatre critic saw it and wrote the good review with the wrong name. Barry Martin was the name he put, Barry being the only other man in the show. Married to a beautiful dancer at the Windmill, the Irving's rival, he was our singer and a future Tevye in *Fiddler on the Roof.* I, as I said, wrote to Harol Hobson explaining the mistake and he wrote back telling me to let him know when I was next doing the act. I did and then forgot about it.

One Sunday morning in 1957, I was reading the *Sunday Times* on my bed at Sussex Gardens, a space so cramped, I had to read the paper sideways, when I came across the headline: 'Laurence Olivier as The Entertainer at the Palace. Victor Spinetti as the Entertainer at the Irving.' Harold Hobson had gone and done it, and the rest of the review was very good. 'If I were a theatre manager, I would employ him,' it finished. I ran down with the paper, well, a dozen papers, and found Mr Chaudhuri outside the Irving pinning up this notice. Beside him, the usual queue of men in macs was crowding round to read it. From that moment on, it was a case of one thing leading to another.

In the outside world, Wolf Mankowitz, the author, took a story he'd written for a newspaper, a satire on Tommy Steele's rise to fame, and turned it into a musical, *Expresso Bongo.* It was an attempt to get away from the middle-class Never-Never Land that British musicals tended to take place in at the time. Consequently, the thinking from then on reflected that. The producer was Oscar Lewenstein, whose background was Glasgow Unity Theatre and the Royal Court, not a typical musical person. The star was Paul Scofield, not known for his singing but considered to be the heir to Laurence Olivier, an actor with weight, in other words. Somewhere along that line, I was offered a job in it. Mr Chaudhuri didn't seem put out. We left it that I could always come back.

At the house of the backer, a wealthy biscuit manufacturer, a reading of *Expresso Bongo* was set up. Not all the parts were cast yet and every time we came to an uncast part, the director Billy Chappell said, 'Read it in, will you Victor?' When we came to the end, he looked over and said, 'Well, you might as well play them.' This accounted for me having not one but six parts, some of them following each other on. In quick succession I played a psychiatrist, a chaplain and a doorman at Claridges Hotel. Though I always thought you couldn't see me for dust, this became, by accident, a little turn in the middle of the show. I also got to play a waiter, my performance provoking a critic to write: 'This waiter has the tiredest feet in London.'

Out on the road, trying *Expresso Bongo* out in Nottingham during the Goose Fair, Billy Chappell said to Oscar Lewenstein, 'Victor's very important to the show. His name should be on the bills.'

'But they're already printed,' said Oscar.

'You'll have to reprint them, then,' countered Billy and it gave me a very nice feeling, a few days later, to walk with Graham to the Saville Theatre where we were going to play, and see my first ever billing in London.

Graham was feeling good too because he'd been in a film, *The Horrors of the Black Museum*. The money he'd earned had been put down on a flat in Manchester Street. That's where we'd come from that day, our first real home, with rooms and stairs and stuff.

Expresso Bongo, which did quite well but not that well, was hardly out of the Saville than *Candide,* Leonard Bernstein's musical, moved in. It was all right for me. I was in that too, so I didn't have to go anywhere.

On the first night, I and the other actors, all in hoops and feathers and furbelows designed by Osbert Lancaster stuffed ourselves into the lift that went from the dressing room to the stage. The lift operator, a woman who had been at the Saville for years and years, pressed the button and, as we went down, turned to look at us. 'These old fashioned things,' she said, 'They never run.'

At the same time, out front, high up in a box, sat three men, their heads in their hands. Down in the stalls sat John Gielgud. A friend leant over to him and said, 'Who are those men up there? They look awfully disconsolate.'

'Quite right, dear,' said Gielgud, 'They're the backers.' The lift operator and Gielgud knew what was coming. *Candide* didn't run and, all at once, there were no more shows.

I went to have coffee with one of the girls at the Irving. Mr Chaudhuri came in. His comedian was leaving to do a show in South Africa. Was I available? I was, but hardly had I picked up the reins again than Wolf Mankowitz came round. He'd written a new musical, *Make me An Offer,* and thought I ought to be in it. Joan Littlewood of Theatre Workshop was going to be the director and he was off to have a word.

11

Joan Littlewood: My University

By then, 1959, I'd already been to Stratford East where Theatre Workshop had its base. I was a fan but, 'God, I'm not good enough to work down there,' I'd thought, 'It's too butch for me.' That was flip. The possibility of it actually happening forced me to think harder. Joan Littlewood's auditions were at the Wyndham's Theatre only across the road from the Irving. There was a gap before the six o'clock show. I walked over, using the five minutes to clear my head.

When I'd gone to the theatre with Graham, I'd often thought as I looked at the actors on the stage, 'You're acting. I know you're acting. You're not fooling me.' And then, when I'd gone up for plays, I'd been embarrassed and self-conscious at the thought of seriously becoming someone else. Talking directly to an audience, looking out front, that was another matter.

Then, there'd been the time in 1956 when Betty Kellond had been casting for a production of *Under Milk Wood* in town. She'd needed two boys. Down to Wales I'd gone and found them, no problem, two very natural boys, not from a stage school. David Barnes and Leonard Mitchard were their names. Had I put *myself* up for this production? It didn't even occur to me. Sixteen years would have to pass before I would be in *Under Milk Wood*. It was the film version and even then that was only because Richard Burton said, 'You've got to be in this, boy,' and I'm Welsh!

I thought back to Stratford East. What had happened to me there had been almost alarming. The actors in *Richard the Second* and *Macbeth* had made me believe them. They didn't seem to be acting but could *I* do that? It would be like climbing the North face of the Eiger, not with an icepick but a toothpick. One question was emerging from all this: 'Are you or aren't you an actor?' 'Oh well,' I thought, 'Whatever happens, in fifteen minutes you'll be safely back at the Irving and still in work.' With that I went into the Wyndhams Theatre, not in the least bit nervous.

'Hallo,' said a voice from the back of the stalls but before I could say anything, its owner began to move down through the auditorium. This was unusual. By now, I'd been to quite a few auditions and I was accustomed to voices remaining firmly and anonymously at the back of the stalls. A figure, slighter than I'd expected, appeared at the front of the stage. 'Have we met? I'm Joan.'

The audition remained unusual. This smiling woman in a woolly hat didn't want to know about any piece I might have learned. Instead, to my surprise, she asked, 'What would you give me for this set?' I looked round and saw half a window, a beer barrel and a battered old piano.

'Five quid,' I answered.

'But Sean Kenny designed it,' she said looking rather amused and indeed, Sean had not only designed it but launched his career with it. 'If you owned this theatre,' she continued, 'And somebody offered you a million pounds for it, what would you do with it?'

'Take the money and go round the world.'

'What about the theatre?'

'There are dozens of theatres in London. Most of them are empty or empty headed.'

'Right, you can play Charlie.'

From the back of the stalls, a voice called out, 'But Joan, Charlie's the lead.'

'Oh well then, you've got the lead,' said Joan. 'Are you working?'

'Yes, at the Irving Theatre just down the road. It's a strip club. We do five shows a day. I've got to go back now and do the six o'clock show.'

'Good. I'll come and see you.' And Joan did, surrounded by the bowler-hatted commuters. When the show was over, she came backstage, chatted to the girls and was charm itself. We went for a meal, over which she told me that Dan Massey was actually playing the lead. 'But come and join us anyway,' and that was it.

What was she up to, Joan, this woman who was to feature so strongly in my life? Not the audition, I don't mean that. You could say she was grasping those vague feelings about theatre that not just I, but a bunch of others, were having – feelings of something not being right, and shaking them into focus in order to turn them into action.

She'd come from a working-class family in South London and won a scholarship to RADA but left early because she didn't like it. She then founded Theatre Workshop in Manchester after the war and toured the UK and Europe with both the classics and new topical work. Next she set up home at the Theatre Royal Stratford East in 1953, and had gone on producing the classics but added the plays of Brendan Behan, Shelagh Delaney and Frank Norman – that's *The Quare Fellow, A Taste of Honey* and *Fings Ain't Wot They Used T'Be* – drawing the town with a fresh, direct style which everyone could enjoy.

At first, this style had been achieved by long periods of training but by the time of my audition, things had changed. The pressure on Joan to come up with new hits to make money to keep Stratford East going was immense. Rehearsal periods were devoted not so much to training as to taking raw material and fashioning pieces that were performable. This was achieved by getting the actors to play games and improvise, strictly supervised by Joan, of course, who then took the day's work home at night and wrote it up for the next day.

As Joan could no longer spend as much time on training as she wanted to, she instinctively looked for shorthands. One of these was the introduction of performers who worked in cabaret, people who sang, danced and played comedy, sometimes to very tough audiences, and who could bring an energy and a directness to the stage that a drama-school-trained actor couldn't. That accounts for Barbara Windsor (who'd stopped the show in *Fings Ain't Wot They Used T'Be*), myself and a bunch of terrific girls who used to work alongside Danny La Rue. Well, Barbara and I did too but we're not quite there yet. With us there was less time taken up with what Joan called shit shovelling. That meant stopping drama-school-type actors from being, well, drama-school actors.

At the same time, there were actors around who had had this drama-school training but who, like Joan at RADA, were not content. They knew there had to be something better. Some also knew that they didn't have the looks, the shape or the accent to get them anything but the most limited range of parts, comic maids and stupid coppers, that sort of thing. They were keen to learn and if they could think on their feet, they did, quite quickly. In other words, during the second half of the 1950s, there was a natural convergence at Theatre Workshop.

The company of *Make Me An Offer*, had in it two different types: those who'd been with Joan for ages and those who'd been drafted in specially for this one, some never to come back but some to stay on, like Roy Kinnear and myself, for example. Also among the latter were two interesting one-offs: Meir Tselniker from Yiddish theatre, not young at all but fascinated by the way Joan worked and Sheila Hancock, the perfect example of the discontented drama-school student, who was convinced they didn't fit. This was the show that really got her started and, like Barbara Windsor, she too stopped the show.

Rehearsals took place at Stratford East, where we ran for a couple of months before transferring to the New Theatre, now the Coward, in December 1959. What happened at rehearsals? I can tell you this.

Joan had a mischievous way of testing actors by yoking them with a sidekick. 'If you can cope with that, you can cope with anything,' was the idea. I had a yoke and spent so much of my time coping with him I can hardly remember a thing about rehearsals. Meir cheered me up. 'Votever you play, vezza it's a kink or a schnorrer, keep your shoes clean.' And then there was a murder . . .

Wolf Mankowitz, the author, had a large fleshy face, a built-in sneer and eyes fixed at half closed. It was a bit of an act. His real name was Cyril but as 'Cyril', nothing had happened for him, so he'd gone to a psychiatrist who'd come up with Wolf. The aim was to dig out some aggression. During rehearsals, he sat in the stalls but, during rehearsals, Joan normally never allowed anyone to sit in any part of the auditorium. 'No judges, no critics,' she would say. Occasionally people crept in but always without her knowing and they had to be utterly silent. Wolf was not silent and his comments tended to be put-downs. It couldn't go on. Out of the blue, Joan flew into a rage, but was it out of the blue and was it a rage? Quite matter of factly, that morning she had said to me, 'Darling, I've got to commit a murder today.' Anyway, her voice dropped to a thunder which rolled on until she had ground Wolf to a fine powder. 'Instead of criticising, come up here and do it!' was the gist of it. Then, in the twinkling of an eye, she skipped off the stage, put her arm round Wolf's shoulder and walked with him to the door all the time talking away sweetly. She was kicking the author out of the rehearsals of his own show. Seconds later, I found her by the little door between the stage and the foyer, roaring with laughter and, a few moments after that, she was back at work.

Although Joan preferred to keep her actors (her children as she called them) on their feet, she also had very intense periods of script work and it's this that produced my most vivid memory.

I couldn't bear to be away from rehearsals. If I wasn't called, I was disappointed. Each day, long before I was wanted, I used to go down to Stratford just to find out what was going on and, one day, I came in on this. The actors were sitting in a circle lit by a pink stage light but there was nothing passive about what was going on. Despite the quietness, voices hardly above a whisper, it was almost dangerous. The actors' concentration was so fierce, it gave off an energy that infected you. They were thinking, trying this, trying that, not just reading their own parts but other characters' too. In this way, they discovered what was missing. Any fault was then put right, either by an improvisation Joan suggested, or pencil work which could be elaborate. 'This speech goes down here. That one moves up there. You take the first half. You take the second.' That done, the actors went over it and over it to get the tempo and rhythm right, Joan all the while pacing round, smoking her Gauloise cigarette. It was mesmerising and the whole chiaroscuro look of it reminded me of a Rembrandt. Obviously it hadn't been done specially for me. That was an accident. Joan had done it to make the actors feel good because she knew that if actors feel good, they do good work.

Now if Gerry Raffles, the theatre manager and also Joan's partner, had come down from his office and seen this, he'd have had a fit. A stage light as opposed to a drab rehearsal light costs a fortune to have on. At that moment, though, it was what Joan wanted and what she wanted she usually got.

One day, I became aware of other white faces in the stalls all staring, hypnotised, and I thought: 'Oh God, worshipping at the shrine of Littlewood, I don't know about this. I think I'm going to go, go to the pictures.' So I came in for my call, late, and you were never late for Joan.

'Where the fuck have you been?' she said.

'I've been to the pictures.'

'You've been to the pictures?'

'Yeah, I was here earlier and I sat watching and I thought "Fuck this, I'll go to the pictures."'

'Oh,' she said and coolly, like my father, blew out smoke but this time it was with amusement, not menace. 'You're learning.'

The thrust of *Make Me an Offer* was a young stallholder in the Portobello Market tortured at having to part with his treasures. Wolf was an authority on Spode chinaware, so at least he knew his stuff. I played the hero's worst nightmare, a rich American tourist who sang a song that immediately told you where he was coming from:

You've got to have capital with a capital 'D',
The American dollar from the land of the free.
Just as long as the backs are green,
They don't have any qualms.
We always find the native culture with open arms.

When I'm given a song, I just go at it. Dan Massey, like Paul Scofield, a straight actor unaccustomed to musicals, was a little more self-conscious. We shared a dressing room at Stratford East and one evening before the show, he started doing vocal exercises: 'Ma, ma, ma, ma. Ba, ba, ba, ba. Da, da, da, da!' which was odd because he'd never done them before.

'What's up with you?' I asked.

'I'm very nervous,' he said, 'My godfather's out front, Noël Coward. Ee-ah, oo-ah, ba-ha, da-ha, ka-ha, sa-ha, ma-ma, mee-ma, moo-ma.' We were going mad, we others. At the end of the show, there was a knock at the dressing-room door. Being nearest, I opened it and came face to face with Noël Coward.

'May I have a pee in your basin? I can't find a lavatory anywhere,' he asked. I'd never met him before in my life. When he'd finished peeing in the basin with the tap running – you could tell he was an old pro – he turned to Dan and wagging his finger, said, 'Dan, you've been taking singing lessons. You've ruined your voice.'

As *Make Me an Offer* finished its run, news came through that – no, let Brendan Behan take over. This great braw Irish man came walking in one day and said, 'Vic, I want you to be in my play *The Hostage*.'

'Brendan,' I said, 'What can a Welsh-Italian play in an Irish play?' he said, 'The fockin' IRA Officer, of course.'

The Hostage, on the set of which I'd auditioned, was going to Broadway. It was Brendan Behan's second play, a riotous piece of *commedia dell'arte* anarchy, held together by a deadly serious IRA man.

And so I found myself on a plane for the first time in my life, going to Broadway. There was a big publicity tie-up as the airline we were to travel on was the Irish airline, Aer Lingus. It was going to be their first direct flight from London to New York. Nineteen hours it took and we ran out of food, booze, shamrocks and holy water. Brendan, who had been on the wagon for six months, was in a teasing mood. Down at the front of the plane was a group of nuns. Brendan shouted: 'Whenever I travel anywhere on a plane, it always seems to be full of f-fockin' nuns. And they take the vow of poverty.'

A tight-lipped Dublin priest who was with them turned round and said, 'Why don't you have one of your plays running at the Dublin Festival, Mr Behan?'

Brendan said, 'Same reason as you're not married, father. Nobody asked me.'

The journey was terrifying. First the plane skimmed the waves, then it rocked and dived. Headwinds blew us back and, direct flight or no direct flight, we had to land and refuel. Brendan said, 'We'd better get up a concert party, all do turns to cheer ourselves up.' So he sang an Irish song and recited one of his poems. For my bit – there was a play on at the time in the West End called *Ross* by Terence Rattigan. It was about T E Lawrence, Lawrence of Arabia. In the film, Peter O'Toole played him but on the stage it was Alec Guinness. My turn was to do an impression of Alec Guinness in *Ross*. The bit I chose, the fallout from Lawrence's treatment at the hands of the Turks, caused the nuns some alarm. I just looked on it as a throwaway. If only.

At the airport in New York, Brendan, still stone cold sober, was besieged. It was a taste of what I would soon witness with the Beatles, a surging fence of microphones and popping flashbulbs. All the press were waiting for him. 'What's the first thing you want to do in New York, Mr Be-han?' a reporter asked shoving a mike into his face.

'Go up to the top of the Empire State Building and hold a memorial service for King Kong,' he answered.

A woman in the crowd, very elegant in a Chanel suit, hair exquisitely coiffed, looking like Glenn Close in *Fatal Attraction*, moved forward. This was Jinx Falconberg, 1930s tennis star, now showbiz reporter. Thrusting her live, on-air microphone at him, she asked, 'And what else do you want to do in New York, Mr Be-han?'

'Go down to the YMHA and take a swim in the pool,' answered Brendan.

'Why the YMHA?' she pressed, 'The Young Men's Hebrew Association? I mean, you aren't Jewish, are you Brendan?'

'No,' he answered, 'But I'm famous down there. Not because I'm a playwright but because I've got the only foreskin in the pool.'

Before publicity, there has, of course, to be work and in my case, that meant the IRA Officer. I really was nothing like him. 'What did she do?' people often ask me about Joan Littlewood's methods. The first thing I say is, 'She freed you.' On her stage, you were totally at home, on a firm foundation which you didn't know she was putting under you because she didn't let you know she was building it. You couldn't hear the hammering. You couldn't hear the nails. With most directors you can hear the hammering, the nails, the circular saw, all the clatter of making an edifice, of making a platform. She never did any of that but it was there. A perfect example comes specifically from those *Hostage* rehearsals.

On day one, Joan said to me: 'I want you to be a bully. I want you to bully *me*. I want you to bully *everybody*. Even when we come to the lunch break, you are to say: "One o'clock, time for lunch. Everybody out. NOW!" If I'm working too late, stop me. If it's time for tea, make breaks. All I want is to hear your squeaky boots and see you bullying.' So I went around with my clipboard that I always carried, and looked at my watch and busied about, stamped about and rapped out orders, and that was my platform and my rehearsal. Opening night, the Cort Theatre, Broadway, autumn 1960: there I stood with my clipboard, my beret, my boots, my mackintosh and my determination.

'Have you got the place well covered, sir?' asked Mr Pat played by Max Shaw.

'I have indeed, why?' I answered.

He said: 'I think it's going to rain.'

This got a big laugh and without thinking, I swung on the audience, flung up my hand and said: 'Silence! This is a serious play!' It brought the house down. I didn't do it to show off. It wasn't an ad-lib I'd worked out before going on. I was simply, in that moment, the IRA Officer, on my platform. And I stopped the show, which is what I had been doing, without thinking, during rehearsals. The next day, the papers said: 'Brendan Behan flings up his hand and commands Broadway to silence.' The phone rang. It was Brendan.

'Vic, that line you p-put in last night. Keep it in. It's one of the funniest f-fockin' lines I never wrote.'

Tennessee Williams, who already admired the work of Joan, adored *The Hostage* and more than that, fell madly in love with Brendan. 'You're a good-looking man, Brendan, you know,' he said, 'You really ought to get yourself some teeth.'

'Who needs fockin' teeth?' said Brendan, 'I took 'em out and threw 'em in the Liffey.' Anyway, he and Tennessee became very close and often went out together, either for dinner or round the bars.

'Vic,' said Brendan, 'Whenever I go out with Tennessee, you'll have to come with me and translate. I can't understand a fockin' word he's talking about.'

So there he was, one evening, still totally sober, sitting in a bar listening to Tennessee. A bunch of sailors in tight, white bell-bottoms walked past. Interrupting himself, Tennessee rocked his hand from side to side and said, 'Tell me Brendan, why is it that all American sailors seem to walk to a Latin-American rhythm – Managua, Nicaragua, it's a beautiful town.' At that moment, I think the 'romance' was over.

Despite this, Tennessee, in honour of Brendan, gave a big party at what was then New York's 'in' place, Nicholson's Cafe. Maybe Tennessee living above the shop had something to do with it as well. Every star you can think of who was playing on Broadway at the time, was at that party. There was Bette Davis, Joan Fontaine, Carol Channing, Helen Hayes, Rosalind Russell, Terence Rattigan – he's the one who wrote *Ross* – and Laurence Olivier, who was playing the king in *Becket*. 'There's a line in the play where I have to say: "I'm bored,"' I heard him say, 'And opposite Anthony Quinn, I can tell you, I am very bored.'

Suddenly Brendan stood up: 'Right, come on, everybody sit down now, shut up and . . . Bette!'

'Hoowhat?' she inquired.

'Sit down,' said Brendan, 'Come on, shut up now.' Naturally, they all thought he was going to do one of his turns, recite or sing, but no: 'My old friend, Victor Spinetti,' he announced, 'Is now going to give us his impression of Sir Alec Guinness being focked by the Turks!'

How I got to my feet, I don't know. On every chair, on every armrest, on every spare patch of carpet, there they sat, all the stars I'd ever seen in my life. The last time I'd seen any of them was on the screen as a child in Cwm. For a split second I was back at one of those Coliseum matinees, looking up and saying to myself, 'One day I'll know you.' Remember? But what to do now? Under those circumstances, there was only one thing. You couldn't say: 'I'm sorry. I forgot my music.' You just had to do it and so I started: 'Ladies and gentlemen, I would now like to do my impression of Sir Alec Guinness —' and at that moment the door opened. Standing there was Tallulah Bankhead.

'What are you doing, dahling?' she gravelled at me. I couldn't speak. She advanced through the room, all eyes upon her. Nobody had seen her for years.

'What are you doing, dahling?' she repeated.

'Oh well, in for a penny,' I thought.

'I'm just about to do my impression of Sir Alec Guinness being fucked by the Turks.'

'Alec is a very great friend of mine. I hope you aren't going to be vishush.'

'Well, yes, I am.'

'Thank God for that,' and, oblivious of the author under her nose, she continued, 'It was a terrible play. Oh, hallo Terry!' and, with that, she sat down next to him.

Now there was nothing for it. Just as I had done on the plane, I performed this little scene between Ross/Alec Guinness and General Allenby, who on the stage had been played by Harry Andrews. Ross, having escaped from the Turks, sidles onto the stage at the back, claps his hands to his buttocks and shuffles stiffly forward right down to the front where, at a desk, sits General Allenby. 'Something's happened to you, Ross?' he inquires, to which Alec Guinness sadly replies,

'No, I fell off a camel and was dragged through some barbed wire.'

'Dahling!' shouted Tallulah Bankhead, 'That's the story of my life.'

Obviously there was the day-to-day business of keeping up the show's fizz to attend to, and Joan, as well as writing us notes, held weekly sessions every Friday afternoon — bitching sessions she called them. Knowing full well what actors got up to in private, she thought it best to get it all out in the open. Maddened by another actor treading on a laugh or coming in late on cue, we go around saying nothing to the actor's face but a lot behind his or her back. In time, we can, if we're not careful, build up quite a poisonous atmosphere. The bitching sessions put an end to all that. Joan ordered us to say exactly what was troubling us right to the actor's face, while he or she did the same back. In seconds we saw how unimportant our niggles were and before a minute was out, the absurdity of the whole thing had us falling about laughing. If only the United Nations could do the same.

New York loved *The Hostage* and we, the company, were feted everywhere. Eli Wallach and Anne Jackson invited us to their home for a party. It was a beautiful apartment on Riverside Drive. When we arrived, we found Tony Richardson and George Devine already there. Tony had just directed Shelagh Delaney's play *A Taste of Honey* for Broadway and George was the boss of the Royal Court Theatre in London, where Tony normally worked. Both were sitting on a kind of dais being presented, like visiting royalty, to the actors from Theatre Workshop. If you know a bit about the Theatre Royal, Stratford, E15 and the Royal Court Theatre, Sloane Square, SW1, you would know that they had very little in common.

A few days later, I was invited to a tea dance given by a World Heavyweight boxer for his boyfriend, a Canadian lumberjack. As I walked in, I heard Tony Richardson's familiar drawl: 'Joan Littlewood ruined Shelagh Delaney's beautiful play. It's not a play. It's a poem set to jazz.' And, as I walked through the door, there he was again, this time dancing with a boxer. To annoy him, after all that regal posturing from before, I cooed, 'Ooh, what are *you* doing here?' and left it at that.

Trying to explain the creation of *A Taste of Honey* to him would have been futile. Joan and her actors had not just done the play. They had taken what Shelagh had written and fashioned it, releasing, not ruining, the poetry Tony Richardson had heard. This was Joan's way of working and the directors at the Royal Court hadn't a clue how she did it. The plays they put on were new but their way of rehearsing was old-fashioned weekly rep. Theatre Workshop was a different kettle of fish and Tony Richardson's remark sprang from a complete lack of awareness.

Lee Strasberg of the Actors' Studio came to see our show. 'How do you do it, you people?' he asked. 'How do you do it? You're on that stage and you look as if you're enjoying yourselves! How can you possibly do that?' He sounded almost irritated. I went to one of his classes and found out why he would ask such a question.

It started at eleven o'clock, in a chapel very like one at home in Wales. Talk was forbidden once you got in, so people stood outside and spoke to each other in whispers before shuffling through to sit in total silence. Just at the point when I thought someone should hand out hymn books, the clock struck eleven. On the last stroke, Lee Strasberg entered, followed by an assistant. There was a big carved chair and there was a little chair. 'What's it to be? Genius or Ascetic?' I thought, 'Orson Welles or monk? If he sits in the big chair, he's OK.' He sat in the little chair. 'Oh, monk,' I thought disappointedly. The assistant, sitting himself in the big carved chair, pressed the switch on a tape recorder. The click was chilling. Quietly, so quietly that his voice hardly reached the pews at the back and you had to strain to hear, Lee Strasberg spoke: 'Begin.'

The actors started to act. Heavy, crushing stuff it was. 'You gotta tell me the truth, you gotta,' improvised one actor, demanding of another if a child was his.

Eventually it came to an end. What a relief. Strasberg, of course, had yet to do his bit. He launched, still quietly, into a great long dissertation: 'Your relationship to the world, your feeling of anxiety when you step through the dark door of Jacobean tragedy from the light of an Elizabethan birth and register that feeling, infused with what you can imagine would be THEATRE, is not happenening here! You should be —' and on and on he went with no pause for breath, all of it on one note and all recorded.

'Thank you, thank you so much,' said the actors. The assistant switched off the tape. Strasberg stood up. The assistant handed the tape to the actors. Strasberg left the chapel. The assistant followed. Only then did people start to talk to each other in an ordinary, gossipy way. It was the antithesis of everything that happened at Theatre Workshop, or anywhere else, I would think.

After its Broadway run, *The Hostage* set off on tour. Fine by me, I'd not seen any of America, but in Chicago, the phone went. 'How soon can you get back?' It was Joan in London. This was almost alarming.

'What do you mean?' I asked.

'*Fings* is dead on its feet.' I still didn't see what this was to do with me. *Fings Ain't Wot They Used T'Be*? Frank Norman's show? What could I do for that? It was set in a Soho spieler and most of the characters spoke Cockney.

'I don't care,' said Joan. 'We haven't got a Tosher and we need some life.' Tosher, a dodger and diver character was created at Stratford East by James Booth and that means *really* created. The part

Frank had originally written was of an old man. Jimmy had made him young, quick-witted, fast talking. Even actors with genuine Cockney accents didn't relish taking over that part. Still, I knew I'd have to go.

As a result of all the fun I'd had in New York, I had quite a collection of bits and bobs when I arrived at O'Hare Airport, books mostly. 'You're overweight,' said the official at baggage control. Because I'd only made one other flight, the one to New York, I didn't understand. The official made me open my cases and, as I had no spare cash on me, I had to leave all this entertaining stuff behind. I didn't leave my heart in San Francisco but I did leave my books in Chicago.

I arrived back on a Good Friday. Gerry Raffles, Joan's partner, invited the cast of *Fings* for a meal. It went from smoked salmon to hot-cross buns and was most enjoyable. On the Monday I was on. 'What about rehearsals?' I asked.

'Make it up,' said Joan, 'It was made up in the first place.' This wasn't as haphazard as it sounds. Joan had a practical side that not everyone was aware of, mainly because she kept it hidden. At great speed, she could break a play down into units and give each unit a title, a good one too, as it would contain action and lead you onto the next title. If you could cram those into your head and learn Lionel Bart's songs – which by then, every milkman in London was whistling, Lionel being such a great tunesmith – you were in with a chance.

On the first night, I didn't know what I was doing, except for certain moments, that is. Tosher makes a lot of telephone calls to a villain called Wozzo Newman, a character James Booth had dreamed up. They were Jimmy's big contribution to the show, these calls, and to keep them fresh, he kept changing them. Needing security, though, he scribbled them on a board next to the phone. Those were the moments when I did know what I was doing. For the rest of the time, it was another matter. 'Darling, there's a laugh of mine you've just ruined,' said Miriam Karlin.

'Don't worry,' I reassured her, 'Only the first row can hear me anyway.' Eventually I did find my way around the part and I stayed at the Garrick Theatre for a year.

'Hallo, Vic. How's it going?' asked James Booth, steely-eyed, when we bumped into each other.

'Fine, fine,' I said in my best Monmouthshire accent, 'Except the whole action of the play now takes place in Aberystwyth.'

Joan's great passion, actually her greatest, was Ben Jonson the Elizabethan playwright. It was, therefore, something of a treat for her, after whipping up froth for the West End, to do *Every Man in his Humour*. Since Tosher was the direct descendant of a Jonsonian fixer, I wasn't too surprised to find myself playing the wily servant Brainworm. Brian Murphy, Roy Kinnear and Bob Grant were in the company too and together we were doing what Joan, in earlier days, loved to do before the hits pulled the company apart. We weren't making it up, not this time. We were tackling a great writer's language in order to *sound* as if we were making it up. Very healthy, you'd think, so it came as quite a shock when Joan's number one actor from those earlier days, Harry H. Corbett, dropped into rehearsals at Stratford East, took me aside and said, 'Don't work with her. Get out. Get away. She'll destroy you.' His best work, as Khlestakhov in *The Government Inspector*, Ould Brennan in *Red Roses for Me* and above all, Richard the Second, had been for Theatre Workshop. I was in a state of shock. I'll guess. He saw us having a kind of fun he'd once known, a fun *Steptoe and Son* was not providing. Simultaneously he was remembering the exhaustion at the end of his Stratford East days brought on by Joan's relentless demands. He'd then combined the two, short-circuited and blown a fuse. I, on the other hand, was at the exhilarated stage. Admittedly it was soon snapped off but that was nothing to do with Harry.

News came through that Claude Planson, who ran the Théâtre des Nations in Paris, where Theatre Workshop had first triumphed, needed a classic and *Every Man* was to be it. All of us were excited. In my particular case, I'd never been to Paris before but an obstacle loomed.

During the run of *Fings*, Barbara Windsor had told me that a fellow performer, Peter Reeves, was leaving Winston's nightclub, where she was in late-night cabaret, to appear in a West End revue, *Pieces of Eight,* with Kenneth Williams and Fenella Fielding. I could replace him. I did and was still doing it during *Every Man* rehearsals. In fact, for a week or two, the routine of leaving the flat in Manchester Square, travelling down to Stratford on the Central Line and rehearsing the Ben Jonson, returning on the Central Line, walking down Bond Street to Winston's and then walking back to my flat in Manchester Street gave me a warm feeling of security. But now Paris. When I was told about it, I hurried off to Bruce Brace, the club's boss, hoping he would be amenable. After all, it was only four nights. He wasn't. If I went to Paris, I could forget going back to Winston's. Joan was going to be furious. She was never going to give me another job. I went and told her. She wasn't furious. She was just disappointed. Actors have to earn a living, she knew that, and anyway, she had a soft spot for the Winston's team. This was the club, after all, from which she drew the cabaret artistes to do that shorthand she so badly needed. Not only was Barbara performing there, its star was Danny La Rue and around him were Toni Palmer who had formed a very funny partnership with Barbara in *Fings,* and Barbara Ferris who was going to join Theatre Workshop in a few weeks' time. In a few years time, both Ronnie Corbett, who was there too, and Danny himself would work for Joan. I hope you can now see my point.

We drew quite a collection of characters there, all the way from polite gangsters who, when my mother entered, stood up and pulled back her chair, to Margot Fonteyn, Rudolph Nureyev and John Gielgud, who came together on the same night, the night a terrible fight broke out, the first and last I ever saw at the club. I was fearfully embarrassed. Gielgud wasn't. 'Wonderful, wonderful,' he said afterwards, 'So exciting. I've never seen anything like it in my life. Not that your cabaret wasn't exciting too, of course, but cabaret I've seen before.'

Murray Melvin, keen to stretch himself after *A Taste of Honey*, took over as Brainworm and *Every Man* went off to Paris where Theatre Workshop, as usual, won a prize, the Théâtre des Nation's Best Performance. Bob Grant got it as the merchant, Kitely. During the time I *was* in the show, I met the Kray twins on Stratford Broadway. They were fans of Joan's. ''Ullo. Vic, 'ow's it going?' they asked.

'Not so well, as it happens,' I answered. That night the theatre was packed.

Although I knew Joan understood my predicament, £35 a week doing cabaret and only £15 a week at Stratford, I still had the feeling that I would never work with her again. It was lucky for me, in an odd sort of way, that she had her own problems. Weary of batting hits into the West End, frustrated at constantly losing her actors and fed up with the building itself, she left Theatre Workshop. She also left Gerry Raffles but then that was all part and parcel of the same problem. For

a while she hurled herself around London, famous and successful but
not happy, frequently winding up in strange places at night, mine
being one of the less strange ones. Her mind was filled with an idea
she'd had since childhood, The Fun Palace, a beautiful riverside
structure where anyone could go to study or find entertainment. She
didn't get her dream but from then onwards it never stopped
occupying her thoughts. Immediately to hand, though, was the offer
of films. She and Stephen Lewis took a play of his and wrote the
screenplay of *Sparrers Can't Sing*. James Booth and Barbara Windsor
were going to star and I was going to be a Jewish baker.

What a relief, a job with Joan again and one I could do while staying
on at the club. The evening before the first day of shooting I went to
the club as usual, but hardly was I through the door when Bruce Brace
hurried over. ''Ere, there's someone oo wants to talk to you. 'E's a
Swedish shippin' millionaire.' Sitting at a table was a huge man who
had already made himself comfortable with two of the hostesses, Janie
and Mitzi.

'I like what you do in the show,' he said.

'Thank you,' I said.

'I would like very much for you to have a drink with me.'

'That would be nice. When would be a good time?'

'Tonight. After the show.'

'Well,' I said, thinking of the film, 'I er –'

'Yeah, yeah, that'll be fine,' said Bruce Brace. 'Go with him,' he
whispered, 'E's already spent five 'undred quid. 'E's bought the band
cigars. 'E's paid the girls –'

'I'm a hostess now?' I interrupted.

'Go with him,' insisted Bruce. The show ended at two in the
morning and I had to be on the set at seven. Well, at two, the Swedish
shipping millionaire, Mitzi, Janie and myself stepped out of the club
and got into a waiting taxi. ''Ullo,' said the cabby, obviously au fait,
and off he drove in the direction of Hyde Park.

Huge paintings of garish nudes lined the walls of an obviously
rented house. Reclining in suggestive poses, they appeared to be
soaping themselves lasciviously. In the drawing room, a large cocktail
cabinet, on being opened, played Swedish drinking songs. The girls
poured me a drink before sitting and chatting. The Swedish shipping
millionaire was nowhere to be seen. As if on cue, one of the girls got

up, went over to the record player and put on a disc. It was David Rose's 'The Stripper.' As the first familiar notes rang out, the drawing-room doors sprang open and there, huge and completely naked was the Swedish shipping millionaire. From beneath the overhang of a smoother smooth belly peeped his winkle, around which was tied a little ribbon. He was wearing high-heeled shoes and from his ears hung diamond drop earrings. His arms were outstretched and in his hands were candlesticks. Behind him was the leary cabby also wearing diamond drop earrings, high-heeled shoes and carrying candlesticks. A *cache-sexe*, rather chic, had been improvised from a feathered 1950s cocktail hat. Both danced in together and around the room. It was three o'clock in the morning and I'd been working all day. 'Am I going mad?' I thought, hysteria mounting.

'Don't laugh, don't laugh,' said the girls, 'They're wonderful. They never rehearse.' Hysteria seized me totally then but, as I tried to gain control, the dance came to an end.

'You like it?' asked the millionaire.

With a great effort, I managed,

'You move very well for a big man.'

'Oh good,' he said, 'I do another,' and buttocks a-quiver, launched into *L'Après-midi d'un Faune*. The candlesticks sat that one out, leaving his arms to be more expressive.

As he subsided into his final pose I said: 'Good Lord, look at the time. I have to be at the studios.'

'My driver will take you,' said the millionaire.

'Thank you so much,' I said and fled to the cab.

As we pulled away the cabby slid his window back. 'Marvellous man,' he said, 'Marvellous. Not queer, of course.'

'No, no, of course not,' I said as he continued talking.

'D'you know, when he arrives in this country, I put my clock on and it stays on until he leaves. Could be days, could be a week even. I'd do anything for him, well almost anything.' With the image of the elephantine *L'Après-midi d'un Faune* now firmly impressed upon my brain, I wondered what he meant. At the studios, I stumbled gratefully to a caravan and managed to get a little sleep before filming.

A few weeks later, Bruce Brace said: ''Ere, 'e's in again, that shippin' millionaire.' I walked over to greet him.

'Ah, Victor,' he said, 'I want you to meet David and Robin.' I nodded at them. 'And this is the wife of David and this is the wife of Robin.'

'How do you do?' I said.

'David and Robin,' he added, 'Are policemen. Excellent dancers!' and with that he gave me a big wink. I looked at the wives. They were wearing diamond drop earrings. A little later I caught up with Bruce Brace.

'What goes on?' I said.

'Didn't you fuckin' dance?'

'No.'

'Yer silly bastard, if yer dance, yer get to keep the diamond earrings. They're worth thousands.' If only I'd known. I went to a party and nobody asked me to dance.

This was all going on at the same time as the shooting of *Sparrers Can't Sing,* of course. It was only a small part, the Jewish baker, but it was a gesture of inclusion, Joan's way of saying, 'We're all making this film and you've got to be in it.' Even so, catching sight of me as I walked onto the set for my first day's work, James Booth, volatile and edgy, remembering how I'd muscled in on his *Fings* role, stood up and, before the whole cast and crew, said loudly, 'What's a fucking pouf like you doing on this picture?'

Barbara Windsor jumped up.

''Ere, don't call 'im a pouf, darling. 'E can do it when 'e's sober. You can't do it unless you're drunk.'

12

Oh What A Lovely War

During the editing of *Sparrers Can't Sing*, Joan was being urged by
Gerry Raffles – they were now reunited – to come up with an outline
for a new show he wanted to do. His attitude to the Theatre Royal
was not the same as hers. For the year and a half she had been away,
he had clung onto it and waited. My phone rang.

On a winter's day early in 1963, we gathered in the green room at
the Theatre Royal Stratford East. Among those greeting each other
were Brian Murphy, Ann Beach, Griffith Davies, Fanny Carby and
Murray Melvin. All had been in the Ben Jonson. Why we were there,
we had only the haziest idea.

Gerry Raffles switched on a tape recorder. It was a radio programme
of Bud Flanagan introducing songs from the First World War. As I
listened, a knot started to form in my stomach. All my life, the First
World War had brought a frozen horror to my system. In Cwm, I'd
wanted to throw up on Remembrance Day when I saw the spray of
poppies on our headmaster's car. There it stood, Lieutenant Colonel
Tom Morgan's Rover, by the War Memorial while towards it
marched the British Legion, carrying flags and singing hymns. When
they came to a halt, the vicar, his robes blowing in the wind, said
prayers before bowing his head at the sound of the last post. I didn't
want to cry. I just felt a tremendous revulsion. As the tape ran on, that
revulsion, that depression, that nausea returned.

'God, I hate those songs,' I said when the programme ended.

'Good,' said Joan, 'You can be the MC. You'll never have to sing
one.' She was casting on attitude. Any other director would have
sacked me on the spot. I searched in my mind. 'Why are these songs
upsetting me like this?' I realised it was the class-structure thing, the
forelock tugging, the 'We'll get by, we'll see it through, thumbs up, as
long as there's a cup of tea' thing. 'Mostly gamekeepers and servants,'
Lord Haig had written in his diary when presented with the figure of

a hundred thousand deaths for a gain of ten yards. That was it. I was born on Lord Tredegar's estate. We were the natural forelock tuggers. It was only because I had a grandfather who was a freethinker and because my uncles and cousins didn't subscribe to any of this that we didn't play that part.

The image to me of Britain, not just in the First World War, was of being in the trenches permanently, never putting your head above the parapet in case you got shot. 'Keep your head down. Don't get into trouble. Keep quiet.' There in the trench with your head down, you listened to hooves thundering past. Occasionally a rider might lean over and drop some honours and medals into the mud to make sure you didn't raise your head over the parapet. And what did you see if you did? Not a cavalry charge but a polo match. They were playing a game. That, to me, was Britain's class structure. It was also similar to my own circumstances as a child, unable to say what I wanted, unable to join the Boys' Brigade.

'Oh, Victor,' said Myvanwy Jenn who was also in the company, 'What about 'Keep the Home Fires Burning'?' She was remembering the song composed by Ivor Novello, a fellow Welshman.

'You can sing it, Myf,' said Joan, again casting on attitude.

It probably helped that Joan hated those songs too, or rather, the sentimental way they were sung. Gerry had persuaded her to look through the sentimentality to the mocking words the soldiers had put to the old tunes. Once you got that, you could use those songs as pegs on which to hang the events of the First World War.

After that depressing morning, things perked up. On a table, Joan laid out history books, memoirs, personal recollections both of generals and of general dogsbodies, magazines of the time, photographs and statistics, in other words, research. 'If you want to work in theatre,' Joan often said, 'First learn to read.' I loved that and it's why I call Joan my university.

She had an expression: 'the collective mind'. It came from reading about scientists pooling their thoughts to solve a problem. This interest in things apart from theatre made her so much more intriguing than other directors. Where she was curious about science, architecture and paintings, they could only talk about theatre and while actors gossiped, she was off listening to Dr Gordon Pask talking about cybernetics.

Our rehearsals consisted of taking information and, bit by bit, turning it into little scenes, an unnerving process because you don't know what you are going to end up with, nothing perhaps. Some days we were excited, others, we were utterly in the doldrums.

People dropped by to talk to us, people who had been in the Great War. That would be impossible now. Then, we were still able to make it live around us. Lord Haig's batman came. As he told us what a lovely, gentle man Haig was, who liked his boots well polished, we simply listened. When he'd finished, I asked him how he had felt when a fellow soldier, maybe a friend from boyhood, was shot dead next to him. 'What do you do?' I asked.

'Put a hand out, touch him and say "Goodbye,"' he answered gently. I remembered that.

The point is, stuff came from all directions and that suited Joan fine. 'Bring her the raw material, she'll make the play,' Gerry Raffles used to say. Not that it was a play in the understood sense, a handful of characters acting out a single shaped story. Gerry had already turned down two attempts like that. Joan was drawing on her experience of agitprop, a stringing together of sharp, stylised scenes that made a political point. She'd done that in the 1930s. What kind of stylisation was Joan going to use this time? She and Gerry wanted the show to be about life, not death. How do you do that? The answer came from Joan's childhood and a Pierrot show she'd seen on a beach, a little group of entertainers who sang, danced and performed sketches, wearing floppy white costumes and conical hats. If you did the whole thing as a Pierrot show, very popular in Edwardian times, at one stroke you got rid of khaki, blood, real guns, soldiers dying painful deaths on stage and miles of grave stones. And that is why Joan had said: 'You can be the MC.' because those shows always had one.

Later on in rehearsals, I said that there must have been some brave officers. 'Christ!' said Joan, 'All right, you can bloody well play them,' and so, in the second half, I became an adjutant.

'Turn out all the lights in the theatre,' said Joan, 'The exit signs too.' It was the first go at a scene that took place in a trench. When all the lights were out, only a faint greyness filtered down from the flies. That's where the rain came in.

'Half of you go to the back of the stalls,' said Joan and, when they'd got there, 'Make a noise.' In turn, each actor at the back of the auditorium made a tiny noise with their voice. 'Who was that?' Joan asked after each one. A few of us onstage guessed, some even guessed right. 'Now listen again. What can you hear outside?'

We told her, one by one. Someone actually heard the traffic on Stratford Broadway, a quarter of a mile away.

'Well, that's how it would be when a soldier says: "They're coppin' it down Railway Wood tonight."' Very matter of fact, quite unemotional. The sound he was in fact hearing, and which would take some effort to distinguish, was 'Stille Nacht' being sung by a German soldier. To achieve the distance, Joan sent the tenor Colin Kemball up a ladder right to the top of the flies.

This work was so fascinating I wanted to devote myself to it utterly but I was still performing at Winston's Nightclub. 'Find a job you like if you can but first and foremost, earn your living.' Throughout my career, that had been my thinking. At Stratford East, I'd found a job I liked but I wasn't earning a living. What could I do? I spoke to my friend, Peter Shaffer the playwright, and he made a gesture of extraordinary generosity. He asked me how much a week I earned at Winston's and then gave me exactly the same for the rest of the rehearsal period. To pay him back I introduced him to Joan and he wound up writing the Christmas show, *The Merry Roosters Panto*. She was astonished how this West End playwright could listen to improvisations at rehearsals, go away and in no time come back with pages of dialogue.

Although she had an outline for *Oh What a Lovely War*, Joan needed to enrich it. One of the first things she asked us to do was act out what we knew of the First World War. This could be anything from the reminiscences of a relative to films with stiff-upper-lip actors. I liked doing those. We even did *Journey's End*, a play Joan so detested, she used to lose her temper when someone simply mentioned it. This way we warmed up the invention muscle while simultaneously clearing stuff out of the system.

It was time to get closer. 'Anybody here been in the army?' she asked. I told her I had. Leaving out the stuff about soldiers fancying me, I listed bayonet drill and padre's half hour. As Joan took notes, I told her about sticking my bayonet into a stuffed sack as our sergeant threw a cup of pig's blood into my face. When you stick something in, something comes out, that's what he was teaching us.

Straight after that, covered in blood and with no time to wash, we were marched off to padre's half hour, where this little Welsh chap said: 'Now boys, three things you've got to remember in the army. Don't drink. Don't use bad language in front of women. Don't do anything you wouldn't do in front of your mother.'

'I've just been trained to disembowel a man,' I said, 'I wouldn't do that in front of anybody, let alone my mother.'

'That's a question of ethics, that is,' he snapped and threw me out. As I stood there, like a schoolboy outside the headmaster's study, with pig's blood still on my face, along came our platoon commander.

'Hallo, Spinetti,' he said, 'What are you doing here?' I told him. 'I see,' he said, 'Look, on the whole, I think it's best if you don't bother with padre's half hour. You don't have to.' And I never went again. Laughing away, Joan made a note to do a church service with a padre. That left the bayonet practice.

Gerry Raffles, wanting it done properly, sent for RSM Brittain, the drill sergeant of all time. When he arrived, he was not particularly pleased to discover that we had no rifles. However, the sight of us picking up props from an earlier scene, walking sticks, canes and parasols, reminded him that the early recruits had been forced to practise with the very same substitutes. They too had had no weapons.

Before the off, RSM Brittain asked all the women to leave the stage, which they did, Joan muttering, 'I can't bear those licensed killers.' I've been told that in fact the women went up to the gallery to watch but I didn't know. After the sergeant had barked away at us until the air was blue and Murray Melvin had cut his finger, Joan came back down. It was unusable, this drill. The Lord Chamberlain, who still had five years to go, would have allowed not one word of it. 'What did he say?' asked Joan.

'I never knew,' I said, thinking back to our sergeant at Brecon. 'It sounded like this,' and I imitated what my dodgy ear had picked up all those years ago, a semi-gibberish where only bits of words poked through. Onstage, my fellow actors were correctly bewildered while out front, Joan could hear utter filth but no filthy words. With tears streaming down her cheeks she said:

'You bastard, why are you working for me? That's a thousand pound a week act at the London Palladium,' and then: 'Don't ever rehearse it.'

On doldrum days a cheer up had to come from outside. Our rehearsal pay was meagre but little extravagances, when they were really needed, did appear. 'Gerry, how much have we got in the kitty?' Joan asked, 'Let's have some smoked salmon and champagne.' And we got it. Nor did I forget that.

Three years later, at a stressful moment in filming with Richard Burton, I said, 'Where's the smoked salmon and champagne?'

'What do you mean, smoked salmon and champagne?' said Richard, 'Bloody Theatre Workshop actor.' Obviously I then had to explain.

'A bottle of Dom Perignon for Mr Spinetti,' he ordered, 'Some smoked-salmon sandwiches and two glasses.'

When Joan had finished the trench scene, she looked around almost irritably. 'Everyone's onstage and there's 'Good-Bye-ee, to sing.' Her eye alighted on me. 'Oh, you're not on, are you? You'll have to sing it,' and I did, remembering the words of Haig's batman: 'Put your hand out, touch him, and say "Goodbye"' That's how I sang it, quite gently, as the sound of gunfire grew louder and louder and brought the first half to an end. Eighteen months later in New York, Rosalind Russell burst into my dressing room.

'You threw that song away! There should have been ships' hooters going, flags waving, soldiers marching up the gangplank. GOODBYE-EE! GOODBYE-EE!' I told her my story.

Work was at times so joyous at Stratford East, that when it was going well, I felt as if I were a child making a model out of plasticine, not wanting to make the sound of sucking up stray spittle for fear of breaking concentration. A child is born with the gift of being where they are and nowhere else. We too had that sometimes, almost a state of meditation, very satisfying. Again, in sex, at the moment of coming, it's so intense you are nowhere else. People striving to get that back turn to drugs. How lucky I was to find it in work, a work where everything is brought into play, particularly the imagination. Some people thought I found it easy. It wasn't that. I liked inventing, true, but you can't do it without freedom. That's what Joan gave me. I was allowed to play. I had permission to make a fool of myself.

Laurence Olivier, a few years later, watching me encourage young National Theatre actors to play, said, 'I wish I could work in this way, my dear baby, but I cannot. I am nothing but a trained par-ROT.'

And a casting director once talked of the marvellous parts Joan gave me. There weren't any parts. We brought Joan presents. That's how it worked and the more presents we brought the more she loved it.

Understanding her is like pulling back the camera. First you see the part of London where the theatre is, then the whole city, then this island and finally, the whole world.

On the opening night, before the show, I was in the wings. I like to be close to where things are happening. Actors nervously joking in the dressing room make me uneasy. Good luck cards and 'Break a leg!' don't help. I was feeling the silence in the auditorium before the audience came in, when I saw a glow of a cigarette. It was Joan.

'We don't have an opening for the show.'

'Yes, you do,' I said, 'You've got 'Row, Row, Row,.'

'That's a song. It's not an opening. Go out and talk to the audience.'

'What about?'

'Don't ask me. You'll talk to anybody. Go naked on the stage. Just don't make jokes.'

She turned to go but then, in true Colombo fashion, paused and turned back.

'Oh, by the way . . .'

'Yes?'

'I can see your bald spot from the gallery.'

I went out and, as the audience drifted in, talked about the simplest things, the seat they'd got, where they could get a good view, subjects that stayed within the four walls of the theatre. I never said, 'Pretend we're in 1914.' It was not a performance. I had nothing to sell. Interestingly, Joan hadn't told me that the MC of a Pierrot show used to come out to see how many seats were sold and choose the moment when to start. It was enough for her to say, 'Go out and talk.'

What I was doing, without knowing it, was drawing the audience in, so that when we got to the horrors, it couldn't escape. The mistake people make in other productions is to have the MC go out and be funny. That keeps the audience in its place. I was demolishing the proscenium arch. Other directors, like Peter Brook, would give you the history of the proscenium arch in its entirety. After that, the task of demolishing it would seem very daunting.

The audience that night received the performance extremely well.

Relief was my main feeling. I wouldn't have to go and work in the nightclub.

On Sunday in the *Observer*, Ken Tynan the theatre critic, wrote that he'd got so worked up, he'd stormed from the theatre in a rage. That was good. The last thing Joan wanted was an audience that was depressed. More wrily, Basil Rathbone wrote to me, when we played New York: '2nd Lieutenant Rathbone, Royal Fusiliers, British Expeditionary Forces. I came to see the show last night and suddenly I realised how I was fooled.'

At Stratford East, things moved quickly. During the course of one day, something like seven West End managements asked Gerry if they could transfer the show. He was grinning from ear to ear. In the end, he settled for Donald Albery and the Wyndhams Theatre. Donald had already transferred other plays of Theatre Workshop and the Wyndhams was about the closest West End theatre in shape to the Theatre Royal. None of us felt that Donald actually liked us. For Gerry, it was a case of the devil you know. In the meanwhile, someone who did like us and of whom Joan was very fond, Claude Planson, wanted us too. We were to go to Paris.

In Paris, at the Sarah Bernhardt Theatre there was hardly any reaction to the drill scene as the audience simply thought I was speaking very quickly. Lanrezac, the French general, came next. It was important for him not to be understood by the English generals, so I did him in gibberish too, French gibberish. A roar of applause went up. Had my trousers fallen down? No, that wouldn't have got any applause. The penny had dropped. Ginette Spanier, directrice of Balmain fashion house, was there that evening and, the following day, she came rushing round waving a copy of *Le Figaro*. 'Have you read this?' she asked. Of course I hadn't because I couldn't read French. Ginette, being also a British TV personality, had good English. She translated:

'*Par son debit seul* . . . Merely by his delivery, Victor Spinetti communicates to us −' and on it went at great length. 'Amazing,' she said, 'Jean-Jacques Gauthier has never written like that about anybody.' Gratified as I was by such a rave, what really struck me was the fact that he had got the point.

In the middle of the night the phone rang. A quiet voice said, 'You're bloody marvellous.'

'Who's that?' I asked but the caller hung up and only then did I realise it was Joan. She never said that to anybody. It was like getting the Croix de Guerre. It was also alarming. Was the axe about to fall? It didn't but I wondered.

Oh What a Lovely War shared the Théâtre des Nations' prize with Peter Brook's production of *King Lear*. Paul Scofield had it for six months. I had it for the other six, not that there was anything to have. We were simply told. Back in London, the show transferred to the Wyndhams Theatre in June 1963, though not without some rumblings from the Lord Chamberlain's office and the family of Earl Haig. They were quietened by Princess Margaret. Standing in the foyer after a performance, with the then Lord Chamberlain, Lord Cobbold, at her side, she said to Joan, "'What you've said here tonight, Miss Littlewood, should have been said a long time ago. Don't you agree, Lord Cobbold?'

'Yes, Ma'am.'

'That's our permission,' said Joan.

Once in the West End, we won the *Evening Standard* Drama Award. However, not everyone loved the show. Angry audience members got to their feet, crumpled up their programmes and threw them at us. We were accused of dancing on the graves of the soldiers. Joan answered that the soldiers were dancing with us. The Ministry of Defence wrote to tell us that we oughtn't to be saying three hundred thousand men were killed but three hundred thousand *officers* and men. More precise, Miss Littlewood, please. Joan replied that we, the company, were honouring the officers by calling them men. In private, Bernard Levin the critic, said to me, 'You shouldn't be in this show. 'You're making people laugh.' I was surprised. It's as if he hadn't been listening to the words the soldiers had put to the tunes. They were full of fun. Nor had Bernard been in the military wing of a sanatorium surrounded by men who weren't going to make it. I had, and apart from the moment of silence after someone died, the laughter had been constant. I told him that.

A show like *Oh What a Lovely War* only comes along once in a lifetime. Both it and I got a lot of attention and when the show had been running at the Wyndhams Theatre for a while, Hal Wallis, the film producer who'd discovered Shirley MacLaine, Dean Martin, Jerry Lewis and Jack Lemmon offered me a million dollars to go to Hollywood. He even gave me a contract which I showed to Harry Secombe at a Royal Variety Performance we were both in. 'Aw, let me touch it for luck,' he said. Again, this was all very gratifying but it was round that time I heard that *Oh What a Lovely War* was transferring to Broadway. Hal would have to know. When I told him, he became impatient.

'I don't want you to do this show in New York. Anybody who's anybody will have already seen you here in London.'

'But I'm an integral part of the show,' I explained, 'I can't leave now.'

'It's up to you,' he said. As I'd never kept up with the Joneses, would have been hopeless at Gene Kelly's tennis parties (if I'd been invited that is), and was only too aware of the producer, Ross Hunter, being forced to pretend his boyfriend was his cousin, I didn't go. Hal Wallis went back to Hollywood. I went to Broadway and, hand on heart, I've never once regretted it.

It was the autumn of 1964 when *Oh What a Lovely War* went to Broadway, the Broadhurst Theatre to be precise, but first we went to Philadelphia for a warm-up. 'Who needs you? Fucking star!' It was the interval and Joan was nose to nose with me. 'Gerry, give him his ticket. Send him home.' Barbara Windsor burst into tears. 'If he's upset you —' said Joan.

'No,' said Barbara, 'You've upset us, coming round in the interval —'

'I wouldn't upset you for all the world,' said Joan.

'It's all right,' I said, handing my hat from the show to Joan, 'Here's my mortarboard. You do the second half. After all, we do the show in light. You sit there in the dark. Why don't you have your seat raised six inches and illuminated and we'll know you're there.'

'How dare you talk to the director like that!' said Joan, which was unusual, as she'd always denied being a director.

What brought all this about? A review in the local paper had appeared saying: 'Last night, Joan Littlewood and Victor Spinetti brought to the Walnut Theatre . . .' My name and hers in the same sentence — I was doomed. That night, as it happened, I'd forgotten something. I was supposed to lead the girls on after my opening talk with the audience but Joan had said, 'Don't rehearse it. Remember it.' I didn't. The next night, the night of the row, I did remember but it took Joan by surprise. 'What was all that prancing around with the girls?' I'd been doing it for eighteen months in London but Joan had thought I was showing off and so I got 'Fucking star!' Gerry didn't give me my ticket but, for the rest of the run in Philadelphia, I heard not a word from Joan. At note sessions, she occasionally glanced my way but then turned to another actor. It was the same in New York, not a word. Barbara Windsor tried to cheer me up.

'If we don't find anyone we fancy, let's have each other.' Barbara said:

'What?' I said.

'But if we do, don't tell our Ronnie.' That was Ronnie Knight, her husband.

'Why?' I asked.

'He'll be jealous because he fancies you.'

'He's not gay, is he?'

'No, darling. He's been in the nick. He'll fuck anything.' I laughed so much I could do nothing else. As for the show, by then, I couldn't have cared less. This was just as Joan intended. It was a double bluff, an enormous risk, though. I could have gone to pieces during that row in Philadelphia and left the show but Joan knew me better. I was utterly fed up but I carried on. 'Fuck the show. Fuck New York. Fuck the opening night and fuck you.' That was my attitude, so when the opening night did come, I walked out onto the stage, totally free, 'Why are you late?' I asked a member of the audience. He explained that he'd got stuck in traffic.

'And what do you do?'

'I'm a critic.'

'Well, you should have been here when we were here. If we'd gone up on time, you'd have missed my best bit.'

As with the IRA Officer in *The Hostage*, Joan had built me a platform, but this time of teak. In Philadelphia, she had taken the whole of Broadway, the whole of an opening night, all the Broadway critics and how savage they could be, thrown them right in my face and said, 'Cope with that.'

I won a Tony Award but when Carol Channing handed it to me, I knew immediately that I didn't want to make one of those grisly acceptance speeches. I did make a speech but remembering the adjudicator of the amateur dramatics from my teens, I made it in Welsh. As I still didn't know a word of it, this was my usual gibberish. The audience was bowled over.

13

A Hard Day's Night

Before Broadway, there was the eighteen-month run of *Oh What a Lovely War* at the Wyndhams Theatre. Almost everything that happened in my career led from that time. Big personalities who were to colour my life, work that would take me abroad, glossy dead-cert productions that weren't, even some of the gaffes I made, you can trace them back to then. However, if it's true when people say to me now, 'Oh, you know everyone,' it is because of Joan. She was the passport. At the height of her fame, all sorts of people were drawn to her work, some she liked, some she didn't – before becoming admirers, they'd probably been hostile – but still they came, so the fact that I'd met Noël Coward, Tennessee Williams, Terence Rattigan, Laurence Olivier and those Hollywood stars on Broadway was through working with Joan. *The Hostage* started it. *Oh What a Lovely War* brought the rest and, this time, I was to work with some of those big personalities, not just meet them. Even so, it could still be a social thing.

So there was Marlene Dietrich, in my dressing room, having seen the show, telling me that she wanted to have dinner with Miss Littlewood. I rang Joan. We fixed a day. 'But she won't want to be pestered by a lot of people in a restaurant,' Joan added, 'It would be better if she came here,' and off she went to buy lots of food. 'Here' was the flat she shared with Gerry Raffles at Blackheath.

'Sweetheart, I can't make Thursday.' It was Marlene on the phone to me. I rang Joan.

'All that food, you'll have to come round and eat it.' I did and we fixed on another day, Tuesday.

'Oh sweetheart, I'm in the studio recording on Tuesday.' Marlene was postponing again. By now Joan was getting irritated.

'It'll have to be in town. Friday.' And Friday it was, at a restaurant, Chez Solange.

'Trust her to choose that one,' said Joan, 'It's where dykes go.' I came in after the performance with Joan. Marlene was already there. She wore a base make-up but no more than that and her hair was held back in a kind of scarf. On her wrists were not only tidemarks but elastic bands. She'd collected them from the stone floor she'd been scrubbing in preparation for the arrival of her daughter, Maria. Joan, on the other hand, had not only been to the hairdressers but had for the first, certainly the first time I'd ever seen it, put on some make-up. As this was completely untypical, the effect was rather alarming – Elsa Lanchester in the Bride of Frankenstein, if anything.

'I saw your show,' said Marlene, 'It's wonderful but who did your lighting, Henry the Eighth?'

'Lighting? What do you know about theatre?'

'Don't forget, I sing every night in the theatre.'

'Sing? You're nothing but a faded old movie star. You've never had a voice in your life.'

'Of course not, sweetheart. That's why I wear the dwess, to take their minds off my voice.' With that they both cackled and fell about. They'd sparred. They'd broken the ice.

On the work front, a thrilling new energy came into my life, one that has never really gone away. For the sake of the young, who ask me questions like, 'Was Richard Burton Welsh?' maybe this energy needs a little bit of explaining. Those of you who know not only that Richard Burton was Welsh but that he invented Welshness, can either suffer in silence or skip the next four paragraphs.

While Joan Littlewood was blowing a nice big hole in accepted British theatre, four young men were preparing to do something similar to pop music. During the 1950s in the charts, there had been soupy ballads harking back to the Second World War, tiresome novelty numbers and, thank God, Rock and Roll. Altogether, the sounds that came from America were either slicker or more energetic and our artistes had no choice but to imitate them. It was what the public wanted. Anonymous songwriters, mimics of whatever was fashionable, Tin Pan Alley in other words, came up with the stuff, while singers just sang it. We needed a shot in the arm.

It was in the early 1960s that those four young men jumped onto the scene – the Beatles. Even they, before we got to hear 'I Want To Hold Your Hand' and 'Love, Love Me, Do', played Rhythm and Blues and so were also under the influence of America. And to look at, they were no different from lots of other British teenaged boys: Brylcreemed hair, leather jackets, drainpipe jeans and winklepicker shoes; what triggered the difference was the town they came from, Liverpool. Under the influence of America they may have been, under the influence of the London entertainment scene they were not. Their manager, a public-schooly type, Brian Epstein, was also from Liverpool and the Beatles' emergence as something new first happened up there. 'Eppy' gave them the look: mops of shining hair, narrow-lapelled jackets with high top buttons and soft leather boots with cuban heels.

The contribution to pop that was historic came from the boys themselves. For a start, they wrote their own songs. That was already unusual. Furthermore, home grown as these songs were, nothing quite like them had ever been heard before. If you want to find their origins, sail across the Irish sea and listen to a true Dubliner talking. The accent is not 'Oirish'. It's nasal and cynical. The word city sounds like 'cizzy', just like in Liverpool. You then realise that the influence of Dublin on Liverpool was once all pervading, and it made for tunes that were bittersweet. That's what the Beatles picked up on.

As for their lyrics, they're the echo of chants you can hear in children's playgrounds. And when the boys stopped singing and spoke, it was in their Liverpool accents. Up until the Beatles' arrival, the strongest voice the world had heard coming from England was the voice of the ruling class, the voice of command, the voice that governed the empire. Performers from the regions had been forced to iron out – that was the expression then – their accents. If they didn't, they didn't get on. The Beatles got on fine altering nothing. For almost the first time, the world heard and learned a genuine British regional accent and it was love at first sound.

In 1963, with Beatlemania at fever pitch in the UK, the lads needed to do something to get themselves known in America.

A few years earlier, Cliff Richard's success and boyish good looks had led him to star in a series of film musicals, a genre the UK hardly touched. Again, we relied on America for those. They were pretty traditional, though, those Cliff films: plots stuck to 'Boy Meets Girl'; songs were Tin Pan Alley and show dancers, as they always do, bust a gut in big production numbers. Nevertheless, the mere making of those musicals in this country was innovative.

The Beatles – my God, the hysteria by then, the screaming, it was phenomenal, my ears still ring today – wanted to make a film too, but what would theirs be like? What sort of story would it have? Who would write it? Who would direct? The Cliff Richard model was quite wrong. It didn't suit them. In any case, the budget was tight. The Beatles may have been big in the UK but, as I said, were not yet in America. Walter Shenson, the producer, an American living in London, only had £180,000 to play with. He had two ideas, though. One, the subject, which was already staring him in the face: fame imprisons you. Two, the director, another American living in London, Dick Lester. He had made a rather feeble comedy for Walter Shenson, *The Mouse on the Moon* but he had also made an eleven-minute short, *The Running, Jumping and Standing Still Film*. Dick and two of the Goons, Peter Sellers and Spike Milligan – had gone out into a field one Sunday morning and shot it on 16mm film for £70. It was a series of surreal gags with speeded-up action and jump cuts. Characters suddenly appeared in one place and then another, with no logic. Really, it was a glorified home movie but at the time, people were tickled by its originality. The Beatles loved it and Walter Shenson, carefully failing to mention the feeble comedy, sold them Dick Lester on the strength of it.

Certain ingredients were beginning to emerge. The Beatles would not be playing characters. They were going to be themselves. Shoehorning them into a carefully worked-out plot wasn't going to be possible. 'Boy Meets Girl' was out of the question and so were production numbers. When the Beatles sang on screen, it would be because they were performing as the Beatles. For the audience to see this 'imprisoned' thing, all it had to do was follow the boys as they travelled to London by train to give a concert. Sure, you could throw in some gags and diversions along the way but that would be it, pretty much. So what style would you use? If you think about it, you might come to the conclusion that the film ought to look like the news on TV, black and white with the camera dodging about – following, not dictating, the boys' moves. All right, you'd need some sort of script, an invisible one preferably. Dick Lester, while working in television, had met Alun Owen, the writer. They'd presented a jazz programme together and Alun was a Liverpudlian. Things were falling into place. I've spent all this time talking about the Beatles and their film because, if you didn't already know, I was in it!

Back to *Oh What a Lovely War* at the Wyndhams for a moment. As you know, each evening before the show started, I walked out on to the stage and talked to the audience. Even at Stratford East, this was unusual. In the West End, it was unheard of. However, one person who would have been familiar with Joan Littlewood's work was Alun Owen. He'd had a play of his, *Progress to the Park*, performed at Stratford East. So it's easy to imagine that it was he who first spoke to Walter Shenson and Dick Lester and that, as a result, both had come along to the Wyndhams. My pre-show chat would have given Dick a clue as to what sort of actor could get on with four chaps who had no acting experience. The character he was after was a nervy, testy television director who just wanted to get everything done on time. The clash between him and the Beatles could be good fun. I can stop imagining now. That's the part I was asked to play.

It was time to find something to wear. Obviously it had to be right for the TV director but comfortable too. Perhaps I could use something I already had. I looked in the cupboard and there it was, a fluffy mohair sweater. I'd never worn it before. Peter Shaffer had given it to me, or perhaps he'd dumped it because he didn't want it. There was, I admit, something faintly ridiculous about it but then maybe for the TV director . . .? 'Perfect,' said both Dick Lester and the designer. The sweater was in.

The climax of *A Hard Day's Night* was the TV broadcast I was supposed to be directing. A live audience of young fans was going to watch it in a real London theatre. The location, therefore, had to be a theatre that was empty, but all the well-known ones had shows in them – except the Scala. Once a year at Christmas this theatre in Charlotte Street opened for *Peter Pan*. The rest of the time it was dark, so it was there I went for my first day's work.

Most feature films are shot with a single camera. A scene is played over and over again but each time, that single camera is moved from one position to another in order to capture a different angle. The snippets of film that you get as a result are then cut together so that it looks as if the scene is happening all at once. Occasionally, when it's a question of an explosion or a stunt, one go at a scene is all that's possible and for that, several cameras are used. Arriving on the set I saw that there were at least three. Dick Lester obviously wanted to catch the Beatles' first, spontaneous reactions to whatever happened.

Repeating the scenes would only dull their responses or worse, make them self-conscious. I was thinking to myself that I would have to keep my wits about me when the Beatles appeared. If I thought of saying 'hallo' nicely or giving way to a gush, it wasn't for long, a milli-second at most. It would have been useless. Instead, I looked at them sternly and said, 'I am the director. You're late for rehearsal.' John Lennon snapped right back, 'You're not a director. You're Victor Spinetti playing the part of a director.' From the corner of my eye, I could see that the cameras had started filming and not only that, they were moving around between us. The important thing was to ignore them and keep going.

'I am a director,' I insisted, 'I have an award on the wall in my office.'

'Office?' said John, 'You haven't even got a dressing room.' Pretending to be miffed, I turned to go and accidentally brushed against Ringo's cymbals.

'Eh, John,' he said, 'He's fingering me cymbals.'

'Then he must be a director,' said John, 'because all directors are famous cymbal fingerers.' We were away. The boys had relaxed. As we walked off to do the next scene, I heard them joshing each other, like schoolboys on the way to class. 'Are those jeans tight, Paul?' That was John.

'What do you mean tight?'

'I can see your suspender belt through 'em and your stockings. You've got ladders in them.'

A while back, I talked about seeing West End theatre for the first time and admiring the actors but not believing them. It looked as if the Beatles believed me. A few evenings later, I walked into a theatre restaurant, well known at the time, called the Pickwick Club. Alun Owen was there. 'I've seen the rushes,' he said, 'You're fucking great in this.' Encouraged as I was, I hadn't been thinking like that. I had not been aware of giving a performance. I was a TV director whose job was to get these four young men to rehearse. That's all. I simply talked to them, like I talked to the audience at the Wyndhams Theatre. I didn't need a pipe and glasses. The point is, the Beatles were slightly in awe of professional actors but also suspicious of them because they could sense that same artifice I had sensed in those West End actors.

You can sum it up like this. Once filming was well under way, John

Lennon said to me, 'When Dick shouts action, the other actors jump up and become different people but you stay the same. Does that mean you're as terrible as we are?'

The banter that I heard on my first day never stopped. Between takes, the Beatles didn't go to their dressing rooms like film stars. They sat behind the set, chatting away. I've made lots of films but I've only worked with two other people like that, Richard Burton and Orson Welles. Richard recited poetry while Orson told stories. Soon I found myself sitting with these four young men, talking to them as if they and I had known each other our whole lives. It was something to do with all of us being provincials. I'd come up from Wales and they'd come down from Liverpool. We were conjoined in the sense of, 'What was the journey like to come here?'

I'll give you an example. They told me about driving from Liverpool for one gig, one gig only, down to Porthcawl in South Wales. It was midwinter. They played the gig but on the way back the windscreen shattered and by then it was snowing. Together with Mal Evans their roadie, who was driving, they put newspapers up and made two little holes so they could see. That way, they drove on, through the snow, at five miles an hour, eventually stopping at a house to ask for help, and where this women let them stay – sit, that is, not sleep – until the weather improved. It was the kind of memory we could shudder over together – George Harrison, in particular. 'Do you remember that house we were in?' he used to say, 'That woman, she had a dog with no legs. She took it out every morning for a slide.' He wasn't one for talking much, George, but when he did, he was either quietly witty or to the point. John may have been famous for his chat, though I'm sure if he'd been telling that story he'd have said, 'Eet eez a dachshund, Schweinhund!' but George, he was for the connoisseurs.

The banter they kept up behind the set slid straight into the film, as it was supposed to do, and every day I looked forward to work, just as I looked forward to rehearsals with Joan Littlewood. The sense of discovery was joyous.

What did I notice about the Beatles during those weeks of filming? A maelstrom raged round them but they were the still, small centre of the storm. The picture of them sitting there together conjured up a couple of images from way back.

Firstly I remembered miners and steelworkers who, amidst all the drilling and the clanging, invariably created a space, a comfort spot when it came to breaktime. Tea could be brewed, cigarettes smoked, and peace and cosiness created. The Beatles were the same on a film set but there was more to it than that and here's the second image. As a boy, I often saw young lads, mates, sitting, talking together in the warmest part of the house, the kitchen. Among them, I always saw a closeness. It came from growing up together, playing in the same streets, knowing the same things. The Beatles had that. I'm not being fanciful. One day, Paul invited me back to his aunty's house for 'Scouse' with the other three, so I saw for myself. 'Scouse' is the Liverpool version of Irish stew.

On the film set, the boys, in what I saw as their kitchen of the mind, were solid, loving and non-stop sender-uppers of each other. But it wasn't merely a place of leisure, this kitchen. 'Kitchen Cabinet' was an expression made famous, at the time, by Harold Wilson, the then prime minister because he arrived at his most important decisions in his kitchen. The boys too made their kitchen into a cabinet. What's more, as theirs was only in the mind, it could be taken wherever they went. In it was security and strength and, once there, they didn't need anyone else.

Wives never went down the mine in Cwm or entered the steelworks and rarely did they enter their husbands' place of leisure. When the Beatles were together in their kitchen, it was the same thing. If a woman did appear, though, she wasn't whistled at or ogled. She was talked to, properly. Actually, in or out of the kitchen, decent behaviour was important to the boys. When, on looking out into the auditorium of the Scala Theatre, they heard and saw stage-school children swearing and smoking and not only that but sitting amongst real children, they were shocked. The red children, after all, were real fans.

How did I get to be a guest in this kitchen? Although I was ten years older than the boys, there was stuff we shared: not only the provincial boy's journey to London but the 'kitchen' thing as well. I suspect the Beatles could tell that I was familiar with it. Immediately, we could all be unselfconscious and relax. Oh, and I also think it was because I didn't ask anything of them, apart from once, a request for a candle off George's 21st birthday cake and even then, I was asking for someone else. One last memory from Wales on this subject. When a new, young wife entered the laddish kitchen scene, that kitchen relationship soon ended. 'I'm not having your friends sitting about all day.'

'What did they talk about?' people kept asking me. They still do today. 'Everything' is the answer. The Beatles were inquisitive. They wanted to know stuff. Snobs, convinced that they could have nothing to say, even asked, 'What on *earth* do they talk about?' Well, here's an example. John had been reading a book about Carl Jung and got really interested, so we found ourselves comparing the Jungian interpretation of dreams with the Freudian interpretation of dreams. Another day it was the writing of Christopher Marlowe. Really, the main thing was the ceaseless inquiring.

'I wonder what kind of music Beethoven wrote for himself instead of for his patron,' George asked once. 'Do you think he had secret music for himself?' John in particular, could get so intrigued, he often had to be dragged away for his own safety, either from his latest obsession or, worse, some nutcase who was trying to gain power over him.

The boys, nevertheless, remained unpretentious. Given their interest in India and the Maharishi Mahesh Yogi, you may think this sounds surprising. People certainly poked fun at all that back then but think, what if the boys had been Oxford undergraduates who'd decided to do up their rooms in Chinese style? Nobody would have questioned it. Four lads from Liverpool? Ah, well, that wasn't allowed.

To be honest, I had my doubts about the Maharishi too but the Beatles wouldn't have it, 'You've got to meet him, Vic.' So, when he gave a talk on Transcendental Meditation at the Plaza hotel in New York, there I was. He sat on a dais in a darkened room, surrounded by flowers and candles, his audience hardly daring to breathe, as airy-fairy as I expected, but when he finished and a woman asked, 'Excuse me, your Highness, how do you teach Transcendental Meditation to children?' he roared with laughter and said, 'My dear lady, they invented it!' All at once, I pictured a child utterly absorbed in a game of the imagination. That I could understand. In the end, what I'm saying about the Beatles and what they talked about is that you might make a fool of yourself in your search but if you don't ask questions you *are* stupid. The Beatles asked questions.

Anyway, they were good at ordinary stuff too. 'I've got to leave early today,' I said to them one afternoon.

'Yes?'

'You remember my sister? She visited us on the set the other day.'

'With a girlfriend?'

'That's the one, Gianina. Her train gets into Paddington any minute and I've got to be there.'

'What for?'

'I'm giving her a present. She's just got engaged.'

'What's the present?' they asked, growing curious.

'A weekend in London. Dinner at a posh restaurant and a nightclub. Once she's married and settled down, that sort of thing's not going to be so easy.'

'What a great idea,' they said, 'Which club?'

'Danny La Rue's. It's the most popular in London.' That night in Hanover Square, the three of us, Gianina, her fiancé David and I were sitting at a table in Danny's club when in walked the Beatles.

'Hallo, Jan, we've come to have a dance with you for your engagement.'

The club was agog but my sister remained calm. When the dance was over, the boys sat, had a drink with us, chatted and, as suddenly as they arrived, left. Gianina came over and gave me a big hug. 'Thank you!' she said, as if this surprise was my doing but it wasn't. I'd done nothing. It was the Beatles' own gift.

When *A Hard Day's Night* opened on the 6 July 1964, Penelope Gilliat, the *Observer* film critic, wrote, 'It has all the urgency and dash of a popular English daily at its best.'

Before shooting started, the producer Walter Shenson was asked by his Hollywood friends what he was up to. 'Oh, a little low-budget film with a pop group,' he answered but, after the premiere, those same friends couldn't even get him on the phone.

14

Help!

'You've got to be in all our films,' said George, seven months later, as we climbed aboard the plane that was to fly us to the Bahamas for the next Beatles film, *Help!*

'Oh, George, thanks,' I said.

'Well, if you're not in them,' he went on, 'Me Mum won't come and see them because she fancies you.' I treasure that remark, firstly because it came true and secondly, because it was about the nicest thing that happened on that film.

I thought we were the same old team, Walter Shenson, Dick Lester and the Beatles, all of us off to make another freewheeling film together, but that is not how it turned out. The team was the same but something had happened to it. On *A Hard Day's Night* Walter Shenson had been constrained by a small budget and Dick Lester had needed to prove himself. Now the film's success meant that United Artists were falling over themselves to give Walter Shenson money while Dick Lester was feeling free to spread his wings. The screenplay came first. Dick and the playwright, Charles Wood, worked up a nutty plot full of surreal gags and an eastern flavour. We sat around trying out titles. '*Six Arms to Hold You*', somebody called out, 'You know, the God, Kali.'

'Great!' everyone agreed before settling on *Help!*

Although the Beatles were again to play themselves in this story, it was no longer a question of the camera catching them on the wing. Gags, however off the cuff, would have to be worked out and shot in a certain way, otherwise they wouldn't register. Spike Milligan and Peter Sellers of the *Running, Jumping* film knew that. Their whole working lives were devoted to it. However, the Beatles were not Spike and Peter.

OK, I'm getting on this plane to the Bahamas. A beautiful place I know, but that was not the only reason why it was thought to be the right location. The Beatles' accountant, Walter Strach, had worked out that it was a good idea to go there for tax purposes. The chartered plane we were on was also a deal. BOAC, the airline, badly needed the Beatles. Walter Shenson, in choosing it, was assured, along with his family, of free first-class travel for the rest of their lives.

When I got on the plane, I was confronted by a lot of unfamiliar faces. In fact, the only familiar ones belonged to the Beatles. I went over to talk to them. A steward came up and asked me to move to the other end of the plane. This was ridiculous. We had the whole aircraft to ourselves. It didn't matter where we sat. Weren't we in this together? Except for those unfamiliar faces round the Beatles, that is. Who were they? It cheers me up to quote W S Gilbert, 'His sisters and his cousins and his aunts'. That's who they were. Relatives of the producer and the associate producer and so on, coming for the ride, that's all. I glanced down the other end. There were my fellow actors. I wasn't happy. It seemed important to me that if we were going to have the same relaxed atmosphere we'd had on *A Hard Day's Night*, an atmosphere that had helped in the making of the film, we'd better start as we meant to go on.

The aeroplane, a jet, revved but huge as it was, its engines couldn't be heard. The screaming of the fans at the airport was louder. We took off. The Beatles, unable to feel free, surrounded as they were by strangers, played cards, nothing cool or sophisticated, just a jolly, family game. Good. They were managing to stay in the kitchen. I've got to say this. Even in private, I knew that they hadn't become hard bitten because if they were stuck together far away from home, the most daring thing they got up to was a wanking game. There, they'd lie in the darkness like schoolboys in a dormitory and the first to put the others off from coming was the winner. They'd all start and then John would say, 'Madame de Gaulle' and, if the others didn't fall out of bed laughing, he'd try, 'Richard Millhouse Nixon'. With John's permission, that ended up as a sketch in Ken Tynan's show *Oh Calcutta*. It was me who told him. Where was I? People on the plane stood up and moved around. The atmosphere eased but only for a while.

It was a stifling hot evening when we got off. The air in the tin shed of an airport was fetid and humidity dragged us to the floor. We wanted to get to peace and quiet and air conditioning. A limousine drew up. Whoosh! Away went the Beatles. Another one drew up.

Whoosh! Away went Walter Shenson and Dick Lester. A third one drew up. Whoosh! Away went 'the sisters and the cousins and the aunts'. We, the actors, Roy Kinnear, Patrick Cargill and I, stood there waiting and waiting. Eventually, an old, windowless bus trundled up and ground to a halt. The camera crew piled their equipment in and then piled in themselves. Roy, Patrick and I squeezed in as best we could. Off went the bus. I can't tell you what I saw on the way because I couldn't see out.

At a downtown hotel, we were released. Having signed in, Roy and I were shown to an airless room with two beds and no window, only a skylight. This we were expected to share. Roy, the new boy, was ill at ease and uncertain. My mind ran back to the contretemps with the steward on the plane. It triggered thoughts of what was to come: a hierarchy, layers to break through, office doors to knock on, fragmentation, the end of teamwork, no cohesion, no camaraderie, everything that had made the first film a success, gone. My heart sank. Roy, Patrick and I had to be fit for work the next day. 'The sisters and the cousins and the aunts', comfortably installed the other side of town, only had to go and sit by the pool. I'll run on a bit more. In later years, Elizabeth Taylor made a point of asking all of us, when we were shooting in Rome, 'How are your digs?' That's because she understood the need for cohesion when filming abroad. I put a call through to my agent.

'Would you mind ringing the producer,' I said, 'and telling him, I'm on the next plane back to London unless −' There was quite a kerfuffle after that but it ended in me, Roy and Patrick being shown out into a beautiful garden where there were bungalows, one for each of us. I sighed with relief. They had big windows and inside, thank goodness, air conditioning, in the Bahamas an absolute necessity. 'We're lucky to be working,' say British actors. Yes, we are lucky but we have something the producers want and they have something we want. Work.

Putting through an international telephone call, waiting for the result and then moving from one room to another meant there wasn't much night left but, cool at least, I got into bed and turned off the light. A soft scuffling nearby stopped me from going to sleep. What was it? I turned on the light. The sound seemed to be coming from the drawer next to my bed. I pulled it open. A spider the size of a tea plate scuttled up my arm and dropped onto my back. In blind panic I ran out into the garden where, happily, the spider and I parted company. Poor bastard, it was as terrified as I was and no doubt, pretty fed up at being trapped in a drawer. Even so, as I climbed back into bed, I was furious with it for confusing my arm with Sean Connery's. See the film *Dr. No* if you don't know what I'm talking about. Closing my eyes, I took comfort from the thought of the beautiful room but no sooner had my head hit the pillow than it was time to get up and go to work.

For the first day's filming we were on a yacht, far out to sea because there was a big crowd on the beach. At least we knew we were welcome, but right then we needed to be away from all that. We were, where the air was chilly, the sea choppy and the boat bobbing up and down rather more than we wanted.

Films aren't shot in the correct order, as you probably know, so despite it being the first day, we were in the middle of the plot. On deck, Ringo was strapped to an operating table while I stood over him in a surgeon's mask, poised to cut off his finger. Why? Because on his finger was a ring I badly needed. Below deck, Roy my henchman was supposedly turning a crank handle, trying to get a generator to work. My knife was blunt but the sharpener wasn't going round. Maddened by this – 'Sand in the generator!' was my cry – I went below to give assistance to my incompetent assistant. This gave Eleanor Bron, darkly dramatic in a wetsuit, the opportunity to spring on deck, cut Ringo's bonds and free him to dive overboard. The whole of this action, I should point out, needing to be seen in the same shot, required the camera and the crew to be nearly a hundred yards away.

The yacht rode high in the water, so there was a fair drop to the sea where, all around, men swam about with shark nets. We did a take that ended with Ringo's dive. 'Cut!' The swimmers moved in and put him into a little boat so that he could be brought back on deck. There, the hairdresser dried his hair and the wardrobe girl put him in another suit. All the while he didn't stop shivering. The weather may have been fine but it wasn't summer and the water had been very cold.

'Are you ready?' a voice through a loudhailer called out, though it sounded more like a distant seagull. 'Action!' Again, I hurried down to Roy to find out what was wrong with the generator. Again Eleanor sprang on deck. Again Ringo dived that high dive and again he was brought back to the yacht.

'Oh V-v-ic,' he said, as once more, the hairdresser dried his hair. 'D-d-o I have to do this a-g-gain?'

'Why?' I asked him. His answer stunned me.

'I c-c-an't swim.'

'What's the hold-up?' came the voice from the loudhailer.

'Wait a minute!' I shouted.

'Wait a minute! Ringo can't swim!' He could have drowned. Nobody had bothered to ask him if he could swim and if he'd drowned, that would have been the end of the picture, the end of the Beatles, the end of everything. 'Why did you do it?' I asked.

'Well, when you're filming and the director shouts "Action" you have to do it, don't you?'

'No,' I said, and Ringo didn't do it again. The footage already shot was used.

I can't casually mention Eleanor Bron without saying something about her. Like me, she suddenly found herself fashionable in the mid-1960s but her route to that point could not have been more different. It was Oxbridge and satire that had brought her to the fore. The TV satire show, *That Was The Week That Was* had led, in 1964, to another one, *Not So Much A Programme More A Way Of Life*. This had introduced Eleanor plus the three Johns – Fortune, Wells and Bird – and Doug Fisher, who were a second wave of Oxbridge writer-performers after the guys from *Beyond the Fringe*. Eleanor's speciality was to look beautiful and serious, like a Dostoyevsky heroine, while all the time poking fun at the image. Performers like her and I, unknown only two years before, would often find themselves thrown together – *Help!* being a case in point, especially if you add Roy Kinnear who had not only been with Joan Littlewood but had also been a team member of *That Was The Week* . . . on we go.

When you're filming on location and you're famous, you aren't just filming on location. You're an ambassador and that means whatever may be happening on the film, you will be in demand and required to keep up some kind of front. It's unavoidable. The Beatles, obviously, were in constant demand and that's why, one evening, we found ourselves on our way to visit a celebrated sculptor. The house he lived in was known as the Murder House and naturally, John wanted to know why. I told him. Back in the 1940s when the Duke of Windsor was Governor of the Bahamas and, as it happens, on good terms with the owners of the house, a famous aviator and man about town, Harry Oakes, had been murdered there. It appeared he'd been manning about town too much, in particular with a woman whose name was already linked with someone else. The police, needing to act quickly, had arrested a local man, a Bahamian, and got a conviction but, from that time until now, no one had believed it for an instant. The real murderer had to be someone with easy access to the house and knowledge of the murder weapon.

That last bit was what had kept the crime so fresh in people's memories, not the affair. The affair was ordinary. What had really fascinated the islanders was the peculiarly nasty method the murderer had used. I was in the middle of describing it to John when our car pulled up at its destination. 'Don't talk about murder, please,' I just had time to say.

All went well in the house itself. It was when the sculptor ushered us out the back to see his work that I began, for no obvious reason, to feel uneasy. Darkness was falling. Perhaps that was it. He clicked open a gate and down through an overgrown garden we walked, right to the furthest end where some kind of outhouse loomed – his studio. Inside, we were vaguely aware of figures in a row but what were they? As our eyes grew accustomed to the dark, we saw that they were women but something was the matter with them. When I realised what, I stepped back. Tangled up in barbed wire with hair of twisted metal, they were writhing about in agony, their mouths stretched wide, screaming with terror. In themselves they were eerie enough but, as we moved along, they made me more and more anxious that John would start talking about the murder. 'Sorry, it's a bit dim in here,' said the sculptor, making me jump. He moved over to his workbench. 'Actually,' he continued, fiddling with what I hoped was a lantern, 'This is what I use for carving my sculptures.' And with a 'whoomph' he turned round, pointing towards us a lit blowtorch. It cast huge shadows of the writhing women on the wall behind him but they weren't what was troubling me now. Harry Oakes's murderer had used a blowtorch and, to make his point had burned his victim's balls off. I needn't have worried about John. He fled. I wasn't far behind.

On the next outing, John let the ambassador façade crack. We'd been invited to a function at the house of the Minister of Finance in order to meet the Governor. That day, we filmed outside what we thought was a derelict army base but John, inquisitive as ever, walked over and pulled at a wooden shutter. Heat shot out at us – the tin roof had made the place an oven – but worse, a stink came too that turned our stomachs and sent us reeling. John moved forward. 'Look!' he said. We gathered round and peered over his shoulder. It was dark inside and quiet, but it wasn't empty. The place was crammed with beds out of which face after face stared at us. These were the unwanted: the very old, the very young and the disabled. I don't know who was more embarrassed, those in that shed for being found or us for finding them.

After work, we were driven to the home of the Minister of Finance. The guests, Government House officials and their wives, sipped at their drinks and milled about in a group, carefully preserving, I noticed, a gap between themselves and the Beatles. From their vantage point, they stared at the boys and talked, not to them but about them. 'Which one is Ringo?' I heard a voice call out.

'I think it's that one, the one with the big nose,' came a drawled answer as they all continued to stare. One of them, a woman, left the group and wandered across to George,

'Is that hair real?' she asked and, without waiting for an invitation, tugged it. 'Oh yes,' she said, turning in astonishment to the others, 'It is.' These people were looking at the Beatles as if they were prize polo ponies, except that for them, prize polo ponies would have been more interesting.

It wasn't a house of long corridors we were in, with lots of rooms and antechambers, but one with a big space that you stepped into immediately, a living room that on this occasion was also going to serve as a dining room. The decor was sumptuous, with paintings covering every wall. If anything, it was too sumptuous. Someone, out to impress, had been piling Pelion on Ossa. I looked around, expecting Jayne Mansfield to sashay in and drape herself against a pillar. She really should have done. The most sensible feature was a wide window with a panoramic view. It looked out onto a garden around which illuminated Greek statues stood gazing at their reflections in a swimming pool. It was made up of two interlinking circles, this pool, a big one out in the garden and a little one coming under the window into the room where we were, a kind of inlet. Curved around this was the dining table, so you could lift the tablecloth, dive into the water, swim under the window and come up in the garden, if you wanted to. Each place setting was laid with row upon row of gold cutlery and glass after glass. The Beatles played dumb – 'Ooh, what are those?' they asked. The Governor's wife turned to her husband, an Australian – this was all before independence, you see – and murmured, 'They don't know their knives and forks.'

Having found our places, we sat down. John, seeing that he was next to the Minister of Finance, launched straight in. 'We were filming this morning up at a place we thought was a deserted army hut but when we looked in, it was full of old people and spastic kids. How do you reckon that with this?' So saying, he pointed at passing soup plates lined with ice and piled high with caviar.

'Mr Lennon,' answered the Minister of Finance, 'I do not get paid for my work as a Minister of Finance here. I do it entirely voluntarily.'

'Oh,' said John and gestured round the room. 'You're doing better than I thought you were doing.' Despite the fact it wasn't the Governor that John was actually sitting next to, the headlines next day blared out, 'BEATLES INSULT GOVERNOR' and the whole lot of us, when we eventually left, were virtually booed off the island.

A director feeling free to spread his wings is no bad thing in itself. However, when that director flies off to pursue his vision, leaving everyone else behind, puzzlement and grumpiness can set in. Convinced they were adjuncts, little more than extras, the Beatles themselves said filming *Help!* wasn't much fun. The spirit of invention that had seen us through *A Hard Day's Night* had gone. That might be another way of saying it. Tiredness and sullenness permeated the shoot. The only time things perked up was in that magic hour between work's end and dinner, posh or otherwise.

Hoping he could tempt the boys into buying an island, a biscuit millionaire who lived locally invited them to a party, but first gave them sports cars in which to drive round said island. George offered me a lift. Refreshed by the evening breeze, he started to sing, 'When you walk through a storm, hold your head up high'. I hadn't heard him so relaxed in ages. It led to his George Formby impression, 'I'm leaning on a lamppost at the corner of the street'. A few days later, I picked up on this. We were in a boat, travelling back from filming, and it was about time I did some cheering up.

'Let's have a singsong,' I said. 'On Top of Old Smokey,' I sang, 'Come along now.' 'On Top of Old Smokey,' they sang. 'All covered in snow,' I sang, 'All covered in snow,' they sang. Good, we were back in the kitchen again. I don't think the boys were familiar with that kind of charabanc chanting but the novelty of it ended up in 'We All Live in a Yellow Submarine'.

Having been booed off the Bahamas, we had to go backwards in the film's plot – I told you they aren't shot in the right order – to scenes that took place in snow. Our new location was Austria, a ski resort called Obertauern to be precise. The plane, however, landed in Munich and our first night was spent in Salzburg.

That evening, the telephone in my hotel bedroom rang. 'Come and have a look at this,' said John. I went up to his room. He, Paul, George and Ringo were standing on the balcony. Beneath them, spread out as far as the eye could see, were tens of thousands of young Austrian fans. The Beatles took out combs, put them over their lips, raised their hands, gave cod Nazi salutes and barked Hitler gibberish. The crowd roared back with laughter. Only those boys, the Beatles, could have done that. All round the world, kids ceased to be Palestinian, Israeli, Catholic, Protestant, Jewish, Muslim. They became first and foremost Beatle fans, united in their love of the Beatles.

'What you have, your gift,' I said to them, 'is the gift of truth. You don't look like liars.' And then, as an afterthought, I said to John, 'But be careful what you say. They believe you.'

He answered, 'I'm only a songwriter, Vic. I'm no fucking martyr.'

Early next morning we drove in convoy to Obertauern. I say convoy because 'the sisters, the cousins and the aunts' were still with us. Despite that, our journey touched me. The twisting, mountainous road was lined from one end to the other with, not just teenaged fans, but children and old peasants, standing there in the snow, waving and calling out, '*Die Beatles!*' It was like a guard of honour.

There was no question of us skiing on this location. The insurers would have had a heart attack. Nevertheless, things happened. Dick Lester eyed a chair lift he wanted me and Roy to ride on. The lift operator pointed out that it was the kind where the riders kept their skis on and slid them along the snow as the lift moved. It wasn't supposed to carry people up into the air which of course was exactly the picture Dick had in his head. 'It's the one I want,' he insisted. Roy and I were fifty feet up above the snow when the lift stuck. It wouldn't go backwards. It wouldn't go forwards. The anchor-like object we sat on swayed and creaked. The wind howled. It was icy. Roy was dressed for the weather but I only had a blazer and a fur hat. Resignedly, the lift operator wound us back by hand. It was very slow. I could hear every turn of the wheel and every ratchet click. 'Ki-ki-ki-ki, Ki'. Pause. Lurch. 'Ki-ki-ki-ki, Ki'. Brandies were brought for us to sip after that and we didn't do the shot again.

When cut together, those snow scenes worked well. I must make that clear. Unhappiness during filming doesn't necessarily mean the film's going to be bad. In fact, it's often quite the opposite. As for the fur hat, its appearance in *Help!* led it to a glittering career. I last saw it on the internet going for $10,000. The mohair sweater in *A Hard Day's Night* didn't do badly either. It was put on display at the Philadelphia Girls' School. There are years when I think that that hat and sweater have realised more money than I have.

Filming ended at Twickenham studios, where we finally shot the beginning. John decided to cheer himself up by designing a suit. He came onto the set to show it to Dick Lester. Dick was staring straight ahead, his hands clasped together, his head resting on his knuckles which were white with concentration.

'I've designed this suit myself,' said John. 'Could I wear it in the film?'

Dick looked at John, shook his head, felt the material and said, 'No.'

'Get fucked,' said John and walked off the set.

Still, while we were in the studio, Ringo got his revenge on the 'sisters and the cousins and the aunts'. It was in the middle of a scene and, poor man, he was yet again, tied up but this time it wasn't his finger that was the centre of attention but the zip of his fly. A fiendish remote-control ray device was pulling it down. At that moment, Walter Shenson ushered a party of the said 'cousins and aunts' round the corner. Ringo looked up, spotted what they were and called out, ''Ere missus, give us a wank!' If you had shouted 'Fire!' you couldn't have cleared the set quicker.

The first night of *Help!* was at the London Pavilion cinema in Piccadilly Circus. 'Come with us,' said the Beatles, 'We'll pick you up in the car.' As we drove along, we were back in the still, small centre of the storm, back in the kitchen before the maelstrom got whirling again. As the limousine edged through the screaming fans outside the cinema, John said laconically, 'Push Paul out first. He's the prettiest.' When the door, in fact, did open, a girl reached in, grabbed George's hair and tore at it. Out in the crowd, pushing our way through, I noticed blood trickling down his forehead. If you're interested in that kind of frenzy, where love turns to violence, you should read a Greek tragedy called *The Bacchae*. Two thousand years ago, its author, Euripides, could tell you all about Beatles fans, only his hero had not just his hair but his arms and legs pulled off. Mum kept the head.

Working with the Beatles on their films was one thing. Being associated with them in life was another. Over the months and years to come, it led to situations both barmy and pleasurable.

15

The Beatles, by association

When *Oh What a Lovely War* opened on Broadway, Beatlemania in Europe had been amazing but in America, it was mega. People went mad, absolutely insane, and I was now firmly associated with the boys in the public's imagination. When I came out onstage, a group of girls at the back screamed, 'Victor Spinetti! Aaarrgh!' and then, 'He touched George!' Realising that they were Beatles fans, I signalled to the stage manager, 'It's all right. There's a bit of a disturbance but hang on.' 'Listen my darlings,' I said, 'This is a serious musical about the First World War but I'll tell you what, at the end of the performance, after the show, come down and sit in the front row and we'll do a ten-minute seminar on the Beatles, all right?'

'Oh yes,' they shouted. 'Thank you, thank you, thank –'

'OK,' I said. There were two reasons why I did this. One, I wanted them to keep quiet, so we could get on with the show. Two, I knew what it was like to hunger after – to know something about someone you really loved, adored passionately but would never, ever meet. When I was a teenager, if somebody had told me, they knew Rita Hayworth, I'd have said, 'Oh, what's she like?' These kids were the same. At the end of the show, they came and sat in the front row of the stalls, shaking, shivering and crying. 'Tell me about John.' 'Tell me about George.' They knew nothing. No books had been published yet. The Beatles were just four moptops to them but they loved these people they knew nothing about. This is the story I told them.

'We were in Salzburg, filming *Help!*' I would say, 'and I got flu. The Beatles came to my hotel room to visit. The first to arrive was George Harrison. He knocked, came in and said, "I've come to plump your pillows. Whenever anyone's ill in bed they have to have their pillows plumped." He then plumped my pillows and left. John Lennon came in next and marched up and down barking, "*Sieg Heil, Schweinhund!* The doctors are here. They're coming to experiment upon you. *Sieg*

Heil! Heil Hitler!" And he left. Ringo then came in, sat down by the bed, picked up the hotel menu and read out loud, as if to a child, "Once upon a time there were three bears, Mummy bear, Daddy bear and Baby bear." And then he left. Paul opened the door an inch, asked, "Is it catching?" "Yes," I said, on which he shut the door and I never saw him again.' Paul was being the pragmatist as usual. He knew that if he or the others had caught flu, there'd be no filming.

That's the story I told these girls because then at the end of it, they, at last, had some information, some tiny crumbs of comfort, personal details they could take away with them and share with their school friends next day. It became the big thing. Fans came to the show just to hear those stories at the end. Sold a lot of tickets. They came from Detroit, from Chicago, from Philadelphia, flying in for the matinee after which they'd all sit down at the front and we'd do this ten-minute seminar.

It didn't stop there. They'd be outside the stage door afterwards, waiting, 'Oh, Mr Spinetti, what did George Harrison say?'

'Plumped the pillows.'

'Oh no! Oh my God! Isn't that cute! What does it mean?' But then each passed it on to the next down the line.

One afternoon, Warren Beatty was there, backstage in my dressing room. 'Victor,' he said, 'I've a problem here. There's a crowd of teenage girls at the stage door and they're going to tear me apart.' I didn't like to tell him they weren't Beatty fans but Beatle fans, so I said, 'They'll be OK. Don't worry.' As we came out of the stage door, they all shouted, 'Victor Spinetti!' and parted, leaving room for Warren Beatty to walk through. I can see his astonished face even today.

With the Tony Award for *Oh What a Lovely War* and a bit of money coming in, I rang my parents to invite them over. 'Where are you now, then?' asked my mother.

'New York,' I answered.

'Oh, New York. Do you want to talk to the dog?'

'No, no,' I said, 'I want you to come here,' and I sent the tickets. They'd never been on a plane in their lives. In the meanwhile, the Beatles fans I'd chatted to at the theatre, wanting to show their appreciation for the seminars, formed a kind of Victor Spinetti fan club. Brian Epstein even wrote me a letter thanking me for my efforts. Can I find that letter now? Can I —. So it wasn't just me that went to the airport. There was a coachload of these fans as well plus a big banner. They were going to meet my parents too and take them back to the hotel. As Joe and Lily entered the arrivals hall and I went to greet them, hundreds of teenagers ran forward shouting, 'Victor Spinetti!' My father looked around and said, 'What the bloody hell have you been up to then?'

When I was on that BOAC plane with the Beatles, the one flying to the Bahamas location, we landed in New York, just to refuel. We weren't allowed off. Suddenly an immigration officer appeared and said, 'Is there a Victor Spinetti on board?'

'They're deporting you, you bloody wop,' said John, 'Ellis Island awaits.'

'Yes, I am he,' I said to the officer,

'Would you come to the door of the plane, please,' he said, 'And wave. Because your fan club is at the airport.'

'His fan club?' the Beatles said. The next moment I was standing at the door of the plane, waving, with the lads, while the crowd shouted, 'Victor!!' and I was brought jelly babies and teddy bears. It was my friends from the theatre again.

'Eh, Vic,' said John, 'Y'know, we're really impressed with your fan club. Do you think we could join?'

'I don't know,' I said, so I wrote to the lady who was running it and they joined. The Beatles and their manager, Brian Epstein, all received cards saying that they were members of the Official Victor Spinetti Fan Club of America.

After *Help!* I went back to New York to be in a musical called *Skyscraper* with Julie Harris, a wonderful American actress who detested doing the show but that's another story. In the company was a guy called Dick O'Neill, the kind of solid, dependable character actor who has you saying, 'Oh, it's him,' when you see his face on television.

Unfortunately, for all his experience, he couldn't relax. His professionalism had to be fiercely guarded. Outsiders made him suspicious. The only actors he looked up to were American film stars. Actors from elsewhere, even films from elsewhere didn't interest him at all. As for Brits, he hated them, well, he was Irish, and in particular, he hated Brits on Broadway. You can now imagine the scene. Each day, when I came in to rehearsals, he'd call out, 'Good morning,

Limey! How are you, Limey?' or one day, 'Who are you, Limey?' or another, 'I've never heard of you, Limey!' When he yelled, 'Hey, Limey what does it feel like to be in an all-American show?'

I'd had enough and shouted back, 'Talented!'

It was time to knock this on the head. 'Now come on, Dick,' I said, 'This is ridiculous. I'll take you to lunch and I'll tell you the story of my life, all right?'

'Sure' he said, 'Sure. Never heard of him,' he went on, muttering to himself.

A couple of days later, coming out of the Algonquin hotel, I saw a placard that said, 'Beatles arrive today in New York'. 'Good,' I thought, 'Today is the day to tell Dick O'Neill the story of my life.' I knew every Beatle fan would be marauding Manhattan, looking for some sign, some clue as to where the boys might be staying. On their rampage, they'd spot me – they'd seen those films about fifty or sixty times each – and they'd follow me, thinking I'd lead them to the Beatles. I knew that. Dick O'Neill did not know that. As soon as we broke for lunch, he and I set out together. We hadn't gone ten yards when suddenly a group of teenagers, recognising me, screamed, 'Look, there he is, Victor Spinetti!' We turned and ran. Another group came at us, 'Victor Spinetti!' Off in the other direction we sped but from elsewhere came more screams of 'Victor!'

'Jesus Christ!' gasped Dick O'Neill, 'How often does this happen to you?'

'All the time,' I answered, 'Wherever I go!' We were running to the restaurant, to Sardi's, because the Broadhurst Theatre where we'd performed *Oh What a Lovely War* was opposite Sardi's and so it had become our local caff. As we entered, Vincent Sardi, the owner, approached.

'Mister Spinetti, welcome! Your usual table?' This was pretty impressive coming from Vincent Sardi himself but we'd hardly sat down when towards our table walked the top Broadway producer, the man who'd brought *Oh What a Lovely War* to America, David Merrick.

I turned to Dick to introduce him. 'Do you know David Merrick?'

'No' said Dick, standing to attention, 'Hallo, Mr Merrick.'

'Victor, what are you doing in a piece of garbage called *Skyscraper*?' growled David Merrick through his clenched teeth. 'It'll be a flop. If

I hear of anything, I'll let you know,' and off he sauntered, muttering, 'Garbage, a piece of shit, a real flopperooney.' Dick O'Neill visibly relaxed but that wasn't the end of it. A waiter came with a plate. On it was a note:

'Dear Mr Spinetti, I'm having lunch here with my wife. She'd rather sit with you than with me. May we join you? Yours hopefully, Henry Fonda.'

I'd never met the man in my life but I found myself saying, 'Of course, hallo, do come over, May I introduce Dick –' I couldn't find Dick O'Neill. He was a grease spot on the floor. In his confusion over David Merrick, he'd dropped his napkin and was trying to pick it up,

'Hallo Mr Fonda,' he said, banging his head as he got to his feet. Now what Dick didn't know and what I soon found out was that Henry Fonda's wife was a Beatles fan.

'What are they like?' she asked excitedly. I told her the usual story – 'Plumped the pillow, *Sieg heil, Schweinhund*!' and so on. 'Oh, isn't that cute?' she said. At last we were able to order but then a policeman came in.

'Is there a Victor Spinetti here?' he asked.

'Yes,' I said.

'I'm sorry, Mr Fonda,' said the cop, 'But your guests have to leave. We've got big problems out here.'

'What problems?' I asked. 'Come on, we have to move.' said the cop.

'Why?'

'The whole block is jammed with your screaming fans.' I helped Dick O'Neill to his feet and led him to the door. Outside, policemen were beating kids back with what appeared to be rolls of cardboard. Around the restaurant mounted police, their horses rearing, held back the crowds. One of them ordered angry, beep-beeping drivers onto the sidewalk, so that he could carve out a space for a taxicab to come through. We got into the taxi. The fans shook it, 'We love you, Victor, oh yes, we do!' Inside the cab with Dick O'Neill, I began to think, should we go directly to hospital or to rehearsals? But there was more.

At the theatre, I opened the cab door saying, 'Quick Dick, run!' because fans were charging down the street but as we headed for the stage door, a lady came towards us from the other direction.

Dino de Laurentiis Studios, Rome. 1966. The film, *The Taming of the Shrew*. Walking down a fake cobble street are Michael York, as adorable off the set as on, me in my Zeffirelli costume, Richard Burton, by then, in his and Alan Webb. Alan is wearing a codpiece. In Cwm, our slang word for flies was 'coppish'.

The Queen's Theatre, Shaftesbury Avenue. 1966. With Jack Klugman in *The Odd Couple*. Franco Zeffirelli was ringing for ten tickets when a big Hollywood star came into my dressing room. 'I'm a bit busy,' I told him, 'Joan Crawford's here.' 'You bastard!' he yelled. Joan, meanwhile, was saying,'I've seen this show in New York and Los Angeles. You brought vulnerability to the role.'

Shooting the film, *Under Milk Wood* in 1971. I'm Mog Edwards and playing Myfanwy Price is Glynis Johns, 'The mermaid in my lap' you could say. That's if you know your Dylan Thomas and an old film of Glynis's called *Miranda*. Despite masses of big names, this film was made on a tiny budget – the check suit was mine – but then we were very fond of Andrew Sinclair, the director.

With Norman Rossington and John Junkin in *A Hard Day's Night*. It came out in 1964. Of that sweater Peter Shaffer said, 'You have it. I can't wear it.' 'I can't either.' I said but there it is for all the world to see and now people are prepared to pay thousands of dollars for it.

With Katherine Ross in *Voyage of the Damned*. Katherine won an award for her performance. 'I have to thank Victor Spinetti,' she said, 'During my most difficult close-up, he gave me my eyeline and made me cry.'

Marine Street, Cwm. Outside the cafe are Francis the bootmaker, auntie Angelina, 'Is-a terrible, is-a terrible,' Ingeborg, German and employed by my father – that raised a few eyebrows – Shadrach Weeks and his wife, Olwyn, known as Mrs Weeks, the woolshop, the two of them always leading the military two-step at the Miners' Institute, Mam, Adrian my brother and me, the manager.

Leicester Square, With Barbara Windsor. The original owner of that raccoon coat left Carlton Terrace to become Governor of Bermuda. His valet offered it to Dan Massey who thought £20 was too much. That's how I got it. Years later, burglars stole it from my home in Pimlico. The police recovered it all right but then left it by a radiator all night. In the morning, when I picked it up, it fell to pieces.

Fings Ain't Wot They Used T'Be. The Garrick Theatre. 1960. Barbara Windsor as Rosey, Toni Palmer as Betty and me as Tosher, relocated to Aberystwyth.

Graham Lewis Curnow.

A marquee in Grosvenor Square. Another charity do.
Back row: Gary Raymond, me, David Kernan, Gerald Harper, Denis Quilley,
Ned Sherrin, George Sewell, Nicky Henson and Christopher Biggins. Front row:
Patricia Hodge, Gabrielle Drake, Kate O'Mara, Diane Keen, Nyree Dawn Porter, Joan
Collins, Bonnie Langford, Fiona Fullerton, sorry, I don't know and Joyce Blair.

Rome. 1966. *The Taming of the Shrew*. Elizabeth Taylor, Franco Zeffirelli and our make-up man. 'Let me put it on,' said Franco when I was not sure about my wig, 'See, I look lovely in it."

Sean Connery on the set of *Hell Drivers* which was released in 1957. This is the Sean I knew, the man who would fall on the floor, he was laughing so much.

Stratford E.15. 1963. *Oh What a Lovely War!* To change characters, we changed hats. It was as simple as that.

On the set of *Voyage of the Damned*. James Mason took this and when the film was finished, he always kept in touch. 'Let's go and have something to eat.' he'd say whenever he visited London and off we'd go to the Ritz or the Mirabelle.

Me today. Yes, how right Roy Kinnear was.

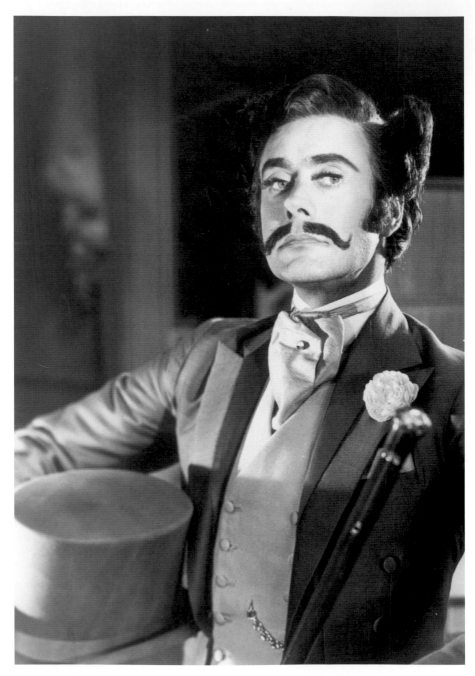

1969. As General Irrigua in *Cat Among the Pigeons* at the Prince of Wales Theatre. Having said, 'You're the only person who understands farce, dear baby, but your make-up is dreadful.' Laurence Olivier designed this, fur fake eyelashes and all.

Beautifully dressed, she looked about – I never know people's ages – say, forty.

'Oh!' she gasped, 'Victor*r* Spinetti? I am your grreat-est fan. I am from Urr-uguay.'

'Uruguay?' said Dick, 'Somebody fucking knows you from Uruguay? Where the fuck is Uruguay?' After that, he carried my bags, opened doors, ordered drinks at the bar and even brought me coffee at rehearsals. Why did he do that? Because he thought he was out with the most famous person in the world and I didn't pretend otherwise. Of course, if you ever meet Dick O'Neill, don't tell him.

16

Skyscraper: A Musical, Not A Building

What about *Skyscraper* itself? I'd never been in a new Broadway musical before so, on hearing I'd got the job, and wanting to do things properly, I booked my passage on the *France*, a transatlantic liner. It was the autumn of 1965. A few days later, the production office in New York rang to say that rehearsals had been brought forward. Another dream up in smoke. I cancelled the four days at sea and booked myself on the next flight. Various drafts of the show, each one printed on different coloured paper, had been sent. The latest, which I'd only just received, I planned to read during the flight. However, sitting next to me on the plane was a lady called Dee, someone I'd met before in New York and of whom I was to become very fond. Naturally, we chatted all the way and the sheer excitement of being in New York, once I'd arrived, the smell of the jet engine at the airport, checking in at the Algonquin hotel, the autumn air with its early-morning hint of the sea, the steam rising from the subway, swept me through the next twenty-four hours with the script still unopened. The next day was the first day's reading.

In a rehearsal room at the end of Broadway just off Seventh Avenue, we gathered. Everyone was introduced to everyone, even if we'd met before. I found myself shaking hands with Sammy Cahn and Jimmy van Heusen, who'd written songs for Sinatra, with Michael Kidd, who'd choreographed *Seven Brides for Seven Brothers,* and with Cy Feuer of Feuer and Martin who'd produced *Guys and Dolls.* Things didn't look too bad.

Skyscraper was based on a play by Elmer Rice, which had been adapted by the screenwriter Peter Stone. By the time he'd finished, I'd become Roger Summerhill, a bookshop owner over whom the Julie Harris character fantasised. For her, he was Tarzan, Rhett Butler, Superman, all these heroes.

I sat down between Julie Harris and the actor who was to play the real hero and opened the script, the one I hadn't seen before. What a surprise. There was my character still speaking on the last page. Obviously the part had grown since all those other drafts on different coloured paper. We started to read. Everyone gave the performance of a lifetime, except me. I simply read. At lunchtime we broke, went for something to eat, came back, chatted and sat down again. The guy playing the hero was not there. 'Where is he?' I asked. 'We fired him on his first day's reading.' The real shock of this was, why hadn't *I* been fired? I hadn't given a reading at all. They must have thought that was how British actors worked.

The producers had been really busy that lunchtime. Another actor, Peter L. Marshall, had already been summoned. He was flying in the next day from Los Angeles. When he arrived he announced: 'Wow! Baby, by the time we open, I'll have Broadway by the balls!' At that moment, I knew we were in for a disaster.

Rehearsals began. Sammy Cahn came up to me and said: 'I've got this great number for you,' and sang it right in my face, nose to nose. 'What do you think?' he asked. I didn't think anything. I was red with embarrassment from him being so close. However, when it came to learning a lyric and I was struggling, he did say: 'You, you've only had a few hours. Frank Sinatra took two weeks.' Apart from that, during the entire rehearsal period, nobody said anything to me.

We flew to Detroit to try the show out. At the New York airport, I was standing in the departure lounge with the rest of the cast, Dick O'Neill amongst them, when a voice shouted out: 'Victor Spinetti!' It was Shelley Winters who was there with Jon Voight. Jon picked me up and whirled me round:

'What are you doing here? Come for a drink.'

'That's OK, you go ahead,' said Dick rather meekly, 'I'll look after the bags,' I almost thought he was going to say, 'Sir.'

The theatre where we were to give these previews was the Fisher. It was vast and because Julie Harris was born in Detroit, it was also packed. Expectations were high. We gave some performances. Still nobody spoke to me. Then the producers said: 'We've been ignoring you so far because Julie isn't landing. When we've sorted out her problems, we'll come to you.' Julie herself was in tears.

'I can't do musicals. I can't.' One number troubled her in particular.

Its lyric went: 'My fabulous legs and thighs.' But her own were not that good.

'You're the star,' I said, 'Go and tell them.' She didn't. She was rather nice.

After a while the director came to me.

'Julie still isn't landing. Let her say your lines tonight and you say hers.'

'Do we change clothes?'

'No, you just change lines. Maybe, we'll find the laughs that way.'

I was fascinated. There, in front of me, was a Broadway musical being made from the ground up, meetings in hotel rooms till four in the morning, lots of black coffee, people scurrying to and fro, desperate rewrites on scraps of paper and I was free to be fascinated because I wasn't involved. Nobody had come to see me. One day they did.

'We've got a great idea for you. We're going to turn your part into a faggot.'

'Why?'

'For laughs.'

'Look, I know what it's like to be a faggot. If you want, I'll do it for real but not for laughs.' I was thinking, the last time I'd been on Broadway, the show had been *Oh What a Lovely War*. I'd won a Tony Award. I didn't want to come back as a two-dimensional queen mincing for laughs.

'I'll play what it means, really, to be a faggot,' I said but that's not what they wanted. 'OK, I won't just walk out,' I said, 'I'll wait and when you find someone, let me know.' At that moment, I remembered seeing Nöel Coward in New York and telling him about this new musical.

'Got lots of lovely frocks?' he asked.

'Yes, I've been fitted for some nice suits.'

'Whatever you do, keep the suits. They'll come in handy.' And that's the deal I struck. A more hard-nosed actor would have said: 'Fire me and pay me for the run of the show.' I settled for the suits.

Over the next few days I carried on performing in the show. Things didn't stand still. I was in the wings waiting to go on, one evening, when Sammy Cahn came up to me. 'Victor, the lyrics for that song I wrote for you, they're not landing. Dorothy Lamour was in last night and she didn't like them.' Dorothy Lamour didn't like them? I didn't know she was still alive. Dorothy Lamour, if you didn't know, was the girl in the Hope and Crosby *Road* movies and was chiefly famous for wearing a sarong. 'I want you to try these new lyrics,' said Sammy and handed me a piece of paper.

'When?' I asked.

'Tonight! Now!'

I went on stage to do a scene with Dick O'Neill and was about to launch into my number when a thought occurred to me. I stopped the orchestra. 'Hold it. Hold it,' I said, 'Ladies and gentlemen, as you know, this is a tryout. The reason why we do that is to see what works and what doesn't. Sammy Cahn,' I pointed to the wings, 'Has just given me some new lyrics for the song I'm about to sing and I'm thinking what a good idea it would be if I first sing the original lyrics and then the new ones. Then you can say which you prefer.' The sweat was pouring off Dick O'Neill. 'OK?' I said to the MD and off we went into the number. At the end, the audience applauded like mad. 'Now, here are the new lyrics,' I said and off we went again. The audience fell about and cheered. 'I've never seen anything like that in my life!' said Sammy Cahn when I got off. 'I can't believe that you just did that. You held up the show!' Yes, but officially I was no longer in it and anyway I thought I was helping out.

As my days in Detroit over the next two weeks were free, I took to visiting the art galleries and if there was anything I learned from being in *Skyscraper* in Detroit, it was this. At the Historical Museum, having walked past miles and miles of rich car manufacturers' bequests, I found in the basement, an exhibition called 'Old Detroit'. This was a street of shop fronts and cobblestones. When I came back upstairs, I didn't feel as tired. Why? Because my feet had been given a problem to solve. Feet get bored and tired in art galleries because the flooring is always the same. Architects forget that you bring the whole of yourself to a museum, not just your eyes. There's your sense of smell and your body too. Different surfaces keep you refreshed.

One evening I went back to the theatre and there, in my dressing room, was my understudy making himself up.

'Hallo,' I said.

'Oh my God! Didn't they tell you I'm on tonight?'

'No, no one's told me.'

'Oh, I'm sorry.'

'That's OK. I'll go out front and watch.'

I went out and sat way, way, back in the vast auditorium. Among the audience I noticed a face that seemed vaguely familiar but, as the lights were dimming, I didn't have time to work out who it was. In any case, I was more intrigued by the prospect of hearing the latest rewrites. Holding up a shoe, on came my understudy and delivered his first line: 'The whole of New York's East Side is covered in dog shit!'

'Hmm,' I thought, 'You're well out of that one, Tallulah.' This was what the actress, Estelle Winwood had said to her friend, Tallulah Bankhead, over cards, on hearing a newsflash about the apprehension of the Lindbergh baby kidnapper.

I went backstage. Everyone must have known what was going on because the cast presented me with a briefcase and a huge book of Michelangelo's drawings as a farewell present. They were quite tearful.

I returned to the hotel. From behind a screen, a telephonist came hurrying. 'Mr Spinetti, I don't know who you are but you're the only person to stay here who's received a call from London, Paris, New York and Hollywood all on the same day.' News had travelled fast.

The next day, I caught the plane to fly back to New York. As I settled into my seat, I heard the sound of crying. I looked round. It was my understudy. 'What's happened?' I asked.

'They told me the part was mine and I told everybody, my family, my friends. I told them I was opening opposite Julie Harris. You saw me. Was I that bad?'

'No, you were very good.'

'Two weeks I've rehearsed but they've been working across town in secret with Charles Nelson Reilly.'

'Ah,' I remembered, 'The familiar face in the audience.' It transpired that Charles Nelson Reilly had indeed been rehearsing across town but had refused to commit himself until he saw the rewrites on their feet. Last night he had and he'd decided to do the show. Consequently, the understudy had been fired. In a book he wrote later, Charles Nelson Reilly said that he'd been hurriedly thrown on because Victor Spinetti had walked out with no warning. Rubbish. He did add, though, that the part had been the making of his career.

In New York, a headline read: 'Pope arrives in New York. Spinetti leaves *Skyscraper*.' The show which opened on 13 November 1965 at the Lunt-Fontanne Theatre ran on Broadway for six months, mainly because Julie Harris was in it. One review finished: 'Victor Spinetti left the show in Detroit. I wish the others had gone with him.'

Of the four telephone calls I'd received in Detroit, the one from Paris had come from the French comedian, Robert Dhéry. I flew to Paris to meet him. There was talk of doing a show of his in New York, *La Grosse Valise*. Robert had made his name creating zany revues like *La Plume de Ma Tante* in which the comedy grew out of things going slightly wrong. I didn't know it but my act, the man who had to keep up with the disobedient sound effects, was rather similar. We got on well and I flew straight back to New York to do the show with Robert directing and his wife Colette Brosset, as with all his shows, doing the choreography. We opened at the 54th Street Theatre on 14 December 1965. For the first-night party, the company was invited to a buffet dinner at the Hilton Hotel. We were standing at the counter, ready with our empty plates, when the producer Joe Kipness, burst in. 'I've just read the reviews and I'm not paying for another thing.' Clang! Down came the shutters and round the corner we had to go to find a deli. Tennessee Williams was at that first night.

'Victor,' he said, 'I'll see you in anything but, please, don't be in this again.'

17

Welcomes to Work: The Burtons and Raquel Welch

Next thing — we're now in 1966 — I was unpacking the *Skyscraper* suits from their new suitcase in my new digs, round the corner from the Spanish Steps, on the Via dei Due Macelli in Rome. An Austrian Contessa was my landlady. '*Meine kleine Puppi Mausi,*' she cooed down the phone to one and all. What it meant, I didn't know but it worked. Over the years, everybody who was anybody stayed at her posh boarding house.

The job was at the Dino de Laurentiis Studios and I was sitting there, in my dressing room, when in burst our director, Franco Zeffirelli. Two days of shooting *The Taming of the Shrew* with the Burtons had gone by and he wasn't happy. 'Is a disasster!' he said.

'What is?' I asked.

'The whole film! Is a disasster!'

'Why?'

'The Burtons have brought some designer, some woman called Irene Sha-RAFF,' he spat on the ground, 'From Hollywood and they're not going to wear my costumes. If they don't wear my costumes, the film is a disasster.'

Irene Sharaff was indeed a Hollywood designer, a distinguished one too, in her Hollywood way. At MGM, she'd dressed Elizabeth Taylor for years and her know-how would have been very reassuring. Clever underpinning to create a sumptuous cleavage was one of her specialities. Her style, however, could not have been further away from Franco's. Whereas he liked nothing fake, she had designed a costume for Richard of silk to look like leather. Coolness under the studio lights was the aim but it made Richard look sort of puny and silly, a big head on a small body. 'Never mind, Franco,' I said, 'Give me the costume that I wear,' and, swirling a huge cloak round me and donning a great big red hat with a long feather in it, I swept into Richard's dressing room.

'Christ! Are you wearing that?' he yelped, 'Good God, what with you and that bloody feather and my wife showing her tits, nobody's going to look at me. Franco! Bring your costumes!'

'Thank you Victor, thank you, you're marvellous,' said Franco. 'Not in the film but on the set.'

For the first weeks we were a tremendous family, Michael Hordern, the young Michael York, Natasha Pyne, Alan Webb, Alfie Lynch and myself. Our dressing-room doors were always open and we were always in and out of each other's rooms. The Burtons themselves were like leading players in a rep company being jolly good to their fellow actors. A surprise dinner or party was always cropping up. 'Come on,' Richard would say, 'We're all going –' and off we'd set to some do or other. Here's one. 'We're all going to see Dino's latest film on his new Cinerama screen,' and cars drove us down to a tall, narrow building in which there was a huge wraparound screen but only two rows of seats. Champagne and caviar were served and we looked up at 'DINO DE LAURENTIIS presents The Bible produced by DINO DE LAURENTIIS.'

When this epic ended and the lights were coming up, I got to my feet, noticing next to me a man I hadn't spotted before. 'Oh yes,' said Richard, 'Victor, this is Dino.'

'But you're so tiny,' I said and then: 'I meant the film, it's so big.' It was hopeless. Richard gave me a wicked smile and whispered in my ear: 'You'll never work in this country again. He hates being told he's short.'

'My sister's getting married next week and I'm the best man.' This was me to Richard in the middle of shooting. The point is, he wasn't just the star. He and Elizabeth, were also the producers. 'You're not bloody going anywhere. This is some bloody scheme of yours,' he said.

'No, it's not –'

'What's going on?' Elizabeth had just come into the room. I told her. 'Oh my God, you've got to be there. It's important for a girl to have all her brothers at a wedding and believe me, I'm an expert at weddings. They're one thing I do know about. You go. I'm a producer of this film as well. You take a day, no, take two days off. Don't rush. Come back the following day.'

'Is that all right with you?' I asked Richard?

'Well, yeah,' he answered 'All right then.'

Into my dressing room the next day, came Elizabeth's two assistants and presented me with a first-class plane ticket. Elizabeth had paid for it. On the day of my flight, a studio car appeared to drive me to the airport and when, back home in Wales I stood up to read out the telegrams from Aunty Poll and Uncle Arthur, there among them, I found one that read: 'If you're as happy with your husband as I am with Richard, you will be very happy. Lots of Love. Elizabeth Taylor.'

Franco was working out the next day's shoot one day when he realised that he would need fifty extras to pass quite close to the camera. They would require make-up. The make-up department threw up its collective hands in horror. 'We'll have to start at 5.30!'

'Don't worry, said Elizabeth, 'I'll do it,' and a marquee was rigged up specially outside the studio where the next morning, first thing, she was to be found making up the fifty extras and it was very stuffy in there. The rest of us had air conditioning. When she'd finished, she came back to the studio make-up room where she found me sitting in the chair.

'Haven't they done yours?'

'No,' I answered.

'Do you mind if I do it?'

'Not at all.' Her violet eyes were inches away, scrutinising my face, when she paused. 'May I give you a beauty tip? Always extend the eyebrows. They set your eyes further apart, which in your case, honey, you need because yours are so close together. Oh, and don't use an eyebrow pencil. Use an ordinary lead one.'

So convivial was the mood the Burtons established, I was inspired to write a short story. It was about an old lady being driven through Richmond Park in an old-fashioned Rolls Royce. 'The Revolutionary', it was called. When I'd finished I went into Richard and Elizabeth's room. Most people, let alone most stars, would have said: 'How interesting,' and got on with something else. They didn't. With them it was: 'Oh, quickly, read it to us.' And, like two children, they sat down to listen hugging themselves with excitement.

'You want to get that published, boy.' said Richard when I stopped reading. 'Tell you what, We'll have a bet. I've just written a short story too. The first one to get theirs published buys the other a crate of champagne.' Having my story published hadn't occurred to me. It was just fun writing it. However, I sent it to *Queen* magazine where it was accepted. Richard's went to the *Observer*. I can't remember who bought it in the end but champagne was definitely drunk.

One afternoon, waiting for an elaborate change of lighting, the cast was twiddling its thumbs. 'Let's have some poetry,' said Richard. Michael Hordern kicked off with a poem by John Betjeman. After that, Richard did some Dylan Thomas. Before, he'd been teasing me about my Welshness or lack of it. 'Of course, you, you're not really Welsh, are you? A bloody Eyetie you are, bloody Bracchi shop.' Bracchi was the first Italian family to open a cafe in Wales and the name had stuck. While he was reciting, I racked my brains and then something floated into my head. It was a poem about a wet day in Wales set by a graveside with mud and tombstones, and mackintoshes and flowers blowing in the wind.

'I'll try that,' I thought and got up to recite it.

'Good God, that's Wales, that is,' said Richard when I reached the end. 'Who wrote it?'

'I did,' I said. I'd written it on my bed shortly after arriving in London. There was a pause.

'Write it out for me, will you?' said Richard and I did.

The next evening, we went to a party given by Anna Magnani, the great actress. 'Oh, Richard, please recite for us,' she said and Richard, with all that banked-down anger of his, recited my poem, by heart. I'd only given it him the day before.

'Who wrote that?' a voice called out and, pointing at me, Richard said, 'That Welsh bastard over there.' Finally I was dubbed Welsh by another prince of Wales.

'You behave yourself when you're in Rome,' said Alan Webb, the old character actor. 'You be careful what you do here. We're representing Great Britain. Don't forget that.' The next day, he came to work in rather a state. He'd been found drunk wandering around Rome with no trousers on. A pick-up had run off with them. Wonderful, all this was wonderful, happy, happy, happy and then the actor who was to play Petruchio's servant, Grumio, arrived on the set, Cyril Cusack.

'How can you chat away like that with Victor and laugh a lot and suddenly go into the scene?' I heard him say to Richard, 'Don't you find it a bit off-putting?'

'We're both Welsh, We're talking about things we love,' answered Richard, but when the scene was finished, he looked across at Cyril, who with his fingers half in his mouth, ever so slightly shook his head. 'Can we have another take here, Franco?' said Richard and it didn't stop there.

'You can't call this Shakespeare, can you?' I heard Cyril say, 'It's "Shakespeare-elli". So, do you think you could manage to ask your man to give a close-up to your poor old friend here? A little close-up would be nice,' and Richard obediently asked Franco to give Cyril this close-up. Not that Franco knew what was going on, not until he bustled off to rushes, one day, and found both Richard and Cyril already watching them.

'No,' said Richard, prompted by Cyril, 'We'll have to re-shoot this.' And re-shot the scene was, because Richard and Elizabeth, as I've said, were the producers.

'He's ruining my film,' said Franco, 'He is a devil. The man is a devil.'

'And all the dressing-room doors are closed,' I added.

'What has he got?' I asked Richard, 'Does he know where the bodies are hidden?'

'Ah,' said Richard, 'He was the greatest Dubedat in *The Doctor's Dilemma* I've ever seen and in that shambling old drunk, I can see my future.'

'What can we do? What can we do?' said Franco.

'I'll tell you what,' I said. 'You know how Richard and Elizabeth love parties?' And so did Franco. He's the most hospitable of men. 'Well, they'd like to go to the Villa D'Este to see the fountains. They can't, though, because of the crowds but you could organise a bus trip with drinks and things and we could go up there on a Sunday night when everyone's gone home.'

'Wonderful!' said Franco.

'Wonderful!' said the Burtons when Franco told them.

'A bus trip!' said Richard, 'I haven't been on one of those since I was a boy.'

'We'll make an evening of it,' said Elizabeth, 'Everybody come up to the villa first. I'll order in hamburgers and hot dogs from Nathan's and we'll eat them before we set off.' Nathan's was *the* hamburger joint in New York. The next Sunday evening up we went to the villa and there, outside, was Elizabeth, glistening with sweat, sizzling hamburgers. When we'd eaten them and the hot dogs with their authentic yellow mustard and drunk cold beer, we were ready to board the bus. It was eight o'clock.

'Wait a minute,' said someone, 'Where's Cyril?'

'I don't know. Isn't he here?'

'No.'

'Try his hotel.'

'He's not there.'

'Where could he be? We can't go without Cyril.' Nine o'clock came and went.

'Maybe he's in that bar he sometimes goes to. Ring and find out.'

'No, he's not there either.' Ten o'clock came and went. At eleven o'clock the bus was cancelled. The trip to restore our camaraderie was off. It was then that the doorbell rang. We all rushed to see who it was. It was Cyril.

'Dear Elizabeth, there you are, the girl who was so kind to me when I was playing my tiny little part in *The Spy Who Came in from the Cold*. You helped me in my little scenes, God bless you. I'm sorry I'm late but I think I've had a bit of a heart attack.'

'Oh my God,' said Elizabeth and rushed off to call the doctor. The rest of us went home and filming was put off for two days. Cyril moved into the villa.

The schedule was organised so that most of the cast finished two weeks before the end. That left Petruchio, Kate and Grumio to do the scenes in Petruchio's house. Despite a much cooler atmosphere on the set, Richard and Elizabeth threw a party for the actors who were flying home. Above the door was a big sign: 'To all the British actors.' Elizabeth came in crying. 'What's the matter?' I asked.

'I'm so embarrassed,' she said, 'Richard won't come to the party.'

'Oh, no?' I said and then to myself, 'No! Enough's enough,' and went to Richard's dressing room. I found him sitting in his chair, behind him, as usual, Cyril. 'Come on, Richard.' I said.

'No,' said Cyril, 'Richard's not going to no party. *I'm* not going to the party. You see, I'm not British. The invitation is to British actors. I'm Irish.'

'Richard,' I said, 'When you were a young man, if the star of the show had given a party and refused to turn up for it, you'd have said he was being a shit, right? Well, you're being a shit now. OK? And you,' I said looking at Cyril, 'Can shove your shillelagh up your arse.'

'You're right Vic, you're bloody right,' said Richard. He then leant on my shoulder because he'd had a few and I led him into the party.

Making a good atmosphere to work in, welcoming actors onto the set, as the Burtons had done, is vital. Even so, my next welcome did take me by surprise. We were into the last days of shooting *The Taming of the Shrew*, when Jo Shaftel, the producer, who was passing through Rome, got in touch. 'Don't go back to London,' he said, 'Go to Marseilles. I have a picture there and a good part for you. Two weeks work.'

I was about to say, 'How nice,' when he rattled on: 'I'll put you into the best hotel and every night you will have a beautiful girl and –'

'Thank you but how much are you going to pay me?' I asked. Two days later, despite that, I was walking down the Canebière in Marseilles. The film, *The Biggest Bundle of Them All*, had a heist plot and starred Raquel Welch and Robert Wagner. I was to be an Italian pilot from whose plane all the bank notes would fly out at the end.

By the time I arrived, most of the other actors had finished filming their parts and had gone home. Vittorio de Sica, who made a big fuss about my working with Joan Littlewood, had one more day. Edward G. Robinson was spending his last spare moments looking at modern art. The two principals, consequently, were pretty much on their own. As I walked towards reception, I glanced sideways and there sitting at the bar was Raquel Welch.

She was wearing something straight from *One Million Years BC*, an early film of hers, the mini-est mini skirt I'd ever seen. 'Hallo!' she called out.

'Oh, hallo,' I answered, 'I'm just checking in.'

'Great!' she said, 'What are you doing this evening? Will you have dinner with me?'

'How marvellous,' I thought, 'I'm hardly through the door and I'm being taken to dinner by one of the most beautiful women in the world. What a welcome to my two weeks on the picture.'

We ate at the hotel. Over dinner, Raquel talked about her life, her early days in amateur dramatics, painting the scenery and waiting for a break. She was enchanting and we talked away happily for the rest of the evening. We were still talking as the waiters were putting the chairs up on the tables. 'I'll show you to your suite,' I said and upstairs we went. As we reached her door, she turned and gave me a long, lingering kiss. 'I can't invite you in,' she said, 'My husband, Patrick, is with me and he's doing a deal, some damn new car he wants but thank you for a wonderful evening,' and silently she closed the door.

The next morning, I walked onto the set and there she was. 'Hallo!' I called out, grinning from ear to ear, almost as though we'd spent the night together.

'What the fuck are you doing here?' she said and, turning, called out: 'Someone please! Get this man off the set! Fuck you, how dare you fucking follow me here?'

'But I'm in the film,' I said.

'Oh my God, I'm so terribly sorry,' she said, 'Please forgive me. I didn't realise. I thought you looked so friendly and I was so lonely.'

18

John Lennon gets Restless

The doorbell rang. Special delivery from Apple Corps. Apple was the Beatles' own company. It even had a shop in Baker Street. Back in bed, I picked at the string and when the paper fell away, I found four books: *The Hobbit* and the three volumes that go to make up *Lord of the Rings*. I had hardly started to read when the telephone rang. It was John Lennon. 'Have you got the books? They're going to do a film. We'll be the Hobbits and you'll be Gandalf.' How on earth had this come about? The answer was quite simple really. The Beatles had a contract with United Artists for three pictures and this was to be the third.

Although the author, J R R Tolkien, had started writing the books in 1937 and finished them in 1955, he hadn't known much popularity until now, the mid-1960s. A quality in the stories that chimed with hippies and hash had made him huge – God knows what that quality was. Tolkien had written the books as a reaction to the First World War while he himself was an Oxford don whose main interest was inventing alphabets. The strongest drug he knew was the tobacco in his pipe. What people were smoking at the newly opened Middle Earth club in the Tottenham Court Road was another matter.

Cards on the table, I can't stand quests. *The Pilgrim's Progress*, The Search for the Holy Grail – all our problems solved by a shiny, silver goblet out there somewhere, it doesn't do it for me. *The Lord of the Rings* had not only a great journey but a massive fight between good and evil. I don't go for that either. Everything that is good and bad is in us. If you want enlightenment, you don't have to travel to find it. That was one subject on which I didn't agree with the Beatles. I'm thinking of that journey they made to India. 'You want enlighten-ment?' I said. 'It's here.' At four o'clock in the morning I'd find myself arguing with John. 'We don't need a religion to lay down rules, tell us what's right and wrong. We already know. Our daily task is to choose, not to pray every three hours or ring a bell. It's as simple as, "Shall I smile at the old lady next door and ask if she wants any shopping done or shall I walk past?" If there's any such thing as civilisation, it's making the choice to do good.' Sorry, I got carried away there. Now this film. I started to read the books but it was no use. I found them turgid and twee. It was time to ring John back.

'What do you think?' he asked.

'Oh John,' I sighed, 'I couldn't finish —'

'That's all right, neither could I, Forget it.'

Look, if there was a way of shaking out the essential, neither of us could see it. Of course there may have been other reasons the film didn't get made, the Beatles wanting a break from Dick Lester or Tolkien withholding the rights. I prefer to think it was our chat on the telephone.

Talking to John was stimulating because he came at me from unexpected angles. In return, I knew it was essential to keep his restless mind exercised. I took him to the Luis Buñuel film, *Belle de Jour*. Our naughty thoughts presented on screen with crystal clarity was not something that John had seen before. Dame Sybil Thorndike and her husband Lewis Casson came to sit in the front row – 'Come along, Lewish, come along' – just as a Japanese punter was smacking Catherine Deneuve's bottom; what these two dear old actors made of it, I didn't find out but Sybil was broad-minded. As for John, he sat through the film again.

'We never go anywhere,' he complained one afternoon. This time, in total contrast, I booked a box at the Palace Theatre for a 1920s operetta *The Desert Song*. It was so wrong, it was right. There we sat – John, his wife Cynthia and I – with a bottle of champagne and a couple of jam sandwiches, enjoying ourselves like excited children. 'You don't need hash do you, Vic?' said John ' you're permanently fucking stoned on life.'

His constant desire to discover something new that he could become addicted to, or someone he could become a disciple of meant that occasionally John could be taken for a ride.

'Vic, come down, for God's sake.' It was Cynthia on the telephone. When I arrived at the house in Weybridge, I found a character called Greek Alex sitting with John in the snug. He had not only installed himself but taken over. Anyone who set foot in the house was subjected to one barked out question after another. The guy was a dog at a gate and testing people was his way of gaining dominance. The solution to the problem was easy. I answered none of his questions. 'Ignorant, that's me,' was my attitude and it worked. There was nothing he could do. Unfortunately, John was so much under the spell of this Greek Alex that he commissioned him to design and build a new sound studio. It didn't work. A tiny transistor radio that everyone could afford, only 10s (50p), was another great idea of Alex's. John poured money into it and saw not one transistor.

At this time of John's frustration, the press began to turn against the Beatles. It was all right while the boys were shiny haired and singing, *I Want To Hold Your Hand* but now they were expressing opinions, trying out new ideas. Altogether, they had too much power. You remember I said it was great while it lasted. That period was over, and in among these new ideas were drugs. Nothing special about that, lots of people were at it but if you were the Beatles, it was open season.

One evening in Weybridge, the singer Donovan had brought round a film. He was just about to show it when the phone rang. 'Oh God,' said John, 'There's going to be a police raid.' It was a tip-off. He rushed round, found what he was looking for, some grass, threw it down the lavatory and pressed the flush. It took forever to float away but then it was a silly place to put it. Back with us, his eyes darted round the room and yes, he spotted something else. Snatching it up, he ran out of the house and buried the object, a box, in the garden. What it contained, I didn't know. We certainly weren't smoking it or, for that matter, eating it or sniffing it. The stuff was just in the house. At that moment, the police barged in, went upstairs, woke Julian, John's son, and shook out his bed, this child's bed! There was nothing hidden in it. After that they went right through the house, ransacking the place. We just sat there. When they finally left, having found nothing, the police asked John for his autograph.

'Is that all there is?' It was a sunny afternoon. John and I were in the garden there at St George's Hill, Weybridge. I know it's a title of a song and maybe John didn't even use those words but it expresses the mood of dissatisfaction that I could feel. You're sitting at home. The kid's in school. The meals are on the table and yet – snatches of a lyric even closer to home came to me: 'Sitting on a cornflake . . . Corporation T-shirt, Stupid bloody Tuesday . . . I am the walrus, Goo, Goo G'Joob.' John used to sing that last bit quite savagely. 'Sitting in an English garden,' it goes on. Yes, in a garden behind a huge privet hedge, just like us then. John pointed at it and said, 'It's as if I'm married to a fookin' privet hedge.' Since it was an apt symbol and being a good improviser, I used what was to hand and ran with it.

'Be careful,' I warned John, 'It isn't just you. Everybody has a privet hedge. You can't say, this is Cynthia or this is my condition and nobody else's. Most people want to make somebody else a prisoner. We all want power over someone else.'

And then who should turn up? This lady who appeared to have no privet hedge whatsoever, just an open space. Actually, she had an even bigger privet hedge. Nevertheless, you still cannot say that was Yoko Ono. I'll repeat. Everybody has a privet hedge and there comes a time when however close, however loving someone is, you come up against theirs and you realise that's as far as you can go. It's quite normal. You just have to be aware of it. Then you can get out the shears and say I'm going to trim this down a bit. Hence, either divorce or a continuation of a marriage. Graham and I spent 44 years living together because we didn't live together. We were together in all things, deep down, but if either he or I wanted to go and see over there, we went and saw over there. We didn't say, 'Can I go and look over there?' which is what happens to most people. Bargaining.

'Can I go out tonight?'

'No!'

'But you're going out on Friday.'

'I haven't been out for two weeks. I've been here with the kids. You can go out Saturday.' That's what was happening to John in Weybridge. At the same time, there were all kinds of people hovering around waiting to take advantage, like Greek Alex, and they were bargaining too. 'I'll do this for you, if you do that for me.' John was not uniquely trapped – that was the point I was trying to make – but trapped he certainly was and when the spacious Japanese garden appeared with no hedge, its appeal was understandable. In fact, there's no doubt that for quite a while, Yoko made John very happy. She challenged him and he found that stimulating.

I have to bring back that kitchen in Wales I talked about and the teenaged boys. When a young wife comes in, I said, the closeness between the pals ends. Laying blame, I now have to add, is pointless.

It's simply what happens, over and over again. Still, I can't stop musing.

'Come up to the studios,' said John to me over the phone, 'We're working.'

'But John, I don't want to bother you.'

'Vic, only the fucking bores turn up.' I knew what he meant. People who really love you don't bother you when you're working. People who come, wanting to be there, don't really love you. But this nice invitation was impossible to resist. I went. It was delightful being there, listening to the boys recording, chatting with them, sitting with George Martin.

'You want a bacon butty, Vic?' they asked. 'Mal,' – Mal Evans, their roadie, was still around – 'Five bacon butties.' and then Yoko appeared.

'No. John only eat food I prepare.' What would have happened, I wonder, if Yoko had prepared a Japanese meal for everyone.

19

The Road to Morocco

H M Tennent Ltd was the name of the theatrical management that dominated post-war West End theatre until the early 1970s. Behind that deliberately uninformative name was a man called Hugh 'Binkie' Beaumont. His own name was little known to the general public; his face was totally unknown and that's exactly what he wanted. Anonymity gave him the freedom to command his empire as he saw fit. This he did from his office at the top of the Globe Theatre, now the Gielgud, by knowing his audience and by finding what would please it. In 1966 he asked me to play Oscar in the Neil Simon comedy *The Odd Couple* alongside Jack Klugman (he who would go on to do the *Odd Couple* TV series and play Dr Quincy in *Quincy ME)*. As the show ran for over four hundred performances, it was only natural that I would come into contact with the social side of Binkie Beaumont's life. He invited me for Sunday lunch.

'Sir John's on his way and we all have to be very kind to him,' said Binkie to his guests, referring to John Gielgud, his old friend and number one star. 'He's coming with a highly unsuitable young man. We all want to meet him.' At that moment the screech of tyres on gravel came to our ears and in walked John Gielgud followed by a young man in T-shirt, jeans and leather jacket, rather like Marlon Brando in *The Wild One*.

'Ah, Victor, there you are,' said John, 'Do make us laugh,' and, without introducing the young man, went to the kitchen to talk to Mrs Rogers, the housekeeper.

After an awkward pause, Binkie offered to show this young fellow round and took him out into the garden. In due course John rejoined us and not long after that, Binkie, alone. 'John, you are impossible,' he said, 'You told me that young man wanted to be an actor. He can't speak the Queen's English. I took him to the swimming pool and said: "Here's the pool, Hector." He just stammered and blushed. I took him to the croquet lawn and said: "Here's the croquet lawn, Hector" He stammered and blushed again.'

'For God's sake, Binkie,' said John, 'I told you. His name's Sebastian. Hector is what he calls his cock.'

Binkie had a partner called John Perry who, over lunch, became very curious about a play John Gielgud had been in on Broadway not long before. It was Edward Albee's *Tiny Alice*, a conflict between the earthly and the spiritual; at one point, John's co-star, Irene Worth, faced upstage, opened her cape before a kneeling John supposedly exposing her nude body and, in so doing, created an emblematic image which left the audience to imagine the rest. 'What were you thinking when you were down there?' asked John Perry.

'Not much,' said John Gielgud, 'It was a very difficult play. I had to have my pages pinned to poor Irene's mound of venus.'

When *The Odd Couple* was well into its run at the Queen's Theatre on Shaftesbury Avenue, a young woman called Adrienne Kennedy came to my dressing room. She was a playwright from Detroit who'd had a success over here at the Royal Court with a play called *The Funny House of the Negro*. So there she was in my dressing room with her latest work. 'I want you to be in my play,' she said.

'What's it about?' I asked.

'It's based on John Lennon's two books, *In His Own Write* and *A Spaniard in the Works*.' I read the script, which was made up of pages cut out of the books, then reordered and pasted into an exercise book.

'John has written fantasy,' I said, 'And to make it work you have to put into this some reality.'

'Oh,' she cried, 'Come and tell Ken Tynan,' who was at the time, Literary Manager of the National Theatre.

So I went and told Ken Tynan and K-k-ken said, 'C-c-come,' (he was famous for his stutter) 'And tell Larry.' Off I went to tell Larry. That's Laurence Olivier.

'John's poems are all about the beginnings of things,' I said, 'The first awareness of cinema, of books, of poetry. Through that, we get a whole picture of his childhood in Liverpool,' and then, remembering what the Maharishi had said, 'What one wants to get is that absorption when children are playing and they're nowhere else.'

'My dear baby,' said Olivier, 'Come and direct it for us. You see, none of *us* will understand it,' and, since there was a stage direction which read: 'A Christmas tree turns into a horse and gallops off the stage,' I wasn't surprised.

'But has anyone got John Lennon's permission?' I asked.

'No,' came the answer. I rang John.

'The National Theatre wants to do a play on your books.'

'They must be fookin' mad.'

'No, I think I can see how to do it.'

'Well, you go ahead, Vic. I'll give you the rights.'

'But why don't we do it together?'

'OK, we'll do it together.'

I told Olivier. 'Ah! I would very much like to meet with Johnny Lennon. I've not met him before. Ask him over for tea or something.' I rang John up.

'Big sir wants to meet you.'

'OK, great, me and Yoke will be over tomorrer.'

Next day, Olivier and I were on the steps of the Old Vic Theatre, waiting, when this Roller with black windows drew up. Out of it got the pair of them, dressed exactly alike: white hats, white suits, dark glasses and herr down to therr.

'Which is which, my dear baby?' asked Olivier.

After tea in his office, he started up: 'My dear Johnny –'

'I haven't been called Johnny since I was at school,' John interrupted. Olivier went on.

'My dear Johnny, I really must tell you that if this play is made into a film and, God knows, with your name and er, dear baby here directing it, if this play is made into a film, I must tell you here and now, as you know nothing at all about theatre, my dear Johnny, if it is made into a film, the theatre will own sixty per cent of the film rights!' And with that, he banged the table. Lord Olivier of the National Theatre had spoken.

John didn't move. He just said: 'Don't you have people that you pay who talk about these kind of things to people that I pay who talk about these kind of things?', a sentence like tickertape.

When they left, Olivier snapped, 'What do they look like, ridiculous pair. And what is this?' He flipped through the script, 'Ah! Yes! Here! Ha! I wandered lonely as a sock!'

'It's John's version of "I Wandered Lonely as a Cloud."' I explained.

'Are you telling me that a Beatle has heard of Wordsworth?'

A moment later, he changed tack. 'The first thing you must do is get rid of that girl. She'll be nothing but trouble.' I was shocked because, if nothing else, it had been Adrienne Kennedy's idea. As it happened, John and I didn't get rid of her – our consciences wouldn't let us – but, sadly, she did become overbearing and had to be barred from rehearsals. During one day I received dozens of telegrams demanding meetings with Olivier and Lennon. 'I know,' said the woman in whose home she was staying. 'You should have seen my telephone bill.' Was Olivier being ruthless or just pragmatic?

Together, John and I worked on the play at the flat in Manchester Street. We were in the middle of writing – well we weren't writing, we were listening to old 78s – when suddenly John said, 'Eh, Vic, let's go somewhere warm.' I thought he meant another room but it wasn't quite that. He picked up the phone and said, 'Sorry, did I wake yer? Vic and I want to go somewhere warm.' He looked up.

'You got your passport?' I nodded.

'Yeah, he's got his passport . . . Marrakech?' I nodded again.

'Yeah, we'll go to Marrakech . . . OK, yeah . . . In about an hour? Yeah.'

'An hour?' I said, 'Don't we pack?'

'No, we don't take anything, just go.'

Well, being a Virgoan, I packed my toilet bag, so at least I had that with me. In the meanwhile John shot off to Weybridge to collect Cynthia, with whom he was still living, despite being seen around with Yoko. The next time I saw him, he and Cynthia were waiting at the airport in Paris, where together, we caught the plane for Casablanca. At Casablanca airport a huge chauffeur-driven limo stood by.

As we drove through the desert, only a few hours after leaving London, on our way to Marrakech, John started to sing. Using the rhythm of 'On the Road to Mandalay' he was making up a new song but then he interrupted himself. 'Hey Vic, you got any money on you?'

'I've got a fiver.' I said, 'Why?'

'No, that's OK,' he said, 'We don't need any money. I'll just sign for everything y'know. It'll be great. Yes, it'll be great here because nobody'll know who I am.' The instant we were out of the limo, three women in yashmaks shimmied past, pulling their yashmaks to one side and squealing: 'Yeah, yeah, yeah!'

At reception there were several messages waiting for John. One in particular caught his eye. 'Vic, there's a party being given tonight by some Gettys, y'know, and we'll have to go, all right? Now be careful Vic, because they eat a lot o' hash here and you're not used to it.' I said, 'OK,' and off we went to this party where they were indeed handing round bowls of – well it looked like mincemeat and tasted like when you lick the bowl after a Christmas pudding, that sort of flavour. I was really into this, eating away.

'That was wonderful,' I said, 'Excuse me. I'll have some more of that.' And suddenly I was into Islamic Design! Round the room it spun. Amazing. I turned to where John's head should have been but he was lying on the floor sick as a dog,

'Oh Vic, I feel awful.' We got him back to the hotel and, luckily, you remember, I had my toilet bag with me. John and Cynthia, having left so quickly, had nothing. In the bag was my thermometer, so I took his temperature.

'You've got flu, John. Never mind. I have the very thing, Beechams Powders. I always travel with them,' and unfolded one of those slips of paper the powders came in. 'There you are. Now stay in bed and keep warm.' Back to the party I floated. The next morning I came in and took John's temperature again. 'Still got flu.' I said and was preparing another Beechams Powder, when the phone rang. John picked up the receiver,

'Hallo? . . . Oh Vic, I feel awful. Some of the Rolling Stones are downstairs.'

'Don't worry,' I said, 'I'll tell them you've got flu.' I went downstairs and there in the lobby of the Mamounia Hotel were indeed some of the Rolling Stones including Brian Jones. All had their faces and hands painted with designs. 'I'm very sorry, I said, 'But John's got flu and he can't come down to see you.'

'That's OK,' they said, 'We've just smashed the car.'

'Oh, that's awful.'

'Yeah, but we've bought another one. We're waiting for it to be delivered.'

'Of course.' And then I noticed that Brian Jones had a terrible cold.

'Don't worry, Bri, I've got the very thing. 'And upstairs I went. 'It's all right,' I said to John, 'They're only here for twenty minutes. They've just smashed the car –'

'And they've bought another one.'

'That's right, yeah, and Brian's got this terrible cold. I'm taking him a Beechams Powder.' So I went back downstairs to the lobby.

'There you are, Bri.'

'Oh, thanks man,' he said, and, snatching the open white paper, snorted the lot. 'It's a Beechams Powder!' I squawked. 'Yeeeah!' he went and gave the paper back to me. With it still in my hand I stood there waving goodbye. 'Drive carefully now. Sorry John couldn't come and see you! He'll be all right in a couple of days. Bye!' and, turning to go back in, found myself nose to nose with the manager.

'Mr Spinetti! Please! Do not give your friends, er, things in the lobby of the Mamounia Hotel.'

'It's a Beechams Powder.'

'Ye-es, that is what they all say.'

I went upstairs and told John who fell on the floor laughing. A couple of days later, he was feeling better. 'Let's go out somewhere, Vic,' he said, 'Perhaps we can go somewhere swinging, y' know, where the action is.'

'OK,' I said, 'I'll find out.' Downstairs I went and said to the chauffeur: 'Take me to where the action is.'

'OK,' he said and ushered me into the limo. We drove to a bar. It was Ramadan, a time of strict fasting, so there were just these five women on a platform, huge women, yashmaks, caps with rings in them, going round and round, undulating to an accompaniment of wordless semitones. Minutes went by. They stopped, moved to another part of the platform and started again. This dance looked as if it would never end and all I had to drink was hot coca-cola. Hot, because I was frightened to add ice in case I caught something. To make conversation, I said to the chauffeur: 'That one on the left has eyes a bit like Elizabeth Taylor.'

'I'm very sorry,' he said, 'I cannot get these women for you.'

'So, what goes in Morocco?' I asked. His eyes lit up.

'You are a true Moroccan. Come with me. We go to this other place.' It was amazing. Everything was going on there and I had what I can only describe as an Arabian Night. Even now, just thinking about it, I get a stirring in the loins. The next day, I emerged, blinking, into the sunlight.

'I must give you something for last night,' I said to the chauffeur.

'No, no, please sir. Please sir, no.'

'God,' I thought, 'The hospitality of these Moroccans.' I persevered. 'I must give you something.'

'No, please,' he said, 'IT'S ALL ON MARRAKECH MOTORS.' Would you ever get that with Avis Rentacar, I wonder.

During work on the play at the Mamounia, I noticed that something was missing. Over my shoulder I said, 'I need a Queen's speech here, John.' Without hesitating, he grabbed a sheet of cardboard from a shirt Cynthia had just bought and wrote: 'My housebound and eyeball take great pressure in denouncing this loyal ship in the blue corner, two stone three ounces,' and he was sitting on the lav at the time.

'Will that do?' he said, shoving it over to me. He hadn't paused. He hadn't crossed anything out. Back at the National Theatre, we were disappointed to hear that, because of censorship, we couldn't include it. So, using its rhythm, I recorded a Queen kind of sound and that's what the audience heard.

Before *In His Own Write* opened, John came to a run through. After it was over, I found him weeping. 'Was it that bad?' I asked.

'No, you cunt,' he said, 'It made me think about all the things I used to think about when I was sixteen.'

'And that is my review,' I thought.

The opening night on 18 June 1968 was sensational, but in an odd way. John and Yoko's presence ensured that the streets round the theatre were thick with journalists. However, the press had no interest in the play. The two of them hadn't been seen together in public before. That's what it was all about. The rest of the audience found it almost impossible to get in.

A while later, I was summoned by Yoko. 'Ah. I want you to direct *my* play.'

'Oh,' I said, 'What is it? Let me see the script.'

'No, no,' she said, 'No script. All audience get in bus.'

'Yes,' I said.

'And allowed to go to house,' she went on. 'Then all people in bus allowed to come out and open door to symbolise beginning awareness. Then everyone get back in bus. Then they go to other house. All allowed to come out. This time allowed to meet one person. Symbolise beginning communication. Then audience get back on bus —'

'Now wait a minute, Yoke,' I said, 'What's the big finish? I mean, what happens?'

'Oh, everyone go into Hyde Park and wait for something to happen.'

'Like what?' I said.

'Like chair falling out of sky.' I turned and looked at John. His face was full of love and wonder.

'Ooh, that's fookin' great, that is, Vic, "chair falling out of sky."' And I didn't know whether he was sending her up or whether he was serious, so I thought I'd better stop this now.

'You don't want to get me to direct it, darling,' I said, 'You want to get Cook's Tours. They're great with the buses.' And she didn't speak to me for months.

'Come to the hospital and visit us,' John was ringing me after Yoko had had a miscarriage, 'Nobody comes till six o'clock in the evening.' Since, each morning, I was passing the hospital to get to work on a TV series with Sid James called *Two in Clover*, I dropped by, sneaking in a packet of cigarettes for John.

Yoko was sitting up in bed typing. John was lying on the floor looking dreadful. 'My God,' I said, 'Which one's had the miscarriage?' John laughed. Yoko got onto the phone.

'Hiya,? . . . Two o'clock? . . . Fine' and on she went, fixing up appointments.. When she'd done that, she returned to her typing. 'I'm writing to my little daughter.'

'Oh, yes?' I said.

'I'm sending her a poem. Here's the poem: *Do not worry, Mummy is only looking for her handprint in the snow.*'

'How old is she?' I asked.

'Five.'

'And when did you last see her?'

'Four years ago.'

'Darling,' I said, 'Send her a doll's house.'

The next time Yoko told me about a venture, I remained silent. 'I have bought ten thousand cups,' she said.

'What are you going to do with ten thousand cups?' I asked.

'John and I take hammer. Smash cup. We sell broken cup and people all over the world will buy it and stick broken cup that John and I break, stick it together, because, you see, now we are married, we are more famous than the Burtons.'

20

Dali, Farce and Princess Margaret

Even before that lunch at Sardi's with Dick O'Neill, David Merrick had been looking out for me, and what happened next started with him back then, just after *Oh What a Lovely War* in *1965*. 'There's a show on in Paris,' he rang to say. 'I might do it in New York and if I might do it, you might be in it. You're booked in at the Hotel Meurice. Your ticket to Paris will be at the airport. I'd like you to go.'

'When?'

'Tomorrow.'

I rang my old friend Marti Stephens, an actress with the air of a young Marlene. 'And I've been given a suite,' I said, 'Would you like to come with me?'

The next night, the two of us were sitting in the bar of the Meurice sipping martinis when Marti said, 'Oh look.'

'What?'

'There's Salvador Dali.'

'Where?'

'There, across the other side of the room. Hallo!'

'You know him?'

'Yes. Hallo! Salvador! Come and join us!' And across the room he came. For a moment, Marti and he talked to each other in rapid Catalan – Marti knows several languages – but then she said, 'Please, you must speak in English, Salvador, because my friend, Victor, cannot understand what you're saying.'

'How *is* your English, señor Dali?' I enquired.

'My English is greatly improv-èd!' he announced.

'Yes?' I said, 'Will you be coming to England soon?'

'*Na!*' he said. '*Di English av di canarish hoon di villibo di anish da canarish hoon mashtubat!*'

'I beg your pardon?' I said. Red in the face, Dali reiterated:

'*Di English av di canarish hoon di villibo di anish da canarish hoon mashtubat*!!' After that he went back to rapid Catalan with Marti, leaving me alone to work out what he'd said. It was this: 'The English have canaries and they put violin bows in the anuses of canaries and masturbate.'

I saw the French play, *Fleur de Cactus,* and loved it. Sophie Desmarets, not afraid to be plump or getting on for middle age, was magnificent. 'Where do I sign?' I asked, as back in New York, I entered David Merrick's office, my pen at the ready.

'Victor, have you met Abe Burrows,' said David, 'He's done the translation.'

'How marvellous,' I said, 'Where do I sign?'

'We have a bit of a problem,' said David, 'Lauren Bacall has just agreed to play the lead and you're too young to play opposite her.'

'But in Paris,' I said, 'The charm of it was the woman being older than the man.'

'We don't do that over here,' said David, 'She wants a man who looks the same age as she is.'

'Get another leading lady,' I said. They fell about and I, having told them what a great time I'd had in Paris, went off and got the *Skyscraper* job. During the Detroit previews, David Merrick sent a telegram. The leading man in *Cactus Flower* wasn't getting on with the leading lady. I had to get out of *Skyscraper*. The part was mine. Since the 'faggot' business in *Skyscraper* was yet to happen, I had to turn the job down. Anyway, if I'd said 'yes', I'd've lasted a day, if that.

Now we get to it. In London, H M Tennent, Binkie Beaumont again, inspired by the success of the Feydeau farce, *A Flea in Her Ear*, at the National Theatre, decided to do another one, *Un Fil à la Patte*. As at the National, John Mortimer was to do the translation and Jacques Charon from the Comédie-Française was to direct. I was asked to be in it. Great, particularly as I didn't have to read or even go for an interview. The character was a flamboyant general whose most prominent characteristic was an impenetrable Spanish accent. As I hadn't been to Spain I thought, 'I know, I'll use the Dali accent.'

Cat Among the Pigeons –, myself I preferred *By The Short Hairs* as a title – opened in Brighton. Laurence Olivier came round. 'You're the only one who understands farce, dear baby, but your make-up is dreadful. Let me design it for you.' I wasn't complaining. First there'd been Elizabeth Taylor doing my make-up in Rome and now there was

Laurence Olivier in Brighton. Fine by me, and he too had a tip: 'When you wear a wig onstage, dear baby, you always wear false eyelashes. For example, when I played Othello. I wore fur eyelashes.'

Our London opening was at the Prince of Wales Theatre in the April of 1969 but before the first night there was a big charity preview with Princess Margaret sitting in the front row of the dress circle. Afterwards we were presented to her. I don't know whether you've ever been involved in this being presented to royalty business but they don't come in on a red carpet. They come in on a carpet of silence. You're standing in a row and, at first, all you can hear at the far end is a high-pitched whispering. This whispering, remaining high pitched, comes closer and clearer and closer until it's piercing. Suddenly, at its most piercing, it became: 'Where did you get that marvellous Spanish accent?'

'Well ma'am,' I said, 'I was in Paris and I met Salvador Dali and what he said to me sounded like *"Di English av di canarish hoon di villibo di anish da canarish hoon mashtubat!"'* Either side of me, the cast stiffened, their faces, like the heads on Mount Rushmore. They knew how this story ended. There was a pause.

'How curious,' said the Princess, 'What did he say?'

'Well, ma'am, erm, the English have canaries, ha, ha, ha, and they put violin bows in the anuses of canaries and masturbate, ha, ha, ha.' The Princess looked at me and a twinkle came into her eye.

'Oh,' she said, 'He spoke a Dali pick-tchah.'

Next morning, the phone rang and a mysterious voice said: 'It's Princess Margaret.'

Thinking it was a member of the cast sending me up after the embarrassment of the night before I said: 'Fuck off.'

'I will not,' said HRH. 'I want you to tell me that marvellous story again, the one about Dali. I can't remember it and I'm dying to tell my sister.'

For a while, the Princess took me up and one evening, we went for dinner at the Rib Room in the Carlton Tower Hotel. Her entrance was spectacular. Loosening her fur coat, she let it drop to the floor, sure that someone would pick it up. Accompanying her was Ruth, Lady Fermoy, her lady-in-waiting for the evening. She'd recently broken her arm while building a wall, so the Princess had to cut her food up for her. While she did, she asked me if I'd heard from 'Dear Verna', Verna Hull, who lived in a beach house next door to the film star Claudette Colbert. I said that I hadn't. The Princess explained that the two, Claudette and Verna, had been the greatest of friends, travelling the world together, that is until a rumour had gone round that they were having a lesbian affair. Claudette Colbert, on hearing this, had immediately built a wall between their two properties going right down to the sea and from then on had never spoken to Verna again. 'Isn't it sad?' said the Princess. 'She lorst the friendship and, apparently, didn't have any of the fun.'

The premiere of the film *Staircase* – at which the Princess was the guest of honour – was when we next met. That was also 1969. *Staircase* the play had been such a hit that a film had been made with Rex Harrison and Richard Burton. 'As this film is about two poufs,' said Richard, 'You can sit in the back of the limo with me and Elizabeth can be in the front with the chauffeur.' So when we arrived at the Carlton Cinema and Richard emerged from the car, it wasn't Elizabeth he handed out but me. Together, we went into the cinema, arm in arm, followed by Elizabeth, carrying two little brown paper bags. We found our seats in the front row of the dress circle where soon the Princess joined us. Looking across at me, as the lights dimmed, she called out:

'Who are your friends?' The film started.

As Rex Harrison came onto the the screen, Rachel Roberts now divorced and not amongst the guests of honour, shouted from the stalls 'Look at her!'

This seemed to be a cue for Elizabeth to produce the contents of the little brown paper bags, bottles of Jack Daniels, which she passed round. Given that the film did not achieve the success of the play, they weren't such a bad idea. At least that evening was riotous.

At the Savoy Hotel, where the post-premiere party was held, the Princess, on finding herself not at our table but at the one next to ours, picked up her chair, plonked it down next to Richard and started the way she meant to go on, that is, monopolising Richard. The only time she included Elizabeth was when she looked over at a ring she was wearing and said: 'What a huge diamond! How vulgar, but I'd love to own it.' After that, she rested her elbow on the table, put her chin in her hand and effectively cut the fuming Elizabeth out. That night Elizabeth and I did a lot of dancing!

21

From Top to Bottoms

David Merrick is often portrayed as a monster. All I can say is, he didn't give up on me. 'You still got that raccoon coat?' he asked on the phone from New York.

'Yes,' I answered. It was something I'd picked up second hand and it made me look like Bud Flanagan in his act.

'I need that coat for my production of *The Philanthropist*,' said David, 'so I suppose you'll have to come with it.'

Together with Alec McCowen and Jane Asher, I went to New York for Christopher Hampton's play. My role was a successful author who liked to dress flamboyantly, hence the coat. Radie Harris, columnist for the *Hollywood Reporter* and noted for having only one leg, was on the Tony Awards panel. 'We're nominating you,' she told me. In England, I would never have been considered for the part. We opened in March 1971 and, as before on Broadway, I got invited out, this time to a party given by Joshua Logan who had directed the original production of *South Pacific*. After food, we were lured into the living room by the sound of a pianist picking out tunes. Josh took charge. 'Ladies and gentlemen, Miss Ethel Merman!' and the pianist struck up, 'There's No Business Like Show Business', which Ethel Merman really did get up and sing. At the end, as she sat down, the applause was tremendous. Josh stood up.

'And now ladies and gentlemen, Miss Diahann Carroll!'

Diahann demurred: 'I'm from California and people there don't ask you to sing for your supper.'

'You're in New York now, honey,' said Joan Fontaine, 'So get off your ass and sing.' Diahann compromised by singing 'The Sweetest Sounds' from her hit musical, *No Strings*, but very softly and only for her lover who was sitting there, David Frost.

'Now, ladies and gentlemen, Victor Spinetti!' It was Josh again. 'The mime act?' I thought. No, that didn't seem right. Oh yes, singing in the pub in Hammersmith but 'Jezebel' was American. That didn't seem right either. Perhaps something both American and universal? I turned to the pianist. 'Do you know 'Swanee' in E flat?'

'Sure.' He said and off we went: 'Swanee, how I love you, how I love you, my dear old Swanee.' When I'd finished, the guests applauded like mad and Ethel Merman rushed over.

'Victor, that was so wonderful, ' she said, 'I want to fuck your nose.' As I turned to thank the pianist I realised it was Leonard Bernstein who said:

'You should have been in my show, *Candide*, in London.

I said: ' I was,'

Along with me that evening came someone I mentioned earlier, the woman on the plane who distracted me from reading my Skyscraper script – Dee. I'd got to know her through her husband, an enchanting, erudite man who'd written me a fan letter during the run of *Oh What A Lovely War*, something he'd apparently never done before. He invited me to his home for dinner, home being a grand appartment full of Aubusson carpets and Waterford crystal chandeliers. Before long, he and his wife became my great friends and, during their London visits, got to know Graham and the family too.

On arriving in New York for *The Philanthropist*, I rang as usual. The secretary answered. My friend had died and Dee, his wife, was distraught. She wouldn't see anyone. She wouldn't go out. She wouldn't do anything. 'Tell her I'm coming to tea,' I said. I felt I owed her something. She and her husband had not only invited me round frequently but had also put an air-conditioned limousine at my parents' disposal for a whole month when they'd come over at the time of the Lovely War Tony Award. Dee looked dreadful. 'Come on,' I said, 'Put on some make-up. Comb your hair. I'm not having tea with you looking like that.' She did, and on her return, asked me where I was staying. 'The Algonquin,' I said, adding, 'But I'm moving to an appartment in two weeks time.' 'Why not stay here until then?' she said and so I did. It was nothing new, after all. I'd stayed there often enough before.

Every evening, during those two weeks, when the show was over, I went back to her place. We ate together. I told her stories about my day and we looked at photos taken in summers gone by, that she had strewn about the floor. Some of them even had me in them. On the night before I was due to move to the appartment, Dee hugged me. 'God sent you to get me out of all this.' she said and would not let go. That night, I ended up in her bedroom. First thing in the morning, though, I went back to mine. I didn't want to alarm the help. Over the days, we turned into two naughty children. At weekends when the help was away, we ran round the house naked. 'Get my breakfast,' I'd say, smacking Dee's bare bottom and off she'd go, giggling, to the kitchen.

It was a delightful time. Every night, in the cab, on my way back to the appartment, I'd feel these urges as I imagined the games we were going to play.

When we weren't occupied with those, Dee carried on her normal life, inviting her top-people-type friends to stay for the weekend, though how normal they actually were was questionable. One guy, a high flyer who worked in the forces kept popping pills.

'What are you taking?' I asked.

'Ritalin.'

'But those are the pills that killed Judy Garland.'

'Victor,' he said impatiently, 'These were prescribed by the Navy doctor. On Monday, I have to be in London. I have to talk to your premier. I cannot afford jetlag.' Needless to say, two years later, he died of a heart attack.

Sometimes the high jinks Dee and I got up to broke into this world. A famous Greek was due for dinner. Knowing how agitated Dee became on these occasions, I rang her on the intercom and, in a very serious voice, told her there was something wrong with the table decoration. Down the stairs she flew, only to find me lying naked in the centre of the table with her emerald necklace twined round my private parts. I'd got the idea from Lady Chatterley's Lover. It seemed a good way to ease her nerves.

'Victor!' she hissed, He'll be here any second!'

'He's Greek. He'll love it.' I said. During the dinner she absent-mindedly fingered her emeralds, which caused her to giggle. She was remembering where they'd been an hour before.

Unfortunately, these children's games became serious for Dee. Me, I just loved the fun and wanted it to carry on but I also knew that the run of *The Philanthropist* was coming to an end and that I would have to think about work. A Green Card seemed a good idea, so I applied for one. Recommendations came from Laurence Olivier, Richard Burton, David Merrick and Jack Paar. If I could stay in America I could keep things going that way. However, as I waited, I began to feel uneasy. Letters sent to me appeared to have been steamed open and resealed. Phone calls I made were often interrupted by a click on the extension.

Over dinner one night, with lots of guests, Dee mentioned the Green Card saying that I was going to get it the very next day. Even at the time, I wished she hadn't. Pill-popper was there and he gave me an odd look. Shortly afterwards, a phone call came for him. It was from President Nixon. To take it, pill-popper stood up. When he'd finished, he said that he had to leave immediately for Washington.

The next day, I was phoned by the Head of Immigration. My application for a Green Card had been turned down. Years later, using the Freedom of Information Act, I tried to get to the bottom of this. My search led to a document saying that the Green Card had been pulled because I was living with a woman, unmarried. The document was in Washington. Pill-popper was a family executor. That odd look meant, 'You're not getting your hands on her money.' If only he'd known I didn't want it. The friendship and the fun were all I cared about.

In hanging around with these top people and getting into trouble, I felt like Icarus, who had flown too near the sun. I told Dee that it was time I went home. She brought me to the ground in a rugby tackle. 'If you leave me, I'll kill myself.' she said. 'I really am a Prisoner on 2nd Avenue,' I thought and then said, 'We can carry on having fun together, can't we? Come to London,' and she did.

I went home first, home to a house in Pimlico. Graham ran to the door and hugged me. Every room was lit up and in all of them were flowers. 'Whatever you've both been up to – he knew about Dee – you look very well on it.' he said and then, 'I thought I'd never see you again.'

When Dee came over, she didn't stop pressing. 'Give everything up and marry me.' she said, 'All that I have will be yours.' 'Why didn't you?' friends asked later. What would I have done with it?' I replied, 'I don't want things.' Anyway, giving everything up meant, not just acting, but also my family and Graham. 'Get rid of that faggot. Sell the house and come with me.' she said. 'I don't do that. I don't give up people,' I said, 'Where were you when Graham cooked meals for me on a gas ring in a bedsitter? Where were you when, with his own money, not mine, he bought a flat in which I lived? For years, I had no other home. He was supporting me.'

And how *was* my relationship with Graham when I said that? Years before, both he and I had decided to give up sleeping together. That side of things wasn't working out. However, I'd said, 'But let's share a life together,' and that is what we had gone on to do. Deep down, I knew that wherever Graham was, that was my real home.

I tried to persuade Dee to settle for a more easy going arrangement. 'Didn't you say last summer was the best summer of your life?' I said. 'It works both ways, sweetie,' she answered, 'You enjoyed the swimming pool.' 'Does she know me?' I thought, 'I can't swim.'

It was one morning in Pimlico when things began to come to a head.

'Graham is downstairs with some man.' said Dee, as she walked into my bedroom.

'I know,' I said, 'He's a plumber.'

'You mean I've been having breakfast with a plumber?'

'Yes, Graham's awfully good. He gets all these people to come and work here and, God knows, whatever they get up to, I'm thrilled.'

'Is that the way for an actor to live?'

'It's the perfect way for an actor to live. That sort of thing, domestic stuff, I don't want to know about it.'

'You don't want to know about anything, so long as somebody pays the bills.'

'Which, at the moment, you aren't paying.' I thought, beginning to get angry.

Flu struck me down a few days later. I rang the doctor. 'Who's that lady?' he asked on seeing Dee. I explained that she was the woman I was with. 'You should be sleeping on your own.' he said, 'You have a high fever.' When he'd gone, Dee came in.

'What did he say?'

'I should be sleeping on my own.'

'Another one of your faggot friends.' That's when blind rage seized me and I tried to throw her down the stairs. The doctor, fortunately still on hand, was able to intercede. Dee moved out and it was like a herd of elephants had left my roof. She hadn't gone far, though. She'd moved in downstairs with Graham, where he told her to take it easy and allow me some space. If she could do that, things would be fine.

Ever practical, he was even hoping she might buy the house a new fridge. However, she couldn't do as he suggested and she went back to New York.

I told Ken Ken Tynan the story of Dee and me. Ken being Ken, it appeared in his diaries as something much less innocent.

Some time later, when I was in the middle of directing a show in Paris, in French – *Jesus Christ Superstar* it was – and trying to cope with an overbearing producer, Dee appeared again. Wearing one of her sable coats and with six pieces of Louis Vuitton luggage, she swept into the foyer of the Pont Royal Hotel. I first heard about it when the concierge rang to say that my wife was there. Who was coming up in the lift? I wondered. Having dismissed the hotel as cheap, which it certainly wasn't, she asked to be taken out to whatever was going on, fashions shows, art galleries, anything to divert her.

It was impossible. Fortunately, I was saved by the arrival in town of Count Uberto Quintavalle, a Milanese steel magnate I knew. His visiting card had a coronet on it which appealed to Dee. So it was he who escorted her round Paris. While there, I had one last go at persuading her to stick around in an easy going way but it was no use. Again, she went back to New York and I haven't seen her since, though, we did talk on the phone once. 'I still love you,' she said. Why did it sound like a threat?

When I look back, I think of that fan letter Dee's husband sent. It was possible it saved my life. With Dee, I enjoyed more sex than I had ever had before and would ever have again, yes, but also in staying under her roof, I was safe. If I'd gone wild in New York, round the bars and other joints, who knows what might have happened? Those were the days when AIDS was incubating. When I get fed up about the Green Card, I remember that and, I wish Dee well. Sometimes, in the fastness of the night, I can hear her laughter.

As I'd been away from London for quite a while, people often asked me what I'd been doing. I had a standard answer but here's one specific example of where I gave it. Joan Collins asked me to do a day's filming for a series she was shooting in Paris. Three years before, I'd been in a film with her called *Can Hieronymus Merkin Ever Forget Mercy Humppe and Find True Happiness?* a pet project of her then husband Anthony Newley, the actor, singer, writer and, on that occasion, director. Despite being in the picture, she had a lot of time off. On top of that her life was at a point where she was feeling that she was more Mrs Anthony Newley than Joan Collins. As we were on location in Malta, it was very jolly for both of us to join up, go round, see the sights and eat together. This also explained why, post-Dee, Joan asked me to do the day's filming. The part was a hairdresser and she didn't want a stranger touching her hair.

When I got to the studio, where did I find Joan? In her caravan being fussed over by make-up and wardrobe? No, in the canteen, with the crew, eating lunch. She never pulled the *grande dame* act. 'What's happened since I saw you last?' she asked.

'I've been in America,' I answered, 'I was someone's bit of rough.' I then went on to tell her how rich Dee was and how she'd wanted to buy me a Rolex watch, jewelled cufflinks and a gold chain. I was also going to tell her how I'd turned it all down but then my eyes slid over to the man sitting next to her. It was the new bloke in her life, Peter Holm, the Swedish singer, and he was covered in everything I'd described. In the nick of time, I stopped myself from putting my foot in it – for me, a triumph – and stayed shtum.

'She sounds very generous,' said Joan.

'Yes, she was,' I said, adding not a word.

Straight after returning from New York, I was flat broke. To economise, I moved into the basement of the Pimlico house and it was there I got a call one Sunday from Shirley Bassey. 'I'm staying in a suite at the Dorchester,' she said, 'It's got a kitchen and I fancy doing some cooking. Are there any shops open round your area?' This was the time when most shops were shut on Sunday.

'There's an Italian deli on the corner,' I said and round she came to buy pasta and garlic and everything for an Italian meal. The shopkeeper was a very happy man. 'Come to my place for a drink,' I said and along the street she walked, bringing her husband, a hotelier. While sipping a Bloody Mary she sniffed.

'What's that smell?'

'Sunday lunch,' I answered.

'Oh, I love Sunday lunch. I haven't had Sunday lunch for ages. What are you having?'

'Roast beef.'

'I love roast beef.' This would have been fine if I hadn't bought an old-age pensioner's rounding of beef, in other words, a piece that was very small. Doing my best, I sliced it up for three and surrounded it with roast potatoes, parsnips, cabbage and cauliflower. Of gravy, at least, there was no shortage, so plenty of that went over everything. 'What a marvellous lunch,' said Shirley when she'd finished. And marvellous it may have been but it was also the lot. For pudding, there was nothing, nothing until I remembered some pears and a piece of cheese. The hotelier, taking in Shirley's contentment and a friendship that had started way back at our Corey Hall broadcast in Cardiff, was seized with jealousy. Staring at the pears and cheese, he said, 'That figures. A typical peasant's dessert.'

For all my economies, I still owed the bank a hefty sum, £20,000. I went to see my agent, Jimmie, in Regent Street. Not only had he no work for me, he saw no prospect of any either.

I was walking down to Piccadilly Circus when who should I bump into but Paul Raymond, the man who all those years before had produced the nude revue on the peeing poster in Crewe. 'I've got a ticket for a show but I can't go,' he said, 'Do you want it?'

'Sure,' I said but, sitting in the theatre, I was so taken up with wondering what on earth I was going to do that twenty minutes had gone by before I realised the show was *Oh Calcutta!* And even then I wasn't concentrating. At that moment, my neighbour, a woman, nudged me.

'Why have you never done a commercial, Mr Spinetti?' she whispered.

'Because nobody has ever asked me,' I whispered back.

'*I'm* asking you. We'll have a drink in the interval.'

'What's the product?' I asked when we were standing at the bar.

'Jaffa Cakes,' said the woman.

'Oh, I quite like those,' I said. 'We can only pay you £20,000 for the first year,' she went on, 'But for that money you'll have to eat them.'

'Madam,' I said, 'For that money, I'll fuck them. Live. On television.' In no time at all, I'd done the first batch and, the next day, I was so early at the bank with my cheque, I fell over the woman scrubbing the steps.

The overdraft was cleared but I still needed work. I'm pretty sure that the theatre ticket Paul Raymond had on him wasn't what was uppermost in his mind when he gave it to me, because he rang later, 'I've g-got this g-girlfriend. It's not enough that I've given her a f-fuckin' car. She wants to go on the f-fuckin' stage. Could you do something about that?' With no prospect of any other work, of course I could. Anyway, hadn't my first break been at the Irving Strip Club? Hadn't Joan Littlewood seen me there?

At Paul's office, he told me that my name could be left off the poster if I wanted. I was shocked. He was resigned. Two well-known people who'd written for him had asked for that and he'd agreed. To me it seemed hypocritical. 'It's the re-opening of the Windmill,' I said, 'It's been a cinema for years and now it's going to be a theatre again with nudes. That's what the place is famous for.' You have to remember, this was long before pole dancing and lap dancing. What we were planning wasn't like that. It was going to be a show on a stage with sets, costumes and lighting. The UK, having no tradition of burlesque, had always been uneasy about nudity. America, which did have it, understood the bringing together of comedians and nudes in a spirit of healthy vulgarity. I'd been reading about it and that's what I wanted to do.

Paul introduced me to his girlfriend, Fiona Richmond. Needless to say, she had a beautiful figure and in fact, still has. What does need saying is how bright and likeable she was.

Although we wanted the show to look like the Folies Bergères, we had to have a structure, however slight, to hold the whole thing together and give opportunities for comedy. We had a script about two innocents abroad who, by chance, find themselves flat-sitting for a James-Bond-type figure. These innocents would be, as in a burlesque show, our comedians. John Inman and Jack Haig, strong performers both, were available. All I had to do was make the girls look fabulous.

At the Royalty Theatre, a drag show, *Birds of a Feather*, fronted by Larry Grayson, had recently folded. Backstage was a cornucopia of costumes doing nothing. 'Take drag and put it back where it came from,' I thought, 'On women,' and I did. The James Bond figure having lots of girlfriends, provided an excuse for long-legged girls in high heels, ropes of pearls, diamond chokers, feathers everywhere, to cross the stage, walk up and down a flight of stairs and parade about to the goggle-eyed amazement of the two innocents. As well as the stairs, we had a big circular bed in the centre of the stage that turned round allowing more pretty girls to pop up. To give them the best look, I used dance lighting – that's done from the side. Instead of flattening things out, as front lighting does, it moulds and gives a distinct silhouette.

The whole thing reached a pinnacle of ridiculousness when a girl in a headdress of feathers going feet up into the air made her stately progress across the stage with John Inman asking: 'Who's that?' and Jack Haig answering: 'The cleaning woman.' Elizabeth Taylor came to the first night which caused a great fuss. She wanted to meet John, Jack and all these beautiful women, so I took her backstage. When Fiona Richmond opened her dressing-room door, she was wearing nothing but a merkin (that's a pubic wig). She looked at Elizabeth and said, 'Er, oh, Victor always brings back weird people t–to s–see us but you're the most beautiful of all the weird people Victor has ever brought back to see us.' Elizabeth didn't bat an eyelid.

'Darling, you're so slim, if you were on the pill it would show.'

Our entertainment ran for two years. During the run, John Inman was spotted and started recording the TV comedy, *Are You Being Served* while, some time after that, Jack joined the *'Allo, 'Allo* team.

Round the corner from the Windmill Theatre, in Shaftesbury Avenue, was the Lyric Theatre. On the wall between the two, side by side, were posters advertising each show. One read: 'The Lyric Theatre. Paul Scofield in . . .' The other read: 'The Windmill Theatre . . . Directed by Victor Spinetti' and, as I had been in *Expresso Bongo* with Paul, that gave me the tiniest of twinges. The same thing happened to John Inman. At the end of each episode of his sitcom, the credits read: 'Trevor Bannister is appearing with the Royal Shakespeare Company. John Inman is appearing in *Let's Get Laid*.' Even so, for Paul Raymond I went on to direct two more Fiona Richmond shows. Then Tony Shaffer, Peter's twin, and author of *Sleuth,* told me that the film producer John Brabourne, son of Lord Mountbatten announced at a party, 'If Victor Spinetti does any more of those Paul Raymond shows, he'll be finished in the West End.' He was casting *Murder on the Orient Express* at the time and, with all those different accents in it, you might have thought there'd have been a phone call. There wasn't. This mixture of snobbery and ignorance – John Brabourne hadn't actually seen the shows – was depressing but I shouldn't have cared. People with more independent minds, like Joan Littlewood, came, were entertained and said so.

In order to follow this thread, I'm going to hop over some years. I don't want people thinking, he's left out the work he's ashamed of. I got flack from working with Paul Raymond and in the 1990s I got flack from working with Jim Davidson.

I had just finished an episode of *Give Us A Clue,* the TV charades programme, when Lionel Blair, one of the two team leaders, asked, 'What are you doing for Christmas, chuch?'

'Nothing,' I answered.

'Do you want to do a pantomime?'

'Yes,' I said and there I was with Windsor Davies, Melvyn Hayes, Mollie Sugden and Clive Dunn at the Palladium, playing King Rat in *Dick Whittington.* Dick was Jim Davidson. I'd never been at the Palladium before and at first, I was uneasy. I'd been given a song 'The Rats Are Creeping Down the Street' which I knew would have the children heading en masse for the lavs. I could even hear the seats flipping up.

Louis Benjamin, who ran the Palladium, said, 'It's your spot, Victor. You've got three minutes there. Do what you want.' I went to Lionel Blair who was directing and told him how miserable I was.

'Why don't you write your own song?' he said, 'And use the tune of the Habañera from Carmen.' I rushed home and with the help of my cousin, Mike Young, wrote:

I am King Rat,
The Evil One,
Who stops all little children from having fun.
It finished:
May your football team never score another goal!

Barump Bump Bum!
I loved doing it. We ran at the Palladium for so long we were selling Easter eggs.

Up at the top of the theatre was my dressing room, a funny little place with a door that opened on to the roof. It became the Noël Coward bar and, on fine days, my fellow performers brought their sandwiches up there between shows. Sitting next to the water tank one afternoon, Jim Davidson said, 'I'm going to do this panto again, Vic, and if I do, I want you to be in it.' Years later, he came to me and said, 'I'm doing Dick Whittington.' He wasn't just thinking about himself, though. He did a whole new production. My King Rat lair, for example, was not just a front-cloth scene. It had a set to itself with thrilling laser beams because Jim wanted it to be both spectacular and modern. Seven times I did that production and again Joan Littlewood came, this time bringing Kirsty MacColl's two sons, who were very excited when Jim showed them round. Joan knew nothing of what people had been saying about Jim. She based her judgment on what she saw.

'Whoever put this on,' she said, 'Is a man of the theatre,' There is something in Jim that wants to appeal to the people who he knows perfectly well don't like him. There's no practical need. His audiences are quite big enough, but he still does.

'Do you want to do one of my wicked ones?' he asked at the end of the seventh *Dick Whittington* production.

'What's that?'

'*Boobs in the Wood.*'

'Ooh, yeah.'

Having done all sorts of shows, posh and less posh, going onstage as Friar Tuck and saying: 'It's fucking pissing down in Sherwood Forest,' was a tremendous relief, like doing the lewd satyr play after the tragedy in Greek drama. Shortly afterwards I was invited to the College of Music and Drama in Cardiff for an award ceremony. As I went in a voice from behind called out.

'Victor Spinetti?' I turned. A couple were sitting in a car eating sandwiches.

'Yes,' I said.

'We'll never forget you in *Boobs in the Wood*!'

I needn't have worried. Upstairs the students already had the video. Recently I went to a gathering of top people in the profession. One of the formost of these top people in making a speech, used incredibly rough language, setting the tables of Lords, knights and bishops aroar, some of them, the very people who damn Jim. He gave me seven year's work. Drawing the line, saying, 'I don't do that,' seemed ungrateful.

22

Funny Business On and Off the Set: Peter Sellers

'Put that cigarette out. I don't smoke in this house. Neither does my-wife-Julie-Andrews.'

'I'm terribly sorry,' I said, slightly taken aback as, in 1974, everyone was still smoking. The man addressing me was the film director, Blake Edwards. He and Peter Sellers were getting together again to make *The Return of the Pink Panther* and it looked as if there might be something for me in it.

'Now, I've never heard of you,' said Blake, 'But the star wants you in the film, so we'll have to humour the star. As it happens, last year my-wife-Julie-Andrews wanted you for a TV special in Hollywood but as I was directing and as I'd never heard of you, there was another job you didn't get.' This one I did get.

Gstaad – the Swiss resort where the scent of Lanvin, Hermès and Givenchy hangs heavy in the alpine air, the shopfronts of Van Cleef & Arpels, Cartier and Bulgari out-sparkle the snow and a laundrette would be hard to find – was the setting.

For my scenes, we were filming and living in the Palace Hotel where, during breaks, I would explore. On one of these rambles, venturing down instead of up, I found a network of tunnels carved in the rock on which the hotel was built. Past carpenters', plumbers', electricians' and upholsterers' workshops I walked, all of them there to maintain the goings on upstairs, but right at the very end, with a number on it, was a room.

I went upstairs to fetch Peter Sellers and off he bustled to fetch Blake Edwards. An idea was forming. When Clouseau asked for 'a rheum', I, the concierge, could produce a key from which I blew dust and send him in the lift, not up but down to that room. Peter was delighted.

That was the good thing about him. New ideas, when he was working, made him joyous.

In one of these jolly moods, he said to me. 'My old darling, we must have dinner together. How are you fixed for tonight?' We had just broken and I was still in my concierge's uniform so I told him I'd go upstairs and change first. 'Marvellous,' said Peter, 'We'll go out.' After my wash and brush up, I returned to the foyer. Peter, by then, was sitting at the bar. He turned round. 'And where've you been?' he said or was it *she* because, if anything, he was sounding like a nagging wife or girlfriend. While I was away, he'd found a voice and the voice was of, God help me, a gangster's moll.

'I'm sorry,' I said with an American accent, 'I had to go up and change.'

'Well, I mean, a lot of men have been looking at me sitting at the bar,' said Peter. Oh no, he *was* a gangster's moll. For a while, I played along but it was causing a problem, this transformation. Peter couldn't stop it.

There was no way I could say, 'Very funny, now let's drop that and go on,' because, when I looked into his eyes, he wasn't there. I could only see this sulking, petulant woman who'd been kept waiting at a bar.

'Well, I suppose we'd better go,' she said, 'Have you booked a table? What? Oh really, I have to do everything,' and off she flounced to the receptionist.

'Book us a table.'

'When for?'

'Immediately!' The restaurant she'd requested was only a few doors up the street but she wasn't happy. 'No cab? We have to walk? Thank God I have sensible shoes on,' and all the way there I was nagged and berated.

At the restaurant, the moment the waiter came over, Peter started flirting with him. 'Hallo, you're lovely. What's your name? Do you ever see yourself in the movies?' It was Judy Holliday in *Born Yesterday* and all through dinner, when not suggestively dipping a potato at the end of a long fork into melted cheese, she was ogling the other diners. I didn't know where to look. By the end of the meal, I was getting desperate but escape was not forthcoming. 'You never take me dancing,' said the moll. 'There's a disco at the hotel. Come on.' And back to the Palace she dragged me. In an utterly straight disco, Peter and I danced the rest of the night away, Peter, all the while, looking around, smiling, waving and chatting to the others.

Eventually I said, 'I have to go to bed. I'm exhausted.'

'But the night is young,' said Peter.

'I'm not,' I said and fled.

A couple of hours later I was in bed asleep when the phone rang. It was Peter but no longer the gangster's moll. 'Peter, what is it?' I asked.

'Oh, my darling. I can't sleep. I've got the most dreadful toothache.'

'Have you got anything you can take?'

'No, and it really is dreadful.'

'Then you have to go to a dentist.'

'It's the middle of the night.'

'Don't remind me but you really will have to go to a dentist.'

'Oh, my dear darling, can you find me one? I'm in agony.' Being me, I did know of a dentist and I looked up his number in the phone book.

'I'm sorry to wake you but Mr Peter Sellers —'

'Bring him over.'

'Come on, Peter,' I said.

What an evening. First the gangster's moll and now this stricken man with a terrible toothache. We got into a taxi. Peter held his face and swayed. 'Oh, God.' The taxi pulled up at a house. Outside stood the dentist, behind him, a lady in curlers and dressing gown, his wife. 'Don't leave me, my poor old darling, don't leave me,' said Peter, 'Hold my hand!' Earlier, I'd had the embarrassment of Peter the moll, trying to pick up the waiter and now I was sitting in a dentist's surgery next to the chair, holding his hand. The dentist did his job and relieved the pain. 'Oh, thank you so much.' And, from that moment on, for many years, whenever he needed anything done to his teeth, Peter went to Gstaad. 'I've got to go to the dentist,' he'd say and people would think he'd gone round the corner. He'd flown to Gstaad.

After we'd finished the entire *Pink Panther* shoot and the film was edited, United Artists said, 'We want more of Sellers and Spinetti.' At Pinewood Studios, the interior of the Palace Hotel was reproduced. It cost a fortune. For two weeks, Peter and I filmed on this set. Over those two weeks, I earned more than I had during the entire picture. In one of the new scenes, I knocked on Clouseau's door with his dry

cleaning and opened the door. Thousands of gallons of water –
Clouseau had left his bathroom tap running – came out and knocked
me back several yards into a pile of boxes. I stood up trying to regain
my dignity but thanks to a fast-shrinking material, my uniform was
doll-sized. 'Wonderful,' said Peter who was standing behind the
camera, 'Your reaction when the door opened was terrific.' In
another, Clouseau's room caught fire. He picked up the fire extin-
guisher but I snatched it from him. 'Give it to me!' and pressed the
button myself. Foam went all over me and as I turned slowly to the
camera, with an extra bit of foam going all along my nose and beyond,
I looked like Scaramouche. Peter was slapping his sides and rolling
about. 'That has to be the funniest scene in the movie.'

Months later, I was invited to the film's premiere, which, to make
it appropriate, was held in Gstaad. Across the main street was stretched
a banner: 'Tonight. Premiere of *The Return of the Pink Panther*. The
stars of the film welcome you! Peter Sellers, Catherine Schell,
Christopher Plummer, Victor Spinetti.'

'This is it,' I thought but at the hotel, the producer told me that
nearly all the gags I'd been in had gone. You only saw Clouseau asking
the concierge, 'Der yer 'ave a rheum?' and the concierge answering:
'A rheum?' That was it! Still, scenes ending up on the cutting-room
floor, it happens all the time. I knew that but if I had known earlier, I
wouldn't have travelled to Switzerland because United Artists had
flown in five hundred of the world's press, TV crews from America,
Australia, Japan, England, everywhere and, the very next day, all
would be wanting interviews. What were they going to ask? 'How did
you build up to your part of "A rheum?"' I became quite depressed. It
was then I remembered that Richard Burton and Elizabeth Taylor had
recently got remarried and were living in Gstaad. I rang them up.
'What are you bloody doing here, boy?' asked Richard.

'Well, there's this premiere today and a big party tonight.'

'They haven't bloody asked us.'

'You sound depressed.' It was Elizabeth, speaking on the extension.

'I am in a way,' I said, 'They've billed me as one of the stars and I've
got all this publicity to do but I've been cut out of the film.'

'It's that bloody Peter,' said Elizabeth, 'He's got final cut of the
movie. I'll tell you what, we'll come to the party just to see you. Fuck
him.' Brrr. She'd rung off.

'Oh my God,' I thought and turned to see Theo Cowan, the film's publicist. With a pipe in his mouth and dressed in a blue blazer, he always looked as if he were on the prow of a ship sailing towards his retirement. 'Theo, Richard and Elizabeth are coming,' I said. He bit on the stem of his pipe.

'Have you told Peter?'

'No.'

'Well I'm not going to tell him. You tell him.'

I went to Peter and told him, adding, ' . . .To see you.'

Stiffly he said, 'How kind of your friends to grace us with their presence.' You could almost hear the drum beats at the end of *EastEnders*.

That night came the party with lots of tables, lots of press, Henry Mancini and a full orchestra. I was sitting at the top table on which were (as indeed were on all the tables), *Return of the Pink Panther* wrist watches, *Return of the Pink Panther* champagne, *Return of the Pink Panther* fondue sets, the lot. Peter was with two blondes and a priest because he was thinking of becoming a Catholic at the time. Accompanied by my-wife-Julie-Andrews, Blake Edwards was there too. I began to think that's how it must read on her passport. As is often the case when you put lots of stars round a table, the conversation was quite desultory. However, in the middle of discussing the merits of Judaism as opposed to Catholicism, we were interrupted.

'Victor!' a voice called out. I turned. At the top of a flight of stairs stood Elizabeth Taylor. However, the woman I'd spoken to only hours before who, because it was Saturday night, would have been in jeans and sweater with her hair down, had used the intervening hours to look out the jewels, have her hair done and dress herself in a long evening gown. So at the top of the stairs, what we saw was Elizabeth Taylor, superstar and behind her, Richard Burton, leaning a little.

'Vic,' he nodded at me.

Wild, the press dived for cameras, leapt up and ran forward, shoving each other out of the way to get the first pictures. Since getting remarried, the Burtons had been seen by no one. I rose to my feet. It was only a few yards to go, but it felt like a hundred miles. As if in a shampoo commercial, I seemed to move in slow motion. In the middle of the room we met and amid the clicking of cameras, the popping of flashbulbs, the hugging and the kissing, I said to Richard,

'Don't do this to me. I'll never work again,' but he seemed not to hear.

'You may have been cut out of the picture, boy, but we'll make sure you get the bloody publicity. We'll see to that.'

From the middle of the room to the top table, we didn't so much walk as get harried, the press still clicking away. When we arrived, the priest and the two blondes had to move up one. Elizabeth sat down, kicked me under the table and murmured, 'We're going to have some fun tonight.' Then, having looked around, cried out, 'Oh Peter! Are you *eating* here?'

'Yes,' said Peter.

'But the food is awful. We never eat here, do we, darling? And that band, it's awfully loud. What are they playing?'

'It's the theme from *The Pink Panther*,' said Peter.

'How gross,' said Elizabeth, 'Could you ask them to be a little quieter please?'

Peter leant across to me: 'Would you tell your friends, the band is playing for me and not for them.' Since my friends were either side of me, they had no trouble hearing for themselves. Nevertheless, I whispered to Elizabeth:

'The band's playing for him, not for you.'

'Oh well,' she said, 'We'll leave.'

'No, no,' said Blake Edwards, 'Don't leave.' Because if they had, that would have been the headline: 'Stars leave party.' Peter, returning to an old accomplishment, got up on the stage, silenced the band and played the drums as loudly as he could.

After dinner, we were ushered into the cabaret room. Up one end were Henry Mancini and his orchestra still playing the theme from *The Pink Panther*. In the middle was the press of the world and at the back, on a banquette, were Richard, Elizabeth and myself with a bottle of champagne, no bucket and three glasses. Blake Edwards came on to the stage. 'My-wife-Julie-Andrews!' he announced and out came Julie to sing 'The Hills are Alive with the Sound of Music'. While she sang, the press turned in their seats to click over their shoulders at Richard and Elizabeth. Richard inclined towards me.

'Listen, we'll see you get the bloody publicity, you know, Vic, but is there anything you can do here tonight? Because the press of the world's here, you know. You might get bloody discovered again. You know what I mean?' I thought for a moment.

'How about Alec Guinness being fucked by the Turks?'

'Oh yes,' said Richard because he liked that one. 'Right, when Julie finishes, I'll put you on.'

As Julie Andrews finished, Richard stood up, clapping over his head. 'Bravo Julie! Wonderful, wonderful. Now ladies and gentlemen, my great friend Victor Spinetti –'

'NO!' came a powerful shout from down at the front. It was Peter on his feet. Richard paused.

'You're quite right, Peter. I do apologise. It is after all, your evening. I'm sorry. I'm sorry. I am very (pause), very (long pause, his famous voice so deep it was almost a growl), very sorry. Come Elizabeth! Come Victor!' and out of the room we swept followed by the press of the world.

The next morning at nine o'clock, the phone rang. It was Richard. 'You're up early,' I said.

'There's bugger all else for reformed drunks to do but get up early,' he said, 'I'm downstairs with the car. Come on, we'll go and get the papers.' As I left my room, I noticed outside all the doors, presents, *Return of the Pink Panther* sweatshirts, *Return of the Pink Panther* T-shirts, *Return of the Pink Panther* tracksuits and *Return of the Pink Panther* running shoes – but outside my door, nothing. I nicked one from each pile and went downstairs to meet Richard. At the newsagent he bought all the European newspapers before driving up to the villa where Elizabeth was fixing lunch. As I came in, she was coming out of the kitchen wiping her hands on her pinny.

'Oh, thank you!' she said as I handed her my stolen presents, 'Let's see the papers.' We settled down. On the front pages of *Le Figaro, Die Zeit, La Stampa, Det Svenske Dagblad* all those European papers, was a huge photograph of Richard, Elizabeth and myself in a great bearhug. 'Last night,' the headline read, 'At the premiere of *The Return of the Pink Panther*, Richard Burton, Elizabeth Taylor and Mel Ferrer.' There was a long pause, the three of us started laughing. 'Oh Christ,' said Richard, 'Your bloody mother won't even believe you were here.'

The next day, the reporters at the film's press conference were very kind. All of them asked me about other things, Joan Littlewood, *Oh What a Lovely War,* the Tony Award I'd won. It wasn't as bad as I'd feared. Lew Grade, whose company, ITC, was involved in the film, invited me to lunch. 'Sorry you were cut out of the picture, old son,' he said, 'It wasn't that you were bad. You were good, too good.' And I suppose my performance must have made an impression on him because a little later, when ITC were producing *Voyage of the Damned* and the director, Stuart Rosenberg, wanted me to play the very serious Dr Strauss, Lew Grade said, 'You can't have him. He's only a comic.'

'Did you see him in *Oh What A Lovely War*?' asked Stuart, 'If you did, you'd know he was an actor. Now, you've got James Mason. You've got Orson Welles. If you won't let me have Victor, I won't direct it.' Stuart Rosenberg got his way. I've not had many champions but he was one.

23

The Magic Word: Mel Brooks, Sean Connery, Sony

On Broadway, you feel the kiss of success very quickly and, for that matter, the slap of failure, as *La Grosse Valise* had taught me. During the runs of both *The Hostage* and *Oh What a Lovely War*, however, it was always: 'Hallo, I'm Kirk Douglas.' 'Hallo, I'm Joan Crawford.' An introduction I like, star or no star. It cuts out the agony of 'Do you remember me?' And at parties you'd hear: 'Judy Garland's just left,' or catch sight of Peter O'Toole slumped in a corner asking, 'Where the fuck am I?' or be told, 'Vincente Minnelli was waiting for you but had to go.' Stars everywhere and we were made to feel as talented and famous as they were. In this champagne atmosphere, Mel Brooks first appeared and he's why I've jumped back. That's how I can introduce him. At nearly every party we went to, Mel and his comedy partner, Carl Reiner, were improvising their *Hundred Year Old Man*, while over the way from us on Broadway, Mel's wife to be, Anne Bancroft, was playing Annie Sullivan in *The Miracle Worker*. Soon after that, I was at home in London when the phone rang. It was Mel.

'Victor, get your ass to California.'

'When?'

'Tomorrow.'

'Who's paying?'

He named a big TV company NBC, CBS, one or the other. I was a little anxious as Graham was out on tour and I didn't like to leave our home empty. Also, in a few days time, my mother and sister were coming up to stay. Who should then appear though, but Dave 'the burglar'. There he was, just out of jail, standard issue brown-paper parcel under his arm, on the doorstep. He was being helped by the New Bridge Society. It gave aid to people just out of jail and Graham was a member. Providing a meal, giving advice or even patching things up with an alienated wife was the sort of work he did, so there was Dave hoping to find him. 'You're just in time,' I said, 'Graham's on tour and tomorrow I've got to go to Los Angeles. You'll have to look after the place until I get back.' There couldn't have been anyone more perfect and, when my mother and sister came, Dave took a huge fancy to my mother.

'God, she's an attractive woman,' he said on my return. I told her, years later, and she said, 'But why didn't you tell me at the time?'

From Los Angeles airport, a chauffeur, who'd been holding up a placard with my name on it, drove me in a limo to the Beverly Hills hotel. There, I was shown out to a bungalow in the grounds which had the sort of rooms in which Scott and Zelda Fitgerald had once stayed. These bungalows were the best rooms in the hotel. A thousand dollars was handed to me in an envelope for 'walking around' money and a message came through that Mel was going to ring.

I went to The Polo Lounge for a drink. In came George Segal. 'Victor Spinetti, what are you doing here? Come for lunch. Meet the family,' which was very kind, particularly as I'd never met him before. I rang round British performers I knew who were in Hollywood, something of a risk as you can't be sure they're going to take your call, but there was Julie Andrews: 'Oh Vic, what are you doing?' and Sean Connery: 'Where are you staying?' and when I told him the Beverly Hills hotel he suggested we meet up there on Friday evening. 'I have a clause in my contract. Once a week, I can show any film I like and they lay on caviar and champagne.' The rendezvous was at the hotel because that's where the films were shown, downstairs in a private cinema. I began to get excited about what we might see, an old Hollywood classic, perhaps. A film with Carole Lombard was what I fancied. I'd only just discovered her on American television and I adored her sense of comedy. On Friday evening, into the lobby came Sean with an entourage: 'This is my director. This is my producer. This is my secretary and this is the editor.' All told, there were about twenty people, an end of the week get together, in other words. And down we went to the screening room where the champagne and caviar were already laid out. 'What are you going to show?' I asked. '*Rashomon* without the subtitles,' said Sean, 'I want to get the real sound of violence.' My heart sank. Many years before, at the Curzon cinema, Mayfair, with a tin of stewed steak in my pocket (all I could afford for dinner that night given the price of the cinema ticket) I had seen Akira Kurosawa's *Rashomon*. It had been long enough then. Now, without subtitles, it would be even longer. It started. The sound of violence was very clear, long wailing vowels leading to staccato consonants. Champagne or no champagne, I couldn't stand them. While the others watched engrossed, Sean all the while giving notes to his secretary, I got to my hands and knees, crawled along the front row to miss the beam, tiptoed up to the door, opened it a crack to prevent any light coming in, slipped out and went back to my lovely bungalow. It was a chilly night, so I lit the fire and aired the sheets.

'What are you doing?' asked a maid rushing in.

I pointed at the sheets draped around the fire, steam rising from them and said 'They're damp.'

'Oh, you're English. Oh, well, that's all right then.'

Ten days of having a ball went by with no call from Mel Brooks and then, 'Sorry, Vic. I had to go to Mexico. I'll pick you up tomorrow and explain everything when we meet.'

The following morning, he collected me in a limo and took me to a big black building on the Universal lot that I'm pleased to say fell down during the film *Earthquake*. 'I've written a series,' said Mel, 'It's called *Get Smart* and it's about a hopeless James Bond figure. I wrote it for you.'

At the big black building we took the lift to the top floor where, in a long corridor, we came upon the head of the TV division practising putting shots. He was down one end. A tin was up the other. 'Pnk!' a ball would go as it rattled into the tin. 'Max,' said Mel, 'This is Victor Spinetti, the guy I wrote *Get Smart* for.'

The man didn't say 'Hallo.' He didn't even look up. While still addressing the ball, he said, 'Mel, are you insane? We never bring anyone in from outside. We use contract players,' and the ball rolled down the corridor, clinking into the tin. 'Pnk!'

'Vic, what can I do? I'm so sorry,' said Mel in the lift going down. 'You see, I'm only a writer. I have no power. I HAVE NO POWER!'

'Never mind,' I said, 'I had ten days in Hollywood,' and I listed what I'd been up to. 'So, thank you very much. It's been a wonderful trip.'

Mel, I'm glad to say had a hit with the series, while I, in a way, was relieved. I've never wanted to drive a car and that would have been de rigueur. What's more, by now, I'd've had ten face lifts, starved myself half to death and worn God knows how many toupées because in Hollywood, you're not allowed to get old. You're not allowed to get fat and you're not allowed to get bald.

With *Blazing Saddles* Mel found power and he wrote me a letter: 'If ever I make a movie in Europe, on Polaroid, you'll be in it.' The next thing, I opened the paper to see that Mel Brooks was arriving in London and would be staying at the Connaught hotel for a couple of days in order to cast a film called *The History of the World, Part Two*. We're now in 1980. I rang:

'Mel, I got your letter.'

'Come on over!' he said.

As I walked through the lobby of the Connaught, I noticed actors looking at scripts. Obviously they were there to read for Mel. I took the lift up and was shown into his suite. He moved towards me awkwardly saying, 'I've got this frozen shoulder,' and clutched at it. 'I must have sat in a draught on the plane. Never mind, you're in the movie. You're playing the Duc de Monet. That's your part, OK? This is the scene. I come in carrying these buckets . . .' Then, frozen shoulder and all, he went through the whole scene. 'That's what you're going to play. Would you like some tea?'

Mindful of the actors downstairs, the two days for casting and the frozen shoulder, I said: 'No Mel, really, thank you so much. I can see you're busy –' The charm vanished, the sweetness disappeared. A cloud of smoke seemed to come from his ears.

'Busy? You don't know what busy means. Up my ass, I'm busy. In my lungs, I'm busy. In my spleen, I'm busy. In my kidneys, I'm busy. In my aorta, I'm busy. In my liver, I'm busy. I AM SO FUCKING BUSY!' He was now shouting in my face, shaking his fist, so angry he'd quite forgotten about the frozen shoulder. Out of the room and down the corridor he chased me, shouting: 'BUSY? YOU DON'T KNOW WHAT BUSY IS! In my eyeballs, I'm fucking busy. Up my nostrils, I'm busy! My teeth are busy. I AM SO FUCKING BUSY!!' By now, I was getting into the lift but as the doors closed, he pounded on them. 'YOU DON'T KNOW what busy me-e-e-ans.'

Down in the lobby, when I passed the actors reading scripts, I stopped and said: 'Don't, whatever you do, mention the word "busy".'

Rooting around to find an explanation for that outburst, I imagine

Mel's friends, after his great success, saying, 'We never see you. You're always so busy.' They must have said it so often it drove him mad and there was I unknowingly driving him madder. I've seen Mel since and he's been as sweet, charming and entertaining as ever but I have not once, in his presence, used the word 'busy' again. When he came over for *The Producers*, I left a message on his answering machine saying: 'Mel, welcome to London. Don't worry. I'm working.'

This Abbott and Costello scene, where the mention of a single word drives someone to apoplexy is something I seem to be rather good at, here's another example.

Graham and I and Joan Littlewood were watching the Oscars on television when Sean Connery won for *The Untouchables*. We cheered and I wrote Sean a note of congratulation. I knew how important the prize was to him. Roderick Mann, the show-business journalist, had written an article in the *Sunday Express,* just when Sean was starting to make pictures, betting that he would never, ever, make a living from acting in the cinema. That had stung. He'd worked so hard. Sean rang. I told him how thrilled I was. He asked me what I was up to. Happily I'd just made a film for television. 'Its based on Anne Franks Diary' I said 'Paul Scofield's in it and Mary Steenburgen and Eleanor Bron and I'm playing the doctor. The producer's told me that if it ever gets the showing it deserves, I should win an Emmy,' but then I thought, 'Vic, pull back. This is Sean's moment,' and said, 'Of course, it'll only be a Supporting Emmy.' There was a sharp intake of breath.

'Right, we'll have a drink sometime,' said Sean and hung up. I thought this rather odd but it wasn't until weeks later that I realised, and it came like a punch to the solar plexus, that what Sean had won was a Supporting Oscar. 'That bitch, that bastard,' he must have thought, 'An old friend, in my hour of triumph, saying "only supporting."' There's nothing I can do about it but I would not, for the world, have knowingly taken anything away from that Oscar moment.

Before I go on, here's Sean, the tonic. When he was making the science fiction film *Zardoz* in Ireland, he gave me a call. 'Why don't you come over for the weekend? You could pick up Jason on the way.' Jason, then a boy, was his son by Diane Cilento. Together we flew over and most enjoyable was the weekend we had, John Boorman, the film's director, and his family, being extremely attentive in their welcome.

That Saturday night, Sean and I were sitting in his hotel suite when the telephone rang. For a few moments the caller talked while Sean listened but then he snapped: 'No way. I wouldn't dream of it. Get knotted.' and hung up. 'What was that about' I asked. He told me that it had been Harry Saltzman, the bond films' co-producer on the phone. *Live and Let Die*, Roger Moore's first go at Bond, had been shooting for some weeks, only for them to arrive at the conclusion he was hopeless. Would Sean come back? Because if he did, they would pay off Roger Moore, scrap the footage shot so far – millions of pound worth – and start again. 'The bastards,' said Sean, 'they won't give him a chance. Now you know what I had to put up with.' It was a case of panic, just like in new York, when the leading man had been fired after the first reading of *Skyscraper*. On this occasion, though, the outcome was happier. Roger moore was able to settle in and make a good job of it.

Years later, I was a dinner guest at Michael Caine's house in Hollywood. Also at the table, was Luisa moore, Roger's wife. What a bastard Sean Connery was, she said, doing *Never Say Never Again* while her husband was still playing James Bond. I bit my tongue. It was hard not to tell her that I was sitting with Sean on the night he could have said 'Fire him. I'll come back,' so bringing her husband's bond career to a sudden and early halt. Sean's innate sense of decency had triumphed.

Now back to putting my foot in it but, this time, it wasn't something I said.

George Martin asked me to recite some of John Lennon's poetry at a concert he was giving at the Barbican with the London Symphony Orchestra. To make it clear, this was after John's death. I went to George's house. In his downstairs lavatory, resting on the floor and all along the wainscoting were his gold discs, and there were a lot. Not one was hanging up. 'Look at this,' he said and pointed to a wardrobe. He'd made it himself. That's what he was proud of. It was his hobby. He had a workshop and in it he made furniture for the house. Lovely man. After a drink, he said, 'Why don't you sing some of the songs?'

'Sing?' I said.

'Yes, I've got a hundred musicians playing the songs. You can do a Rex Harrison and sing-speak. I'll play behind you.' At home I sat up all night with a tape recorder learning 'I am he and you are he . . .' and

'Sitting on a cornflake . . .' and 'Nothing you can do that can't be done . . .' I was very nervous.

The next day I left the flat and hailed a cab. 'Where are you going, wack?' asked the driver.

'Where are you from?' I asked.

'Liverpool,' he answered.

I looked up at the roof of the cab: 'Thanks, John, thanks!' It was a sign.

'In fact,' said the cabby, 'I'm unique. I'm the only Liverpudlian cab driver in London.' His name was Fred Stokes.

By the time I arrived at the Barbican, I wasn't nervous at all. I was cheerful and seeing a man selling stickers outside the artistes' entrance, I bought one. So relaxed was I, that when I got to my dressing room, I lay down and slept, right through the first half in fact. Not that it mattered because I wasn't in that part. I was woken by a voice saying: 'You're on,' and, without even changing my jacket, I walked straight onto the stage.

As I started to recite, it became like a seance. I could hear John's voice in my head, so my only job was to let him do the work. At the end, members of the audience came forward to the edge of the stage and reached up, as if I were a pop singer, and shook my hands. Graham came round to my dressing room with a friend of ours, Jilly Burns, probably the best Nancy in *Oliver!* since her cousin, Georgia Brown, who had created the role. 'We didn't believe it was you,' she said.

Afterwards, there was a drinks party. George Martin came over to me with a Japanese guy from the Sony Corporation. 'You must do this show in To-ki-o,' he said.

'I'd love to. Thank you,' I said but then his eye descended to my lapel and that sticker.

'You in Greenpeace?' he said.

'What?' I said.

'Greenpeace!' I turned my lapel so that I could read the sticker. Yes, it was one of Greenpeace's. 'Save the Whales' it said and what country was most guilty of killing whales, Japan. 'No show in To-ki-o!' said the man from the Sony Corporation.

'You've ruined the gig,' said George. I looked skywards. Obviously it was John again. Not only had he made sure I got there, he'd also made sure I was a political agitator.

24

Marlene: Here, There and Everywhere

When I first mentioned Marlene Dietrich, that time backstage at the Wyndhams theatre after a performance of *Oh What a Lovely War*, I said that it was a social thing. That's how it stayed with her – we never worked together – but it stayed for the rest of her days. How did it work? When you're running in a play, even more so when you're rehearsing one and you're at the point of despair, it's both diverting and reassuring to get a phone call from a colourful character you're fond of who is absolutely nothing to do with what you are doing at that moment. So it was, for many years, with Marlene.

Between *Oh What a Lovely War* at the Wyndhams Theatre and *Oh What a Lovely War* on Broadway came Shakespeare's *Henry the Fourth* at the Edinburgh Festival. I was playing Prince Hal's friend Poins, about whom Joan said, 'Look at the Queen's lady-in-waiting. She's cleverer than the Queen. She's more beautiful than the Queen. She's wittier than the Queen. The trouble is, she isn't the Queen. That's Poins.' Rehearsals were at the Theatre Royal Stratford East but, shortly before leaving for Edinburgh, Joan said, 'I forgot. You're playing Owen Glendower too.'

Owen Glendower is a Welsh insurgent with a touch of the wizard about him. Typical actor, the first thing I said was, 'I haven't got a costume.' We were standing by a settee in the green room at the time.

'Take that off,' said Joan, pointing at the cover, 'And wear it.' Under the lights it looked, when it came to it, magnificent.

'But I haven't learned it,' I said, referring to the actual part. As it happened, the solution to that problem came from Shakespeare himself. In the first place, Owen Glendower does not have much to say and most of that is him blowing his own trumpet and being bogusly mysterious. When he's not doing that, he's talking to his daughter in Welsh because she can't speak English.

'Do it in phoney Welsh,' said Joan and, on the same principle as the Drill Sergeant and Lanrezac in *Oh What a Lovely War,* that's what I did. Given that Glendower's main aim is to bamboozle and mystify, it was right and because it was right, it was funny. The production as a whole though, was detested by the critics, so much so that we had to hold a press conference to explain ourselves. Aiming to demonstrate what she was trying to get away from, Joan gave her impersonation of Vanessa Redgrave as Rosalind in *As You Like It.* I accompanied her with impersonations of famous actors but, as usual, without actual words. The result was that *Henry the Fourth* might have been a flop but the press conference was a huge hit. In the end, *Henry the Fourth* was not a flop. It was packed out every night.

After we opened, a man came up to me in a pub and said: 'You are in ze Joan Littlewood production of *Henry ze Fourth* Part One and Two?'

'Yes,' I said.

'Oh, it's vunderful, one of the best Shakespeare productions I have ever seen. Because you have the stage in the centre of the theatre', (we, did a catwalk that went right across) 'so you not only have schizophrenia, you have total audience alienation. So Brecht, so Brecht I have given it great reviews behind the Iron Curtain!'

At this time I got a garbled message about a telephone call. I didn't follow it up but then the doorman came to me and said: 'It's a "Marleen" for you. Could it be Marleen Dietrich?'

'It might,' I said and went to the phone.

'Why are you not speaking to me? Are you not my fwiend?' It was Marlene. 'I need black paint.' What could she want black paint for? Something to do with make-up? I couldn't think. It turned out to be exactly what she said. She needed a pot of matte-black emulsion. I found one and took it round to the theatre where she had been asked by Lord Harewood, the artistic director of the Edinburgh Festival, to present her one-woman show for the first time. When I arrived, she was up a ladder in her jeans, adjusting a stage lamp. Climbing back down she said, 'Look at those music stands. They're different colours. I can't have different colours. They must only be black behind my dwess.' The band, it has to be established, was not going to be in the pit but behind her on the stage. She began to paint.

Her show opened to excellent reviews. Because of *Henry the Fourth*, though, I couldn't go right away but one Saturday, the stage-door keeper appeared. 'There's that Marleen again on the phone.'

'Sweetheart, why do you not come to see my show?'

'I can't get a ticket.' This by then, was true. The show was a smash.

'I have a ticket for you,' said Marlene, 'For tonight, for my final performance.'

I was staying with a chap called Jimmy Allen at the time. His father had a chain of shoeshops in Scotland, Allen's Shoe Stores. 'I'll drive you,' said Jimmy and after *Henry the Fourth* that night at the Assembly Halls where we were performing, he collected me in his car, a white Rolls Royce. As soon as we arrived at Marlene's theatre, I went backstage. She was standing in her dressing room wearing full make-up and her white dress, which was ever so slightly baggy at the knees. She came right up close. So close I could smell a heady mixture of perfume and alcohol, quite often the scent of a powerful woman.

'Have you ever seen my act?' she asked.

'No,' I answered, nose to nose.

'I will tell you,' she said, 'When I say: "My first film in America," do that to start the applause . . .' and she clapped once, 'When I say: "Now comes the song," do that to start the applause . . .' She clapped again. When I say, "No, no, not that song. This is the song," do that to start the applause . . .' and she drilled me through the entire act.

My seat was in the front row, so no shirking was possible. Marlene could see me. She didn't, however, need me. A flutter of an eyelash or the raising of an eyebrow was enough to provoke a storm of applause. She was simply making sure. That applause had to be there. My palms, as a result, burned with clapping. At the end, the reception was tremendous. A woman next to me took off her ring and threw it onto the stage. 'Marleen!' she shouted, 'I've thrown you my ring!' but at that moment Marlene was looking up in astonishment at rose petals descending around her.

'What a delightful surprise,' she seemed to be saying, when of course, those petals descended every night. Certain gentlemen friends plucked them from bouquets sent by fans and, on cue, threw them down. Still, Marlene's astonishment couldn't have looked more spontaneous.

'I've thrown you my ring, Marleen!' the woman next to me repeated.

'Vot, sweetheart?' said Marlene, leaning forward, 'I can't hear you!'

'My ring, I've thrown it onto the stage.'

'Vot?' and then Marlene heard her, at which point, she walked to the wings and returned with a sweeping brush. The audience went wild, a sound not lost on her. This became a gag that went into the show every night. Oblivious of the audience, she swept at the rose petals until she found the ring, put it on and showed the woman who'd thrown it.

I went backstage. Why Marlene had thought she needed me to start the clack, I couldn't figure out. Everyone was there, the German ambassador, the head of the Arts Council, everyone. Her dressing room was packed. 'Now, sweetheart,' she said when finally, everyone had left, 'I just get changed. Do you have a car?'

'Yes,' I said, 'A white Rolls Royce.'

'I'll come in your car,' said Marlene, 'The luggage can go in mine.'

Outside the stage door, the street was jammed. It could have been a crowd for the Beatles but for one difference. These fans were absolutely silent. Marlene stood underneath the stage-door light in her trench coat, the belt tied casually. It was Lilli Marlene. Slowly, she walked towards the car. The crowd parted, still not making a sound. At the car, she said, 'Help me up.' When I understood what she meant, I lifted her onto the roof of the car. 'Give me that box.' She had with her a box full of signed photographs. Up in the air she flung them. Fans, laughing and shouting dived and grabbed, while those who couldn't reach, clapped. When all the pictures were distributed, I lifted Marlene back down and helped her into the car. 'Open the window,' she said to Jimmy Allen, unaware that he was my friend and not a chauffeur but Jimmy didn't mind. He'd got what he wanted. Marlene stretched her arm through the gap. 'Mind how you go, sweetheart,' she called out, shaking hands as the car moved slowly forward.

'Will you no come back again?' sang the fans.

'Goodbye, sweetheart, goodbye!' Marlene carried on and then suddenly to Jimmy, 'A little faster. They're thinning out.'

We drove along Prince's Street to the Caledonian hotel. As we went, I introduced Jimmy to her and, as we got out, told him that I wouldn't be long. Marlene walked through the lobby of the hotel, smiling to left and right as if she was the Empress of Russia but then, she had played her. Everyone applauded, the guests and the staff. We went up in the lift. We went into her suite. She closed the door. 'Now, sweetheart!' she said, 'Only now, is the performance over!' What did we have to eat – smoked salmon and champagne? No, huge ham sandwiches and steins of beer. As she ate and drank, she talked. 'Do you know how much this is costing me?' She listed everything. So much for the posters, so much for the band, so much for the costumes, the entire venture. I, in the meanwhile, was still thinking about 'Now the performance is over.' It was a lesson. Don't come out of the stage door falling down drunk. Dress. Keep up the performance. It's only over when you get home.

Ages later in Paris, I bumped into Ginette Spanier who was a friend of Marlene's. 'What a wonderful time I had,' I told her, 'She was so sweet, Marlene. She rang me up with a ticket for her last performance –'

'I know, darling,' said Ginette, 'I told her you were in Edinburgh. There was fog at the airport in Paris and I couldn't get there to be the clack on the last night. "Ring Victor," I said.'

The first time Marlene invited me to her Paris apartment at 12 Avenue Montaigne – this was after Ginette had introduced us – as I was going up in the lift, I had to go and lose a button. The loose thread was still round my finger when she opened her front door.

'Come in.'

'I'm terribly sorry, A button's come off my jacket.'

'Take off your jacket. Give it to me.' Out came the glasses. Out came the sewing basket. Out came the cotton. She moistened the cotton. She threaded the needle. She sewed, and all the time she talked. In that way I met the woman, not the legend. It stayed that way. We were able to talk about anything, even my hair which I was beginning to lose. 'I've got the very thing,' she said and climbed some kitchen steps, those shapely legs right in front of me. Reaching up, she brought down a bottle of Joachim's hair tonic. 'For you, sweetheart. Me? I've only ever had five hairs in my life. I always wear wigs.'

I even asked her about her sex life. 'My mother always told me it was rude to say no,' she said. 'For example, I was at a party in New York once and a young man came to me and said, "What are you drinking?" I said, "Dry martini" and he mixed the most wonderful dry martini I've ever drunk. I told him so. "This is wonderful," I said, "What's your name?" and the man said, "You're joking. I'm Frank Sinatra."' Marlene peered over a glass she was sipping from and, to show me what she did next, made an appraising 'Mmm' sound, then carried on. "Come to Vegas," he said. I said, "Sure." We leave the party. We go to the airport. We travel in a private plane to Vegas – you know, sweetheart, how I hate travelling in crowds – we get to the hotel. He gets his key. He gets another one, throws it to me. "That's your suite," he says. It was next to his but then he goes straight in to gamble. I hate seeing money wasted, sweetheart. I'm sitting there watching and he's drinking and I think to myself, he'd better eat something or he's going to be no good to me. "You must eat something, Mr Sinatra," I said. He orders a plate of spaghetti but he leaves it and you know how I hate to see food wasted, so I eat it. After a bit, I say: "You really should eat something," and he orders another plate of spaghetti. I eat that too but I can't finish it. I'm gagging, so I go to bed. Later he comes up and he gets into bed and, sweetheart, he may have been dwunk but he's banging all night. When he's not banging, he's eating cornflakes, so, all night long, it was bang, bang, cwunch, cwunch. The next morning, I get up. I have a shower. I get dwessed. I thwow the key onto the bed and I say: "Goodbye, Mr Sinatwa" and I get the plane back to New York. That, sweetheart,' said Marlene leaning forwards and looking directly into my face, 'Was the one-night stand.'

At her Paris flat, Marlene cooked meals for me. During them she sat talking but not eating, just watching. 'You know, sweetheart,' she said at one, 'Many men have been to my bedroom but not many to my kitchen.'

'They are showing a film of mine on French television and, you know, because I have such an unusual voice they can't dub me. Would you like to see it?' Marlene was on the phone. 'Sure,' I said and round I went. She'd prepared a picnic with dazzling white napery, the best cutlery, all beautifully laid out in front of the television. The film *Dishonoured*, was directed by her mentor, Josef von Sternberg. She talked me through it, but in her own way, nothing about the film itself, only the clothes. 'Those gloves, now those were *my* gloves, sweetheart. That was not wardrobe. My shoes, I still have those shoes. That coat, now that coat was designed for me. "I'm keeping this," I thought. The studio don't know but I still have it.' And if it wasn't clothes she was talking about, it was make-up. That's how it went all the way through to the end when she gets shot and falls into the snow. 'People in films, when they are shot, they do all sorts of things,' she said, 'What you do, is drop. You don't fall back and wave your arms. You drop and I dropped into the snow and I'm lying there. I mustn't breathe. My eyes are closed. I'm waiting for von Sternberg to say "Cut!" Nothing. I'm holding my breath. Nothing. I open one eye. He's moved to another set-up!' and she roared with laughter. People say she didn't have a sense of humour when it came to herself but she did.

After all this hospitality, it was time to ask Marlene out. 'That would be lovely, sweetheart,' she said when I rang and named a little restaurant where she and I would both be at ease. Once we were sat down, I picked up the wine list. I had to choose something good but wine was not a subject I was well up on. All I could do was order the most expensive which was Chateau d'Yquem. 'Oh, sweetheart, how lovely. I haven't had Yquem in years. This is delicious,' said Marlene and drank it all through her meal of steak and chips. Yquem is a dessert wine, very sweet, not nice with steak and chips. At the end of the meal, she thanked me very much and breathed no word of criticism.

'Would you like to go to the pictures with me?' It was another day and I was in the middle of directing a show I wasn't having much fun with. Marlene's use of the word 'pictures' intrigued me. With her long stay in America, I would have expected 'movies'.

'Yes, wonderful,' I said, 'What are we going to see?'

'*Boom!*'

'Boom?'

'Do you remember, there was a play –' I did remember. It was by Tennessee Williams, only then it was called *The Milk Train Doesn't Stop Here Anymore*. The British actress, Hermione Baddeley, had scored a personal hit with it on Broadway. The film starred Elizabeth Taylor. This was puzzling, as I knew Marlene didn't like her. It was something to do with Mike Todd, the producer, having had an affair with Marlene then going off to marry Elizabeth. In any case, I'd seen Marlene with a certain book. It contained pictures of great beauties caught at a bad moment. Elizabeth was in it, probably at an airport, shouting at someone. Marlene loved to chuckle over this.

We took a cab up the Champs Elysées. It was dusk and there was a lot of traffic. All the way up, in front of us, were red rear lights and all the way coming down were white headlights. I was panicking about time. 'Oh, look at all this traffic,' I said.

'But, sweetheart, isn't it beautiful?' said Marlene.

'What?' I said, seeing nothing but an appalling jam.

'Yes, sweetheart, look, rubies going up, diamonds coming down.' I've never heard such a Cartier description of a traffic jam.

At the cinema, as soon as Marlene had sat down, she brought out a big bag of sweets. All the time the film was going on, she was unwrapping those sweets, chewing them and talking. 'Sh,' went people all around but it was no use. She wouldn't stop, not that is, until Noël Coward appeared on the screen.

'Ah,' said Marlene, 'This is why I wanted to see the film. Look, there's Noël.'

'Isn't that touching,' I thought. 'She's come specially to see her old friend Noël Coward.' She even stopped chewing, put on her glasses and leant forward.

'My God, sweetheart, I'd heard he'd had a face–lift for the film. I wanted to see it. Look. Oh my God! He's got two ears on each side.' She then cackled with laughter and left the cinema.

When my friend, the actress Marti Stephens, the one who looked like a young Marlene, opened on Broadway in the musical, *Company*, Marlene wanted to go. She too was a friend of Marti's. Hardly had we sat down in the stalls when we heard: 'Miss Dietrich, I can't believe it!' A woman in the next seat had recognised her. 'Will you sign my programme?'

'Sure, sweetheart,' said Marlene.

'Oh, this is the happiest night of my life!' said the woman. At the interval, we went to the bar.

'My God!' It was another fan. 'I saw your one-woman show. I was there the night you fell down. Did you cut anything?'

'A number,' said Marlene. After the show, we went to Marti's dressing room.

'I couldn't work out out how you did it,' said Marlene, 'Now I know. It was the wig. Oh and there was a woman out front who said, this was the happiest night of her life.'

'She enjoyed it that much?' said Marti.

'She meant meeting me.' said Marlene.

For all that, Marti was good friends with Marlene and together, she and I went to the first night of her one-woman show in New York. Just as in Edinburgh, the band was visible on stage and just as in Edinburgh, it started the show by playing *Falling in Love Again*. The audience waited for Marlene to make her entrance, and it waited. This was not like Edinburgh. *Falling in Love Again* came round again. I turned to Marti. 'Why doesn't she come on?'

'She's waiting.'

'What for?'

'Applause.' My mind flashed back to Edinburgh. Pinned up in the wings had been Marlene's running order and indeed, it had read: 'Applause. Song. Applause. Song.' At the bottom it had also said: 'Xerox. Xerox. Xerox.' That was nothing to do with the act, of course, but it might just as well have been. Every performance had to be exactly the same and was. At the theatre in New York, with the audience still waiting, things were about to get awkward when a drape, at the side of the stage, twitched. That did the trick. The audience woke up and clapped. No sooner had this applause started than Marlene made her entrance. The stage was wide but she walked the full width of it, going right past the microphone. Only when she had done that did she come back to the centre. There, she turned, looked the audience full in the face and said, 'Hallo.' That provoked another storm of applause. After the show, we drove to Sardi's. Sitting at the back of the car, Marlene was in ecstasy. 'Sweetheart, did you hear that applause?' Then, clutching herself, she rocked backwards and forwards and came to a climax.

At Sardi's, when the meal was over, the waiter approached with the bill. 'What's this?' said Marlene.

'The bill,' said the waiter.

'Sweetheart, what do you mean? It's enough that I'm here.' And she tore it up, throwing the pieces to the floor.

That was the naked ego of the star, which in itself, is neither good nor bad, merely instinct. It certainly didn't mean that Marlene couldn't be kind or considerate. The unwanted Yquem had shown me that. She proved it again during the time when I was directing in Paris. I like to involve my family in anything I do. My sister Gianina at Danny La Rue's, my parents' flying to New York after I'd won the Tony Award, they were examples. Here is where the family and the whole star thing came together. Spotting which was which might not be so easy, though.

I was just about to set off for rehearsals – that *Jesus Christ Superstar* I mentioned earlier – when the phone rang. 'Sweetheart, you know, tomowow is your birthday?' It was Marlene. 'I'll take you to dinner, to Maxim's.'

'Oh,' I said, 'I can't. My family's coming – my mother, my father, my sister, my brother-in-law.'

'I'll take them all,' said Marlene and rang off.

They arrived at the hotel, led by my mother. 'Oh, that bloody boat. I'm never going on that boat again.'

'Pull yourself together,' I said, 'Because you're having dinner with Marlene Dietrich.'

'Right-o,' she said and started to unpack. Being the youngest of nine children, she'd had to learn to do all sorts of things for herself but making clothes was what she loved. She made them for the whole family. All she needed was a photograph in a magazine. Just by looking at it, she could make a pattern, cut out the material and make a dress. For this trip, she'd made one in red with a décolletage and a slit for her leg to come through. Even the detail was there, bows and ribbons, and when she'd done that, she'd made another one for my sister, exactly the same, only in green. Together, they looked like a set of traffic lights. My father was in his grey seersucker jacket that I'd bought him in New York and my brother-in-law was wearing his rugby blazer with his Tredegar Ironsides badge on the breast pocket.

Into Maxim's sashayed these four 'stars'. Marlene was already sitting there with her old friend Ginette Spanier, but when we appeared, she stood up in shock. She was expecting to see those ladies from Llangollen in tall hats and shawls. You see them on ashtrays. 'Mrs Spinetti!' said Marlene, 'That dwess, is it a Balenciaga?'

'Yes,' said my mother, 'I saw this photograph in a magazine and I thought, that'll suit me, so I cut it out and made it myself. Five pounds it cost, well, £5.50 with the buttons. I got the material in Abergavenny market.' We sat down.

'Sweetheart,' said Marlene to my sister, 'That hairstyle you've got, it's the latest style in Paris. It's called Gauloise Bleue.'

'Yes, I know,' said my sister, 'I copied it from a picture I saw in *Elle*.' My mother peered over at Marlene.

'What do you put on your face, love?' Slightly taken aback, Marlene answered:

'A little Ultima II. Sometimes Erase all over, why?'

'No, your make-up is beautiful but before you put your make-up on, what do you do?'

'I wash.'

'In soap and water? Never. You want to use rose water from Gerwyn Jones, the chemist, up in Ebbw Vale. It's 50p the bottle. You get the bottle and you shake it and you get the cotton wool –' and now she was giving this woman beauty hints. The two of then were patting away at their faces, Marlene loving it. My brother-in-law leant forward. David Hughes is his name and, at the time, he was the Heathcliff of the Valleys, a handsome rugby playing hunk with blue eyes and a shock of black hair, a lock of which fell across his forehead as he leaned.

'Fair play, Marleen,' he said, 'I've never seen you in the pictures because I'm too young but, for your age, you're bloody marvellous.'

'Marlene turned to my sister and said, 'Sweetheart, I love him,' and my sister said,

'Well, have him and I can tell everybody.'

Towards the end of her life, Marlene told me: 'From now on, I'm going to live for me and not for Dietrich. If I want to get dwunk, I get dwunk. If I want to get old, I get old. If I want to get fat, I get fat.' She then took down all her photos and put Dietrich away. Once more, she became Maria Magdalena von Losch, which was her real name. Sending flowers to her was no use. She dropped them on the floor. Her wishes were no longer the same. 'Sweetheart, can you get me some pot?' she rang to ask, 'I think I'm dwinking too much.'

25

The Last Tourist

'You're an established actor.' Other people say that. I don't. I've never felt it. A jobbing actor, perhaps, one who tells drama students: 'If you can't cope with the three Rs – Rejection, Redundancy and Resting – don't start.' But, really, for the past three decades, it's been a case of finding welcomes where I hadn't expected them and sometimes the opposite.

Yes, in 1975 Stuart Rosenberg wanted me to be in *Voyage of The Damned*, but I didn't know what to expect from James Mason and Orson Welles who were also in it.

My first day was with James Mason. 'I don't want to worry you,' said Stuart, 'But we have to lose James today. He's on a daily rate and he mustn't go over. Really, we've only got him for this morning.' In the script, it said of my character: 'Dr Strauss is now a broken man,' before launching him into a long, painful tale, related to James Mason's character, about trying to save the lives of his little daughters. As usual, the scene came in the middle of the plot, so there was no chance to work up to this moment. 'Action!' said Stuart. Well, what a good thing I'd worked hard at my lines because I got through it all right, even finding myself in tears. All the while, James Mason was standing by a window, smoking and listening. At the end of the take, he walked Stuart a few paces away from the camera and said: 'Marvellous casting, old boy. He's going to make me work.'

We did one more take for safety and then Stuart turned the camera round to get James Mason's reactions. There was a pause for lighting. In the corner of the room was a piano. 'Do you remember *The Seventh Veil* with Ann Todd,' I said to James, 'When she was a pianist and you were a psychiatrist and you struck her over the hands with a stick?'

'I do,' he said.

'Well, when I was a teenager and I saw that film back in Wales, I was able to go straight to the piano and pick out that tune. I can do it now.'

'Let's do the scene!' said James. I sat at the piano and picked out the tune. It was Beethoven. As I did, James grabbed a stick of wood from the floor, strode over and said, 'Francesca, if you won't play for me, you won't play for anyone else, ever again!' and brought the stick down with a terrific flourish, thankfully, avoiding my fingers. The crew burst into applause. That was James Mason, a charming man, whose enthusiasm was the same as the Burtons' when I'd read my short story to them.

'Ah but James Mason is a pussycat,' said someone on the crew, 'You wait till Orson arrives.' We were on location in Barcelona and I spent the next three days running over the lines I would be saying to him while looking at Gaudi's architecture. Back at the hotel, on the third evening, the phone rang.

'Victor?'

'Yes?'

'Orson. Come down to my suite.' He was on the ground floor because by that time in his life, he couldn't get into the lift. As I entered his suite, he rose with difficulty from a settee, walked over and hugged me. He too loved Joan Littlewood. 'I'm so glad you're doing this,' he said and turned to Stuart who was also there. 'You see. I've rewritten the scenes.'

'Oh my God,' I thought. I'd already learnt them. Relearning them would be hell.

'The scene is about Victor's character, not about mine,' explained Orson. So what Orson had done in his rewrite was bounce things around so that you had to keep seeing how I was reacting. That meant, the following day I got one close-up after another. He was handing me the scene.

At break time, he gave me an example of the opposite. It had happened while he was playing Le Chiffre, the villain in *Casino Royale* with Peter Sellers as one of the James Bonds. Peter had given him no reaction at all and said his lines in a flat voice, so that Orson had had nothing to come back to. Afterwards Peter had dubbed himself with a completely different voice, reducing Orson to nothing.

'Don't leave me. Give me strength. Don't go for lunch. We'll have food sent to the set,' said Orson as work progressed. I liked that. At mealtimes, we were both happy to stay around our place of work and tell each other stories. Once, just before the start of shooting, he became terribly nervous. I told him about a movie nut who used to follow me around.

'Come on,' I'd said to this nut, 'You must have seen every film ever made. Which one made the biggest impression?'

'Well,' he'd answered, '*Yankee Doodle Dandy* was a fair picture but the best was *Bomba on Panther Island*.'

'So,' I said to Orson, 'However good you are, when my friend goes to see you, you'll never be as good as *Bomba on Panther Island*.' Orson laughed, relaxed and got on with the scene.

That's what I mean by welcomes that were unexpected. When, in 1995, I played Lord Foppington in *The Relapse* at Stratford-upon-Avon, it was the opposite. I was really looking forward to that. I thought we'd do the kind of exploring that we'd done with Joan Littlewood, work together to find out how people lived in Restoration times, find Vanbrugh's rippling line.

'Pages 15 to 19,' it said on the noticeboard by the rehearsal room. 'If you are not in those pages, remain in the green room until you are called.' That might have suited the director but on the opening night, I still didn't know the names of half the cast and, if we didn't know each other, how could we do good work? Joan, when talking about the Elizabethan era, used to tell us that you had to watch your back at all times. Somebody might be about to knife you. Now, I wonder whether she was talking about Shakespeare or the Royal Shakespeare Company. Just as I was about to make my entrance on that first night, standing there in towering peruke and frothing with lace, I heard an actor hiss in my ear, 'You'll never get this right. You're not English.'

I put my name down to get my ten minutes with the artistic director, Adrian Noble. That was the system. On entering his office, I found him leaning back in his chair, his legs stretched out in front of him, his hands behind his head like Jonathan Miller doing a TV interview. 'What do I call you, Vic or Victor?' he asked. I charged straight in.

'What do you want first, the good news or the bad news? The good news is that you have a wonderful infrastructure. Your backstage staff's amazing. *Richard the Third* comes down in the afternoon and up goes *Romeo and Juliet* all ready for the evening and they're both big productions. If I have to go and talk to someone at a university because that's part of my job here, there's always someone to make sure I get there all right and get back.'

'What's the bad news?' asked Adrian.

'Where the fuck are *you*? I have to put my name down to talk to you? I've been here nearly a year and, I don't mean just me, you should talk to everybody. When I first came here, you introduced us all to a woman who was going to produce *The Relapse*. We never saw her again. What does she do?'

'She has to make sure the costumes and the set arrive on time,' he answered.

'You all forget one thing,' I said, 'You forget the actors. Without us this building means nothing. It doesn't matter what sets you put on the stage, what costumes, Unless there's someone in them, people won't come. I've been through the most ghastly rehearsal process. I never thought anybody would rehearse like this, let alone the Royal Shakespeare Company but where were you?'

'I couldn't very well walk into my directors' rehearsals,' said Adrian.

'Olivier used to –'

'I *know* you were at the National,' interrupted Adrian.

'Well, whatever you may think of him, Olivier used to pop his head round the door and say "How are you doing, my dear baby?" and then we had to throw him out because he'd sit and talk with everybody and waste rehearsal time but you can see what I'm driving at. Where were you?'

Adrian thought for a moment and said, 'I suppose I am the boss.'

'Well, be it,' I said.

The doorbell rang. It was 2005. I'd recently finished a tour playing Baron Mirko Zeta in *The Merry Widow* and before that, a year playing Baron Bomburst in *Chitty Chitty Bang Bang* at the London Palladium. Two children were standing there. 'It must be Trick or Treat,' I thought.

'We want you to be in our play,' they said. It subsequently turned out that these were not two children but two young men, one a director, Max Lewendel, the other James Graham, a writer. They were putting on James's play, *Albert's Boy*, a two-hander about the life of Einstein. They were going to do it at the Finborough, a tiny theatre, above a pub off the Fulham Road and they wanted me to play Einstein opposite a young actor called Gerald Monaco. I tried to get rid of them but after a good dinner and more than a little flattery, I accepted the part. For it, I grew a moustache which has now turned into a beard because another young man came along and asked me to play Prospero in *The Tempest*, which is work in progress.

As an – in other people's eyes of course – established actor, as a Welshman and as someone who worked with the Beatles, I am invited to and welcomed at various celebrations and events. Performing John Lennon's poetry at the Barbican and talking at The College of Music and Drama in Cardiff were examples. One of these events has a special resonance. In 1981 I went to unveil a statue of John Lennon in Liverpool where, by coincidence, I met Paul McCartney who was up there too. He drove me around in his car, took me to Penny Lane and Strawberry Fields, all the time playing tapes of old Beatles songs. 'They sound great don't they, Vic?'

'Wonderful,' I said.

'I'm not allowed to play them in the house,' said Paul.

I can only imagine that his wife, Linda, was more interested in Paul's group, Wings, that was on the go at the time and of which she was part, while his past, she probably found slightly irritating. Paul parked the car and pointed. 'There you are. That's the house where I was born.' A man tapped on the window. 'Hey, mister,' he said, 'Paul McCartney was born in there.'

On one occasion, there was a welcome even simpler than the Einstein one. For a start, there was no play at all. 'Do you think you could manage to do an evening on a Friday in three months time?' It was no more than that, a casual question asked in 1983 by Andrew Empson, the stage manager of a musical I was in, *Windy City* at the Victoria Palace. He had taken a lease at the New End Theatre in Hampstead and was asking people, mostly people who were starting out like French and Saunders and John Sessions, to do late-night shows there. Nevertheless that question led to a job, that on and off, has kept me busy to the present day. I agreed, at the time, because it was a good way of raising money to bring an American student to London to study theatre. My old friend, Burt Shevelove, the American director and co-author of *A Funny Thing Happened on the Way to the Forum* had died just as he was about to start rehearsing *Windy City*. Using his name for this charity would commemorate him. Admittedly, I forgot about the whole thing almost at once but then on a Wednesday three months later, I got a call. 'Friday night, you're on.'

'On what?' I asked.

'Your one-man show.'

'You'd better let me have some tickets for my friends then.'

'I can't, we're sold out.'

When the time came, I put a carnation into my button hole, stepped onto the stage at New End and said, 'It's taken me thirty years to walk from the dark into the light,' and then went on to talk about my childhood in Wales, working in a factory and quite a lot of things I've told you in this book. As I never wear a watch, I had no way of judging the length of it. All I know is that Andrew Empson said if we wanted a drink before the theatre closed that night, we'd better stop. I went to the bar thinking no more than, 'Thank God, I've got away with it,' but someone said:

'Why don't you do this at the Edinburgh Festival?'

'Do what?' I asked. 'What have I done?' It wasn't as if a word had been written down.

At the Assembly Rooms in Edinburgh, it was a sell-out. The *Scotsman's* critic and Jack Tinker of the *Daily Mail* gave it good reviews but I still didn't know what I'd done. It was me just talking to people, much like when Joan Littlewood had said, 'Go out and talk to the audience. You'll talk to anyone.'

Six years went by, during which there were murmurings about doing the show again, and then I was, at the Donmar Warehouse. 'But it needs somebody to shape it,' I said, 'How about Ned Sherrin?'

'Yes, fine,' said Ned, 'I've heard most of your stories, I might as well direct it,' and we met for lunch over which, as he would put it, I conjured up all these people, Olivier, Gielgud, Richard Burton, the Beatles, and they became the show. Ned's skill was in asking the odd pertinent question like: 'Where are you in this?' I thought for a moment and found myself reciting some of the poems I'd written over the years. 'Right,' he said when I'd finished, 'Those are your tent poles and the Richard Burton one can be the interval.' He knew that was important to me. Other people use the second half of one-man shows for a session of Question and Answers. I wanted to do two halves. It worked.

Louis Benjamin, who'd been helpful during the Palladium panto, got wind of the show and gave me the Apollo Theatre in Shaftesbury Avenue, rent free. When the run there finished, I toured the UK and wound up in Australia, where I did very well in Sydney and less well in Adelaide, which was odd because I knew it had a sizeable Welsh community. Its chairwoman invited me for lunch and the mystery was solved.

Back in Cwm, I and other children used to slide down the steep hills either side of the village on pieces of cardboard. I can hear the grass squeaking now. One of the other children was Jenty Stephens, whose family lived over the road. Until Dad was declared an enemy alien, they were OK with my family but after that they walked two blocks in the rain to avoid meeting us. The chairwoman of the Welsh contingency in Adelaide was the same Jenty Stephens. Our lunch was in a fish-and-chip shop. 'I thought it would make you feel more at home,' she said. We ate and I asked her why there had been such a lack of support from the Welsh in Adelaide. She'd drummed up trade for Harry Secombe, hadn't she? 'But you're not really Welsh, are you?' said Jenty.'

So, forty years on, I could be confident of one thing. Her bigotry and narrow-mindedness were still thriving. Perhaps that's why, even today, I'm constantly being reminded that I'm at a frontier with my papers not in order, my nose, pressed up against the window of life. At other times, I'm convinced I've gone through life missing the holiday season because I didn't know it was on and that actually happened once. It was not my imagination. It just about sums me up too.

During the run of *Fings Ain't Wot They Used T'Be*, when I was playing Tosher, round about 1961, my back gave way. Gerry Raffles led me out of the Garrick Theatre, put me in his car and drove me to Harley Street where an osteopath said, 'Oh dear, you've slipped a disc. You'll have to wear a corset for the rest of your life.' A little more encouragingly, he went on, 'But what you need to do right now, is rest your back. When you've done that, come and see me again.'

'Ischia,' said Peter Shaffer when I told him, 'It's volcanic. Hot springs, thermal baths, the only place for you,' and he booked me a holiday. Before I knew it, I was on the ferry from Naples to Porto d'Ischia and very excited. Half-Italian I may have been but never, in my adult life, had I been to Italy before. In a holiday mood, I'd chosen a holiday suit, white, and to go with it, a white hat. However, as I looked around the deck, I realised that there was only one holidaymaker there, me. The rest were long gone. It was early October. Those on the deck were locals, peasants with their animals, mostly. I began to feel conspicuous, if anything, like Alec Guinness as *The Man in the White Suit*.

When the ferry docked, I was almost mobbed as my cases were grabbed and I was put into a *carozzella*, chatter coming at me from all sides, none of which I understood because I didn't know Italian. How welcoming though, and how refreshing the evening air as this vehicle, a motor cycle with a hooded seat at the back, bounced over the cobbles on its way to the hotel. The bouncing was less refreshing. Oo, my ba-a-ack.

In the town, the streets were dark. In fact, there was no sign of light until we reached the front, where coloured fairy lights along the promenade tinkled in the wind. No lights were on in the hotel windows either. I looked through the door. One light shone dimly. I went in. A woman with blond hair appeared. 'Ah, Mr Spinetti, yes, of course.' She was German. 'The hotel is closed but we honour your booking. We put you in the annexe. We will give you meals. If you want, we will give you packed lunch. We will send meals to the annexe. You will have your own apartment. You will be comfortable there.' 'Ping!' She rang her bell. 'Peppino!' A little *facchino* came out, a porter, blond too. Was he her son? That's what I assumed. Walking ahead of me, speaking the odd word of English, he carried my cases across the street. Not difficult as there was absolutely no traffic at all. At the annexe we climbed the stairs to the first floor and walked along a corridor past three apartments. Mine was at the end, the fourth. Peppino showed me in. I gave him a tip.

'Thank you,' he said and closed the door.

'I'm here!' I thought, 'I'm in Italy for the first time! How wonderful! Yes, I can feel it in my blood.' I was hugging myself with the thrill of it. What's more, the room, when I looked, really was comfortable. 'Have an early night,' I told myself, 'And get up first thing in the morning. Isn't this exciting?'

During the night, I awoke, very thirsty. The drinks on the plane must have made me dry. I went to the bathroom. Nobody had told me: 'Don't drink the water.' At this time, the only other occasion I'd been abroad, you have to realise, was New York where drinking the water was quite safe. I turned the tap on. In the darkness what came out looked like Guinness but I was so thirsty I drank it. Drifting off to sleep again, I heard the most terrible noise. Machine-gun fire. Great explosions. A riot, it had to be but when I opened the shutters. Nobody. Nothing. Only the distant tinkling of the lights along the promenade. It was then I realised my room was over the local cinema where they were showing *The Guns of Navarone* dubbed into Italian. 'Ha, ha, ha, how typical,' I thought and climbed back into bed.

Two hours later I woke up again, very ill. So ill, the room was spinning. From then on, I was on the lavatory. I was vomiting. I was on the lavatory and, all the time, the bathroom would not stop swaying. When I managed to get to the shutters and open them for a breath of fresh air, it was daylight. Help, I needed help. I rang across to the hotel proper. A woman's voice answered but it wasn't one I knew.

'*Pronto!*'

'Help, I'm –'

'*Pronto!*'

'I need –'

'*Pronto!*'

Christ. What was the Italian for German? No, German woman. Ah yes.

'*Tedesca.*'

'Day off!'

Oh God, and then I remembered Peppino. He spoke a bit of English, didn't he?

'Peppino, please.'

'Peppino? You English?'

'Yes.'

'Ha, ha, ha,' cackled the woman and hung up.

I was back lying on the bed when I heard a knock. The door opened and in came a six-foot-four fisherman, woollen hat, big jumper, fish scales on his boots, reeking of the day's catch.

'I am Peppino.'

'No, no, there must be some mistake.'

'Peppino, me Peppino!' And, coming into the room, he clapped his hand into the crook of his elbow and jerked up his forearm.

'Peppino got big dick!'

'Oh, God,' I rushed to throw up in the bathroom. 'There's a mistake,' I said when I got back.

'You know Terence Rattigan? He love Peppino!' and up went the arm again. 'You know John Gielgud? He like Peppino!' Same gesture.

'You know Binkie Beaumont?' same gesture. He was listing everybody who'd ever worked in English theatre. By then, I was pushing him out, or trying to. 'That's a nice camera,' he said as he was going.

'Get out!'

I lay on the bed. What was I to do? Somewhere there had to be a *farmacia*. Yes, I remembered noticing a green light when I looked out of the window. I dressed and crept downstairs, the annexe also swaying, and crawled along the main street. The *farmacista* saw the problem at once and gave me some stuff to take, a drink. I went back to bed. The dizziness subsided. The vomiting stopped. I didn't go to the lavatory anymore. I slept. The next morning, everything was wonderful and, feeling so much better, I opened the shutters. Down below in the street, pointing up at my window was the big fisherman, Peppino. '*Buon giorno*! Good morning!' I closed the shutters and rang down for coffee and panini. It was time to decide what to do for the day. 'Get out of town,' seemed the best idea, perhaps a beach. There was no sign of any thermal baths being open, that was for sure.

In the street, when I left the annexe, I got '*Buon giorno*!' again from Peppino who, with one or two others, was still there. Ignoring him, I made for the hotel where I had another coffee and ordered a packed lunch. That still left me needing to go out into the street again and there was Peppino with his workmates inspecting a boat. A *carozzella* approached. 'Taxi, taxi!' The driver stopped.

'Can you take me to a beach?'

'You English?'

'Yes.'

'I love English. I know Birmingham! I love –'

'Good, can you –'

'Yes, I take you to beach, beach where only Italians go. No tourists. Lovely beach. *Spiaggio*.' That's the Italian for beach. I pressed myself into the back of the *carozzella*, trying to hide from Peppino and his gang as we whizzed past. Out and out and out we drove and then stopped. 'There, proper beach,' said the driver. It was down a slope.

'Thank you very much,' I said, 'Can you come back at – what time is it now, Eleven o'clock – Four o' clock?'

'OK,' he said and off he buzzed. I walked down onto the beach. There was no one there. There was nothing and I don't swim. I sat in the – not baking hot – in the warmish sun. I threw some stones into the water and wondered what to do. 'My lunch, I'll have my lunch,' but when I'd finished eating, it was only twelve o'clock. What was I going to do and where was I, anyway? I waited. Every time I heard a *carozzella* approaching, I rushed up the slope, thinking it was for me. At four o'clock, the driver did come back and drove me to the annexe. I unfolded some lire. 'No, no, I know Birmingham. The English people are good people.'

'You must –'

'No, no, nothing.'

'In that case, what are you doing this evening? Let's go out somewhere to a place and we'll have a meal.'

'OK.'

At eight o'clock he came back and drove me way out of town, past Forio, to, what I can only describe as, the Savoy of Ischia. He was in jeans and grubby T-shirt, this driver. No shoes had he on, no socks and for that matter, there were no teeth in his head either. He spat too. Together, we walked into an airy palm-court atmosphere and sat down at a table. Not one other guest was about. The waiter came over, shook out the napkins and arranged them around us. At that moment, the wistful thought of a little cafe hovered in my imagination. It would have been so much more appropriate but then, I had to remember, the driver had refused my fare. He picked up the menu and began to order and it was, 'I'll have this and I'll have that', the best steak, the best everything. 'Wine? Oh yes, French. No Italian rubbish.' I was getting more and more outraged at this man who was not only taking me literally for a ride but figuratively too when some other people came in, a couple, English. The woman walked across.

'Oh, Mr Spinetti, we saw you last week at the Garrick. *Fings Ain't Wot They Used T'Be.* It was wonderful.'

'Thank you,' I said, 'By the way, this is er, er,'

'That's all right,' said the woman and off she went with the man, both of them looking over their shoulders, trying hard not to giggle and obviously wondering, 'What on earth is he doing with that old man?'

Having drunk most of the French wine, the driver knocked the rest over. He was plastered. Being Italian, he wasn't used to drinking a lot all at once. The bill came. With no credit card to settle it – they didn't exist in those days – I counted out one huge note after another. By then I was seething with rage but I had to get back to the hotel and so I climbed into the *carozzella*. It was like being driven by Albert Steptoe. We drove on, on, into the night until at a deserted spot, the driver pulled up. '*Eh! Inglese!*' he shouted over his shoulder, '*Amore!*'

'What?'

'*Amore!*'

And he pointed down to his crotch. Suddenly from somewhere, I don't know where, I let out a string of Italian profanities. '*Bruto! Viriacho! Maledetto! Va fanculo!*' I don't know what I was shouting but the driver, hearing all this Italian coming from me for the first time, didn't hesitate. He went straight to the annexe. I got out. I slammed the door. He drove off. I stamped up the stairs. Outside my bedroom were the big fisherman and the little porter, the two Peppinos.

'*Cinque mille lire per il due,*' said the big fisherman. Five thousand lire for the pair of us.

'Christ, you Italians, you're appalling!' I yelled, 'Bloody whores! I'm leaving this island! I can't bear it! Get me out of here!' and into my room I went. I started to pack, then rang down: 'Get me my bill. I'm leaving.' There was a knock at the door. Outside, stood a woman. She giggled a little, smiled and started lifting up her skirt. 'Oh, go away!' I thought and pushed her out. I could not believe that bloody place.

I got into a *carozzella*, went to the port and caught the ferry, the last one that night. Holding my bags and seething, I sat there on deck, the last tourist, staring ahead but not seeing. At Naples, where I got off, a young man came up to me.

'Can I help you?'

'No, you can't!'

'Ah. Why not? You are English?'

'Yes, I'm English!'

'But I want to learn English. I would like to talk –'

'Never mind about talking to me. Find me a hotel!'

He found me a hotel, where even though it was October, mosquitoes were still biting. The next morning, I woke up, wondering what the hell I was going to do and then it came to me. My grandmother, up in the north of Italy, I would go and visit her. If I wanted to learn the country of my father's birthplace, now was the time to do it properly. I went down to the Alitalia office.

'I have this return ticket to London. Could you send me via Milan?'

'Sorry, fully booked.'

'How much would it –'

'It's fully booked.'

'But I must visit my grandmother.'

'You have a grandmother?'

'Yes. She lives outside Milan.'

'Ah, well, then.' And he threw someone off the plane. 'Stamp! Stamp! Stamp!' went his rubber stamp over my ticket and onto the plane I climbed. At Milan I caught the train down to Piacenza. It was still light. I hailed a taxi, a proper cab.

'Take me up to Bardi,' I said and up, up we went, twisting round hairpin bend after hairpin bend. It began to grow dark, and all the time the driver would not stop talking over his shoulder. What he was saying I had no idea. All I wanted was for him to face front. As we went higher and higher, I could feel the morning's confidence draining away. Was this journey the most terrible mistake? Still, the chatter though incomprehensible was at least merry.

By the time we arrived, it was late. The only light, I could see, as I paid the driver off, came from a cafe. Outside sat women all dressed in black with black shawls over their heads. I hadn't a clue where my grandmother lived. I had no address. 'Excuse me,' I said, 'Do you know Signora Spinetti, please? Signora Spinetti, *per favore*?' One of the women in black looked up.

'Victor, don't you know me?' she said in a thick Welsh accent. 'Mrs Carpannini from Cardiff. Christ, your grandmother will go bloody mad. She's in bed now. You'd better come back to the *albergo* with me, have something to eat, spend the night and we'll go up together in the morning. My God, she'll be so excited.'

We got to the *albergo*. The bar was full of *contadini*, farm workers, watching *The Marriage of Figaro* on television and laughing at all the jokes. '*Se vuol ballare, signor Contino!*' 'Yes, you tell him!' they shouted at Figaro and clapped him on. Of course, how obvious, Italy, opera, football, that's why my father loved Wales because it was singing and rugby. And my first meal on the soil of mainland Italy? Egg and chips, brown bread and butter, and a pot of tea.

The next morning, it was like an Italian film. A line of cars, like at a wedding or a funeral, followed us as we climbed up and up and up to a farm that used to be an old convent. Standing on the brow of a hill, it overlooked the Po valley. It was a marvellous position and, if you looked down, you could see the Po glistening below. 'Mrs Spinetti! Your grandson's here!' the well-wishers shouted in Italian. A woman came out of the house, clapping her hands together.

'Vittorio, Vittorio, Vittorio!' she cried and throwing her arms around my neck, smothered me in smacking kisses. My shirt was open. '*Pelle come un cavallo*,' she said noticing my hairy chest, 'hair like a horse'. Everyone was clapping and cheering. It was wonderful. Round the building rumbled a muddy bullock cart, leading it, a sturdy young man. 'Your cousin, Renato!' announced my grandmother.

'Vittorio!' He grabbed me, flung me up in the air, squeezed me and kissed me. 'Oh God,' I thought, 'I hope they haven't told him about me from the army.'

'Come on, let me show you our vines. From the grapes, we make our own wine,' and off he carried me with his fellow *contadini* into the vineyard.

There's a PS. Years later, I discovered that, not only theatricals but many other English people, usually sailing on yachts, travelled to Ischia in search of someone like Peppino. I had been staying, I realised, in a place where the inhabitants were accustomed to visitors picking up locals for sex. Now, of course, it is only too easy to imagine the scene downstairs at the hotel. 'Our last chance to make a little bit of extra money but what does he want? We tried big Peppino. We tried little Peppino. He goes and picks up that disgusting old man. How could he? We sent the girl up but none of them he wants, none of them. So, what on earth *does* he want?' In their way, you could see, those people on Ischia were being as hospitable and charming as my relatives in the north but a little more desperate because I was the last tourist of the season.

Postscript

I'm travelling down to Wales by train to visit my 95-year-old mother, Lily. She's raging against the dying of the light. She wants to die. She doesn't want to die. This does not keep my mind from wandering. I love trains. I've spent my life on trains, touring the country, changing at Crewe. As I get nearer and nearer Wales, the excitement, a little less than it used to be perhaps, is still there. It's both physical and spiritual. There's a lilt to the accent that's like an embrace and there's a jungle-drum throb, a brushing aside of dripping leaves that appeals to a part of me that is all below the waist. Up on the mountains looking down into the toy-train valley, it's spiritual. Put both together and you have the energy of a nine-year-old and the sexual capacity of a nineteen-year-old.

As the train rolls on I think about my family. Mario is dead. Adrian, who works at Spar, rises at six every morning to drive up into the mountain with food past its Best Before date for animals who line up at a farm, their heads resting on the wall, waiting for him. Gianina ran a hairdressing salon, with my mother as receptionist. Henry, for six years, drummed for Eric Clapton. Now he drums for Katie Melua, and Paul who is car crazy, drives for a living. My cousin Megan, the one who loved to tell ghost stories, bore a son, Michael, who wrote a children's book, *SuperTed*, and turned it into a cartoon series. I'm the voice of Texas Pete. Michael has his own animation studio in Hollywood now.

Other Spinettis? All over the world, I've looked in telephone books to find them and found hardly any. The most you'll find all together are in Cardiff and Merthyr Tydfil. I questioned my Auntie Angelina. 'Ah,' she said, 'The Spinettis, she don't-a marry too much.'

The train is about to go into the Severn Tunnel. When I won the Tony Award in 1964 and brought it down to Wales, it was at this moment I went to the lavatory, took all my clothes off, held the Tony aloft and, waving an imaginary lasso, went 'Yahoo!' I then put my clothes back on, returned to the compartment and sat in my seat, perfectly composed. At the station, the local press took photographs of me holding the award. The next day, it said in the paper: 'Victor Spinetti arrived last night with New York's coveted Tubby Award.' In the street, a woman called out,

'What's that Tubby Award, love? You're not that fat.'

'No, no. It's not Tubby,' I said, 'It's Tony.'

'Toni?' she said, thinking of the popular home perm of the time, 'Are you into hairdressing now?'

Five Poems

This is the poem I recited during the filming of *The Taming of The Shrew*, the one which Richard Burton recited the next day at Anna Magnani's party.

This is a day for gravestones, wet gravel paths and high, black,
    ornamental railings.
This is a day for the solidity of non-conformist solidity

And heavy four-sided tombs
And wet, carved angels
And rows and rows of RIPs.

This is a day for mud, mud at the graveside,
An umbrellaed, cassocked clergy
And mackintosh mourners
And dark, wet widows
And all the purple trappings of man's peaceful and ultimate
    resting place.

This is a day for the corpse to be left in his deep
and muddy-cold resting place
With the rain washing the 'Deepest Regrets' off the cards

II

And the wind blowing the flowers over the wet gravel paths.
In short, descriptive passages put aside,
This is a day, a godawful, God Almighty, dank, darkday for a
    funeral.

I wrote that on a black, storm brewing day looking out of the window of my bedsit in London but it's really the cemetery at Cwm.

Having lunch at Bert and May Scagnelli's Café L'Ange in Angel Lane, while rehearsing at the Theatre Royal Stratford E15, I thought: "Don't wait. Write."

> I make a mark.
> That mark is understood as something I wish to say or do
> But there is no need,
> For our internal communication makes the truest mark.
> Look deep.
> See the patterns we have traced when there's been no pen,
> The intricate measures we have danced, when there's been no
> music,

III

> The patterns that leave no outward trace
> Except, perhaps, the lines that inner sadness makes upon a
> face.

Early one morning in 1963, shortly after *Oh What A Lovely War* had opened, Joan Littlewood rang. 'I'm giving a breakfast in honour of Princess Alexandra's's wedding day. I've taken a room at the top of the London Hilton looking away from the procession. Would you like to come? I haven't woken you, have I?' 'No,' I said. I've been up for hours writing a poem.' 'Don't tell me you're fucking writing poetry as well. Well, you'd better bring your poem.'

I went. All sorts of people were there including the Labour MPs, Tom Driberg and Michael Foot. After we'd all had champagne and bacon and eggs, Joan said: 'Now, Victor's poem.' 'This is dedicated to the watchers along the Mall.' I said.

> Time has no place where it can exist alone.
> It needs us
> To mark it out and give it space in which to tick.
> That which we call history happens now.

IV

The past is waiting to be born
And the future is already burdened with age.
I know this
By our changeless, barbarous ways,
By the endless inquisition of greed and creed,
By the next Holy War in which I shall surely die, fighting the
    Saracens,
By a royal wedding where feudal lords and ladies ride out
And passers by are made gratified that they have proudly
    shown themselves to us
As we polish our pikes and prepare for Agincourt.

Nowhere yet, has a man rid himself of anything but the fact
    of his manhood,
Thereby rendering unto himself the gift of timelessness.

He must always, the pity of it, always,
Measure out his days and fastidious nights
And synchronise his watch with death each waking hour.
Yet, it is possible to stand outside time
And cease to be prehistoric, which we are

V

Or electronically computered, which we are
And just to be men and women, which we are
And as such, truly eternal.

Michael Foot published that in *Tribune* as its poem to celebrate Princess
Alexandra's wedding.

The management of the show I was in had run off with the takings.
I couldn't pay my hotel bill — always affected, I shouldn't have been
there in the first place — and I had to pay off my debt by working as a
waiter. More money came to me in tips, that summer of 1956, than
would have if I'd been acting. One Sunday, looking out of the
window of the Seaford House Hotel where Tennyson had spent his
holidays, I wrote this.

Wet promenade steps, wind blown, paper strown,
Come up from the pebble beach to the concrete front,
Where the families sit in their family cars, miserably eating,
Looking out to where the sea meets sky,
A dim, distant, misty meeting.

VI

A bather stands and dries himself huddled to the wet sea wall
And as I go by, I wonder why,
Whenever one is by the sea
And the weather is wet and cold,
There is always a solitary bather,
Who is always incredibly old.

I recited that to Tennessee Williams who said: 'Victor, I am that solitary bather.'

A year later, on tour up north, in digs, waiting for lunch, I wrote this.

Muffled from the kitchen, the radio news seeps through,
Lots of visiting diplomats, a riot, a war or two,
Bandits in Malaya, floods in Singapore,
Airforce in Alaska, Royalty on a tour,
People eat and listen, cutting a slice of bread.
'Ooh, another plane crash. Forty-eight are dead.'
What about this world of ours? Trouble, greed and strife,
Switch on Mrs. Dale, dear, and live your second hand life.

VI

Draw the chintzy curtains, have a cup of tea
And leave the world to darkness and TV.

The point of that is, nothing's changed. Calling the news 'The news' is a misnomer. The news is never the news. A few names change but the news itself remains the same and that's why I called the poem *T'was Ever Thus.*

Stage and Screen

Awards and Honorary Fellowships
Oh What a Lovely War!, Théâtre des Nations, Paris, shared with Paul Scofield for
  King Lear. (1963)
Oh What a Lovely War!, Tony Award, Broadway, (1964)
Honorary Fellow of the Royal Welsh College of Music and Drama.
Honorary Fellow of the University of Wales, (Newport).

Stage
South Pacific, UK and Ireland, (1954)
Expresso Bongo, Saville Theatre, (1958)
Candide, Saville Theatre, (1958)
Make Me an Offer, Theatre Royal Stratford E.15 and New (Noël Coward) Theatre,
  (1959)
The Hostage, Cort Theatre, New York, (1960)
Fings Ain't Wot They Used T'Be, Garrick Theatre, (1960)
Every Man in His Humour, Theatre Royal, Stratford E.15, (1960)
Oh What a Lovely War!, Theatre Royal, Stratford E.15,
Sarah Bernhardt Theatre, Paris, and Wyndhams Theatre, (1963)
Henry IV, Assembly Hall, Edinburgh, (1964)
Oh What a Lovely War!, Broadhurst Theatre, New York, (1964)
The Odd Couple, Queen's Theatre, (1966)
In His Own Write (Director), National Theatre, (1968)
Cat Among the Pigeons, Prince of Wales Theatre, (1969)
The Philanthropist, Ethel Barrymore Theatre, New York, (1971)
Let's Get Laid, Windmill Theatre, (1974)
Dick Whittington, London Palladium, (1980)
Windy City, Victoria Palace Theatre, (1983)
A Very Private Diary, Donmar Warehouse and Apollo Theatre, (1989)
Also during the 1980s, UK tours of *The Pirates of Penzance*, *Oliver!* and *One for the
  Pot.*
The Relapse, RSC Swan Theatre and Barbican, (1995)
See How They Run, Bournemouth Pier, 1998
Boobs in the Wood, Wimbledon Theatre, (1998)
The Ladykillers, UK tour, (1999)
Pride and Prejudice, UK tour, (2000)
The Lady Vanishes, UK tour, (2001)

The Lavender Hill Mob, UK tour, (2002)
Chitty Chitty Bang Bang, The London Palladium, (2003)
The Merry Widow, UK tour, (2004)
Albert's Boy, Finborough Theatre, (2005)
The Ghost Train, UK tour, (Autumn 2006)

Screen
Sparrers Can't Sing, (1963)
Becket, (1964)
A Hard Day's Night, (1964)
Help!, (1965)
The Taming of the Shrew, (1967)
The Magical Mystery Tour, (TV) (1967)
The Biggest Bundle of Them All, (1968)
Can Hieronymus Merkin Ever Forget Mercy Humppe and Find True Happiness?, (1969)
Two in Clover, (TV series) (1969)
Start the Revolution Without Me, (1970)
Under Milk Wood, (1972)
Digby, the Biggest Dog in the World, (1973)
The Little Prince, (1974)
The Great McGonagall, (1974)
Return of the Pink Panther, (1975)
Voyage of the Damned, (1976)
Take My Wife, (TV series) (1979)
SuperTed, (Cartoon TV series) (1983)
Mistral's Daughter, (TV miniseries) (1984)
An Actor's Life for Me, (TV series) (1985)
Under the Cherry Moon, (1986)
Attic: The Hiding of Anne Frank, (TV) (1988)
The Krays, (1990)
Secrets, (TV miniseries) (1992)
Young Indiana Jones and the Attack of the Hawkmen, (TV) (1995)
Julie and the Cadillacs, (1999)
Harry and the Wrinklies, (TV series) (1999)
Boobs in the Wood, (Video) (1999)
In the Beginning, (TV miniseries) (2000)
First Degree, (TV series) (2001/2)
New Tricks, (TV) (2005)

Index